Murder at McDonald's

D1569283

Murder at McDonald's

The killers next door

Phonse Jessome

NIMBUS
PUBLISHING

Nimbus Publishing Limited
PO Box 9301, Station A
Halifax, NS B3K 5N5
(902) 455-4286

Design: GDA, Halifax
Cover photo: George Reeves
Printed and bound in Canada

Canadian Cataloguing in Publication Data
Jessome, Phonse.
Murder at McDonald's
ISBN 1-55109-093-7

1. Murder—Nova Scotia—Sydney River—Case studies. 2. Crime and criminals—Nova Scotia—Sydney River—Case studies. 3. Homicide investigation—Nova Scotia—Sydney River—Case studies. 4. Trials (Murder)—Nova Scotia—Sydney River—Case studies. I. Title.

HV6535.C335937 1994   364.1'523'0971695   C94-950198-0

*This book is dedicated to the memory of Donna Warren,
Neil Burroughs, and Jimmy Fagan. You are missed and loved
by many. It is also a tribute to the bravery of
Arlene MacNeil, who continues to struggle to regain
control of her life. You are an inspiration.*

• FOREWORD •

WHILE I WAS WORKING in an embattled Detroit newsroom, I found myself becoming hardened to the horrific stories of violence unfolding around me. Six people shot dead in a crack house; a twelve-year-old girl killed in a drive-by shooting on her way to school; a drug dealer gunned down in a suburban street battle—the stories were frighteningly common. Another human being dead, with no apparent motive and no suspects. There were people trying to stem the tide—trying to take back their neighbourhoods—but there were always the murders.

When I moved to the Maritimes, I found it ironic to see that my former station was being carried on the region's cable system. Its news seemed so out of place, so foreign to the East Coast reality. Surely there couldn't be incidents happening here that were as brutal and senseless as those I remembered from Detroit. Indeed, the commonly held belief was that things like that don't happen here in the Maritimes. The sense of community outrage when it did happen was overwhelming.

ATV's Phonse Jessome was on the scene at the Sydney River McDonald's in the early hours of May 7, 1992, minutes after a hold-up in which three young men from Cape Breton systematically killed three young restaurant employees and left a fourth for dead. This is the story of what happened that night—the police search for the killers, the interrogations, the ordeals of the victims' families, and the volatile trials, punctuated with gripping testimony and outbursts of powerful emotion.

As the story unfolded and the ATV Evening News coverage continued, Phonse Jessome became obsessed with learning every detail of what had happened, and his knowledge expanded with every story he prepared and every person he interviewed. He talked to everyone involved with the tragedy, spending hours discussing the case with the lawyers who prosecuted and defended the three young people charged, and he was able to obtain confidential police information on the investigation of the crime.

This is the true story of the killers next door—and the madness they unleashed.

—Bill Patrick
Network News Director, ATV/ASN

· PREFACE ·

A REPORTER'S JOB is to tell a story. Early on the morning of May 7, 1992, I was awakened by a phone call that led to one of the most difficult stories I have ever had to tell. Four young employees at the Sydney River McDonald's restaurant had just been gunned down during a robbery. Three of the victims died; the fourth remains disabled. Three young men from the Sydney area were arrested and eventually convicted.

I covered this story for a year and a half, from the police investigation that began that morning, through to the trials, held in Sydney and Halifax. I was helped in my work by the investigators, prosecutors, and defence attorneys involved, and by the many people affected by the shootings. I watched as those caught up in this tragedy rode an emotional roller coaster; although shaken to the core by this brutal crime, they had the courage to explain, in public—on the evening news—what they were going through.

Many of the relatives of the victims shared a concern: they wanted to know if anyone would ever have the time to tell the whole story. This book is my attempt to address that concern, and it is my way of thanking the people who let me shed public light on their private pain.

By way of explanation to those who were closest to this story, the names of five people have been changed in the writing of this book: The cousin of Derek Wood, one of the three convicted in the McDonald's murders, is called Mike Campbell; the three men at the centre of the first, ill-fated arrests in the case have been named Gary McIssac, Bill O'Handley, and Glen Delaney; and the sister of one of these suspects is called Cynthia Long. The names have been changed because the suspects were never involved in the crime.

I should also explain that my description, early in the book, of the commission of the crime is presented from the perspective of the victims, by using information in the confessions by the three men convicted in the case. The three confessions have common elements, but they differ in some ways; the disparities become apparent later in the story.

Although this book singles out only a few of the investigators involved in this case, this is in no way an indication that the others were less important a part of the investigating team. Those who are named would be the first to insist that everyone involved in the investigation and subsequent trials deserves equal billing. I would like to thank all the officers involved, for this is also your story. To Kevin Cleary, Pat Murphy, John Trickett, and Dave Roper, thanks for the time you took away from your tasks to talk with me.

Ken Haley, Brian Williston, and Marc Chisholm lived with this tragedy for many months. As the prosecutors responsible for handling the three trials, they showed great dedication and professionalism. Thank you for finding time to answer my questions.

I would also like to thank Dr. Jim Manos of Dalhousie University, who gave me a crash course in adolescent behaviour and the group dynamic.

There are a few people who were not involved in the story, but who were key to seeing it written. Dorothy Blythe, the managing editor at Nimbus, is the one who felt the McDonald's tragedy should be told in book form, and who called to ask me to write it. And although I have been writing professionally for more than thirteen years, it is a Nimbus editor, Liane Heller, who gently guided me in an entirely new craft. Writing news for broadcast is based on conveying information orally, while writing a book is a much more formal process, engaging the eye and the inner ear of a reader's imagination. If this book does not read like an incredibly lengthy newscast, it is because of Liane's professionalism and dedication. I would also like to mention Greg Boone, a colleague and friend for many years. In the months spent preparing this book, he offered support and encouragement bordering on harassment; it helped. Lawrence Bourque is another close friend whose unwavering confidence in my ability to write this book left me believing I could.

There are a number of photographs included here, and for their use I must thank my employer, the Atlantic Television System; most of the photos are prints from ATV video tape. In particular, thanks to Bill Patrick for allowing me to use the tape, and thanks to the camera operators who recorded the shots: Bruce Hennessey, Gary Mansfield, George Reeves, Stuart MacDougall, Sandra Kipis, Cyril Worth, Jim Kvammen, Chris Murphy, Steve Rafuse, and Tom Tynes. I would also like to acknowledge Mike Aitkens, the editor who helped prepare the video tape for recording in still form; and Steve Townsend, who took the photograph of me.

Finally, on a more personal note, I would like to thank my wife, Barbara, for her help and patience as I attempted to juggle two jobs in the preparation of this book. I must also thank our daughter, Barbara Michelle, for sacrificing her "quality time" with Dad; and our son, Paul, for the perspective on the nature of today's adolescents.

One

SHORTLY AFTER MIDNIGHT on Thursday, May 7, 1992, Jimmy Fagan headed out for the last walk of his life. Jimmy did not know that was what he was doing, as he locked the front door of his parents' home and walked down the steps to the sidewalk. His parents didn't know it either, when they went to bed without saying goodnight. Jimmy had been down in the basement watching TV when they retired for the night, after looking in on him to make sure he was still awake to go to work. Not saying goodbye that night was one of the many little things that would haunt them in the difficult months ahead.

Of course Jimmy had every right to expect a normal night at work, and his parents had every right to expect to see their son in the morning. They would see him in about two hours, but he would not be the Jimmy they knew. They would never again see the happy-go-lucky boy they loved so much.

Al and Theresa Fagan had worked hard all their lives to raise and support Jimmy, his five brothers, and his two sisters. Al, who was retired, now had the time to look back on his life—all the years at the Sydney steel plant, and all the weekends when they took off for the cottage in a station wagon loaded with kids. Theresa still worked at a local senior citizens home, but she too enjoyed recalling the memories of a house full of kids, and the couple spent many a happy evening talking over old times. Both were proud of their children and looked forward to years of family gatherings, as the ranks of the Fagan family swelled with sons, and daughters-in-law—and, of course, grandchildren. The old house seemed to come alive when it reverberated with the sounds of children yelling and running, and that was just fine with Al and Theresa. The more, the merrier.

Jimmy had nothing more pressing than the weather on his mind as he walked towards Prince Street, one of Sydney's main thoroughfares.

Jimmy Fagan relaxes in the living room of his parents' home, his irrepressible smile illuminating his dark eyes and strong features. [Print from ATV video tape.]

He didn't even bother looking back at the big white house where he'd shared so much with his family, good times and hard alike. At about five-foot-nine and two hundred pounds, he was stocky and short compared to his brothers, who all edged close to or beyond the six-foot mark. His dark hair, thick eyebrows, and deep-set eyes could have given the twenty-seven-year-old a brooding appearance had it not been for the most dominant feature on his rounded face—his smile. Jimmy had a smile that lit up his entire body, and he was always ready to flash it. He loved life, and it showed. Not that he had much to smile about that night, as he walked along, huddled against a cold, brisk wind. Small piles of snow still clung to the ground beneath the shrubs, trees, and bushes along the way; the arrival of May was no guarantee that a Cape Breton winter was quite ready to surrender to the warmer weeks ahead. Jimmy had a keen interest in the snow and was watching closely each night as the piles got smaller and smaller.

As soon as the last remnants of snow had disappeared for another year, he could say goodbye to the job at McDonald's—and to these midnight strolls—and get back to working outside again, for his brother's landscaping company. It wasn't that Jimmy disliked working at McDonald's; in fact, he really liked it there. For one thing, he was getting a lot more work at the restaurant than he would have by returning to his old job at Zellers. Jimmy had left the department store the previous spring, when his brother offered him the landscaping job—the problem was, landscaping work fell off in the fall, and his brother couldn't afford to keep him on the payroll. Jimmy had complained to the family about the prospect of another winter at the department store; it would be all right until Christmas, but, after that, shifts would be few and far between. It was Marie, his sister-in-law, who came up with the solution; she knew Jimmy wanted to be working full time. Marie was a shift manager at the Sydney River McDonald's, a few kilometres outside the city, and the restaurant needed a back-shift maintenance worker. She would put in a good word for Jimmy if he was interested in the job. It sounded like a good opportunity, but what really sold Jimmy on the idea was that he would not be letting the restaurant down if he quit and went back to landscaping in the spring. Marie told him McDonald's always had a long list of students looking for summer jobs. If Jimmy stayed until the universities let out, he wouldn't be causing a problem by leaving, and she was also fairly certain he could get hired on again in the fall, when the students headed back to school and the landscaping work slowed down again. It was an ideal set-up for Jimmy, who had managed to keep himself working since high school; staying home and collecting unemployment insurance was not something he wanted to get into.

Only a week or so, Jimmy told himself, taking a last glance at the stubborn remains of winter as he continued walking; then he could give his notice at McDonald's and get back to some outdoor daytime work for the short Cape Breton summer. He knew he'd miss some of his new friends at the restaurant, though. Jimmy was quick to make friends; he loved to sit and chat with people, whatever the topic. His father once proudly described Jimmy as someone who never saw ugly people. He just saw people, and he liked them all.

Neil Burroughs, the other night-time maintenance worker at McDonald's, was one of Jimmy's new friends. They enjoyed each other's company on long winter nights, as they got the restaurant ready for the breakfast crew. Fortunately for the two men, their personalities were in sync. The long hours of the back shift can be tough on you, but if the time is spent talking, joking, and sharing the workload with someone you like, well, it doesn't wear on you so much. Jimmy and Neil both enjoyed a good joke or a tall tale, and they exchanged plenty of both as they cleaned, polished, and repaired whatever needed their attention before the customers and morning crew arrived.

Neil was already at the restaurant, working Jimmy's shift. The two maintenance workers had staggered shifts—11:00 p.m. to 7:00 a.m. and 2:00 a.m. to 10:00 a.m. Jimmy was usually on the early shift, but agreed to give it to Neil, who had hurt his back in a car accident a couple of months before. The early shift involved mostly cleaning and light duties; the guy on the second shift did the heavier work. Although he didn't have to be at work for almost two hours, Jimmy always headed to the restaurant early, so he could chat with the early-evening staff for an hour or so, before they went home. He was pretty sure Donna Warren and Arlene MacNeil would still be there when he arrived. Donna was a shift manager like Marie, and Arlene worked the cash counter; the two women were friends and usually left together.

Jimmy stuck his hands deep into his pockets as a blast of cold air from the ice-filled Sydney harbour swept up Prince Street. He decided to stop at Tim Hortons to get a cup of coffee to carry as he walked the rest of the way downtown. The cup would keep his fingers warm, and the coffee would help keep him from getting too tired at work.

As Jimmy waited to order his coffee, his co-workers were busy inside the McDonald's restaurant in Sydney River, a bedroom community on the outskirts of Sydney. Kings Road, the main thoroughfare to and from Sydney, is lined with restaurants, gas stations, and an assortment of other small businesses, of which McDonald's is the farthest from the city. The restaurant is perched on a hill at the point just before Kings Road dips beneath the concrete hulk of the four-lane Sydney bypass and merges with Highway 4, one of two major highways that run the length of Cape Breton Island. It's hard for hungry motorists to miss the restaurant, whether they're driving on Highway 4 or on the newer stretch of the Trans-Canada Highway that links up with the bypass on the north side of Sydney harbour and takes travellers through the centre of Cape Breton, on the northwest side of the Bras d'Or Lakes. Coming in on Highway 4 means driving right by the entrance to the restaurant, while motorists speeding along the bypass need only glance below to see the familiar golden arches.

The restaurant is typical of the single-storey McDonald's design, with its caplike roof, brown brick walls, and large windows and glass doors. The driveway climbs a steep bank to the parking lot, at the rear of the building; beyond the parking area is a field that borders the property and leads to the bypass. Along with the brightly lit glass entrances used by the public, there are two large steel doors. One of them, at the back of the restaurant, opens into the busy kitchen; this door is used by employees. The other, down at the front corner of the building, near the street, is rarely used. Like the employees' entrance, the basement door can only be opened from the inside, and even restaurant workers rarely use it, since they have little occasion to venture into that area of the basement. So there was no reason for anyone to notice, in those early-morning hours of May 7, that the basement door was slightly ajar.

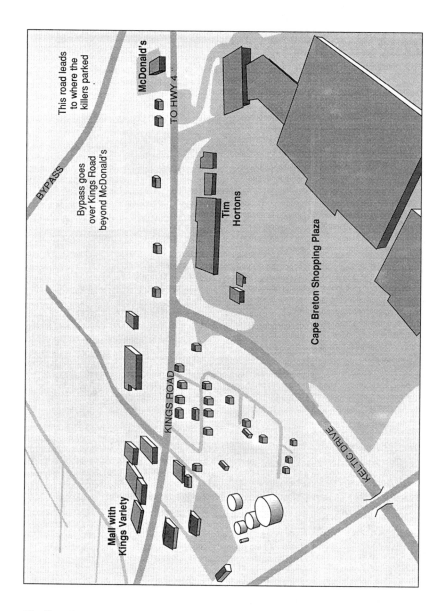

The Kings Road area of Sydney River, near the McDonald's where shooting victims
Arlene MacNeil, Donna Warren, Neil Burroughs, and Jimmy Fagan worked.

Upstairs in the kitchen, Neil Burroughs was chatting with Donna Warren. Donna was in the manager's small office; the door was open, and Neil stood outside, his slim, compact body relaxed as he leaned against the handle of his mop. His thick black hair and moustache accented his smiling eyes and ever-present grin; Neil often saw humour where others did not.

Neil Burroughs celebrates with friends and relatives at a family wedding. The mischievous grin means a friendly quip is not far behind. [Print from ATV video tape.]

"So now I know how you can afford that fancy new car," Neil teased, as Donna looked up from the stacks of bills she was counting out for each daytime worker's float—a cash register insert with compartments for one hundred dollars in various denominations. Preparing the floats and locking them in the safe was one of her last duties before going off shift. "Yep, a loonie here and a quarter there," she said. "You should have seen the look on the salesman's face when I handed him a pillowcase filled with small change."

They both laughed as Neil returned to cleaning the floors. Donna was proud of her new car, a blue Toyota Tercel, and everyone knew it. What they didn't know was how long she had agonized over the purchase, weighing the commitment of a bank loan against her plans to go to law school someday. But the allure of that little car was more than the twenty-two-year-old could resist; besides, Donna had spent years working full time while taking courses she felt would be helpful for her career. In fact, the following week was her high-school graduation—the second one. Although she already had her diploma, Donna had enrolled in the radio and television program at Memorial High School to gain the communications skills she would need in the courtroom when she finally became a defence attorney. It had been a long haul, and she deserved the reward.

These days, Donna was basking in the pride her mother expressed in her accomplishments. Some parents can become impatient with sons or daughters who continually re-evaluate their goals and ambitions—young people who are always looking for more information, more training. But Donna knew her mother would be as proud of her at the graduation ceremony next week as she was the first time Donna "finished" school. Mrs. Warren was as delighted with her daughter's graduation picture as she was with the diploma. Donna, of course, feigned embarrassment every time she looked at the large framed photograph prominently displayed at home, but she secretly agreed with her mom that the picture perfectly conveyed the thoughtful appearance of a future lawyer. In the photo they had chosen from the graduation proofs, Donna's curly brown hair cascades over one shoulder; her chin is raised and her head slightly turned in profile. The look in her eyes, fixed on an object far away from the camera's lens, suggests a determined young woman, preoccupied with something much more important than the photograph for which she is posing. And her soft features add just the right touch of charm.

Donna Warren's Memorial High School graduation photograph shows the purposeful gaze of the lawyer Donna dreamed of becoming. [Print from ATV video tape.]

Downstairs, in the restaurant's basement, Arlene MacNeil was looking for something to do. The attractive twenty-year-old had already punched out on the time clock and changed out of her uniform, but she wouldn't be leaving until Donna was ready. Arlene's last task had been to conduct a stock inventory of the food supplies used on the evening shift and to co-sign the balance sheet for Donna. The inventory had taken less time than usual, because Derek Wood had stayed behind to help her. Wood, a slight young man with dirty-blond hair—still a teenager, really, from the looks of him—was the new cash-counter worker. Arlene hadn't worked with him very often, but she was favourably impressed—it was nice of him to stay after his shift and help her. Even when she was finished, he didn't seem to be in a hurry to leave, Arlene noticed. He had been out in the main restaurant smoking with one of the other cash workers earlier, when she went downstairs. Employees were not allowed to do that, but Donna was a pretty easy manager to work for, and as long as they cleaned the ashtray, she wouldn't complain. Arlene figured the two of them were waiting for a lift.

Well, if the new guy could put in some extra time helping her, she'd return the favour by doing some work for the morning crew. There was going to be a child's birthday party in the restaurant the following morning, so Arlene decided to help get a few things ready while she waited for Donna. As she sorted out the party favours, a gentle smile illuminated her fine-boned face, framed by long, dark curls.

In downtown Sydney, meanwhile, Daniel MacVicar sat behind the wheel of his City Wide taxi. He'd been driving a cab in Sydney for three years now, and liked the freedom the job offered. The tall, thin cabby looked a bit like a teenager whose body had grown too fast and whose co-ordination had not quite made the adjustment. Things were different behind the wheel of a cab, though. His height wasn't an issue, and fares rarely expected much more from him than a quick ride and occasional advice on where to enjoy an evening out.

MacVicar was waiting to hear the 1:00 a.m. news on the car radio as he parked outside the spot he usually recommended to visitors— Smooth Herman's Cabaret. The cabaret licence allowed Smooth Herman's to remain open until three in the morning, making it Sydney's late-night hot spot of choice. In two hours the big spenders would pour out, looking for a drive home; until then MacVicar and the other drivers parked nearby would wait for a radio call or for someone to decide to go home before last call. Maybe he'd get an out-of-town fare and make a few extra bucks on an otherwise slow night. MacVicar was tapping his fingers on the steering wheel and thinking about going for a coffee when the rear door of the cab opened and someone jumped in.

"Hi. Can you take me out to McDonald's in Sydney River?"

"Yeah, sure." MacVicar recognized the fare as a McDonald's employee he'd picked up once or twice before.

"Sure is cold out there," Jimmy Fagan offered.

"Typical Cape Breton spring. I hear it's going to warm up by August, though," MacVicar said, pulling the car out of the parking lot for the short drive to Sydney River. There wasn't much traffic early on a Thursday morning, and the car made good time. As they drove, the two men chatted about sports. Jimmy liked to talk about hockey—not that he followed the game as fanatically as many people did, but he knew enough to get others talking on the subject, and that was fine by him.

Back at McDonald's, Donna Warren was finishing the receipts and preparing the morning cash drawers. She put everything in the safe and locked it. As she stepped out of the office, she looked around the kitchen for Arlene. Walking around the large propane grills, she found Neil working near the sinks.

"Neil, did you see where Arlene went?"

"She went downstairs after she punched out, and I didn't see her come up since."

"Thanks. Oh, look—you missed a spot." Neil turned to look at the sink he was cleaning before he realized Donna was only kidding. She laughed and punched her own code on the time clock before going downstairs to find her friend.

Donna Warren's friend and co-worker at McDonald's, Arlene MacNeil, also graduated from Memorial High School in Sydney Mines. [Print from ATV video tape.]

Arlene was counting long, colourful wooden sticks that would later have Ronald McDonald balloons tied to the tops. The balloons weren't inflated yet, but Arlene was getting enough sticks out for the kids who would attend the party in a few hours. She looked up as Donna walked into the room.

"All done?" she asked.

"Yeah, what are you doing?'

"Just getting a few things ready for the party tomorrow."

"Well, now, aren't you the dedicated employee." Donna glanced at her watch. "The morning crew can handle that. Let's get going."

"O.K. Let me put these sticks out in the crew room so everyone will remember to get them ready before the kids come."

The two friends were in a small office at the rear of the basement, behind the larger room used by the owner, Garfield Lewis. Along the wide hallway outside was a row of green filing cabinets, and a washer and dryer, for employees who did not like to take their uniforms home for cleaning. It was difficult to talk in the area because of the mechanical hum from the huge compressor used to mix syrup and water and pump it to the pop fountain in the restaurant above. Card-board boxes containing heavy bags of syrup were spread out in front of the machine, plastic hoses reaching from each box to carry the coloured fluids into the mixing unit. The whole setup looked like some weird organism from a cheap sci-fi movie. Towards the front of the basement were the crew locker and change rooms, washrooms, a break room, and a large storage area. Beside the storage room was an of-fice used by Lewis's wife, Shirley, who ran her own business from the restaurant; and at the very front of the building was a large room where new employees were welcomed into the McDonald's "family" and received their initial training. Lewis, who owned two other McDonald's restaurants in the Sydney area, liked to consider his employees part of an extended family. About forty full- and part-time workers depended on the Sydney River restaurant for employment; many had been with the company for years, some for more than a decade. Their loyalty was more a comment on the economic conditions in Cape Breton than a testament to what a wonderful place McDonald's was to work.

• • •

"IN MAY 1992, unemployment levels on Cape Breton Island were in the midst of a steady climb that would see them approach 30 per cent. The island, once a prosperous industrial centre, had long before begun a steady decline that would see it become one of Canada's most-depressed economic regions. Don Cameron, premier of Nova Scotia in 1992, referred to the island as "a have-not region in a have-not province." The slide into joblessness and economic uncertainty had not been a quiet evolution. Successive federal and provincial governments had championed economic renewal initiatives aimed at leading Cape Breton away from its historic dependence on failed or failing resource-based industries. None of the programs had succeeded in doing much more than create a minor bump in the steady downward slide. For many Cape Bretoners, life had become a never-ending cycle of short-term work ending in unemployment insurance coverage. Just when their unemployment premiums came close to being exhausted, yet another program would surface, offering yet another temporary job. For many caught in the cycle, planning for the future was as futile as trying to predict it.

An unfortunate side effect of all the political grandstanding on the latest quick fix to the island's economic woes was a general acceptance that the government was responsible for turning things around—not an attitude conducive to the entrepreneurial spirit that local business leaders upheld as the real solution to the economic free-fall. Cape Breton business owners had watched in frustration as millions of tax dollars were thrown at imported solutions. Investors with grand schemes for employing hundreds of Cape Bretoners were given grants, loans, and incentives to build factories on the island, only to leave as soon as the government largesse dried up. The people of North Sydney still have bitter memories of the Ontario-based pro-moter who introduced Cape Breton Chemicals to their community. Hundreds attended a meeting announcing the creation of the plant, listened to promises of hundreds of jobs, and eagerly awaited the opening of the new factory. But government aid was not enough to keep the plastic food-wrap business going; not long after it opened, Cape Breton Chemicals joined the list of failed ventures. Industrial Cape Breton was hard hit by all these plant closings; there were enough oversized vacant buildings in and around the area to make a Hollywood producer in search of sound-stage space jump for joy.

Industrial Cape Breton is a group of small municipalities scattered along the shores of Sydney harbour; Sydney, the only city, is on the south side of the harbour, at its inner limits. On the opposite shore, the towns of North Sydney and Sydney Mines mark the harbour en-trance. Many of the buildings left abandoned in the economic fallout are located in an industrial park between these two small communi-ties. On the south side of the harbour entrance stands the mining town of New Waterford, and two smaller, more-rural communities—New Victoria and South Bar—extend along the harbour between New Waterford and Sydney. Out beyond New Waterford, around the coast to the south, lies the mining town of Glace Bay, and farther down the side of Cape Breton is the historic town of Louisbourg, with its fa-mous reconstructed eighteenth-century fortress.

Towards the end of the 1980s, governments began to pay lip ser-vice at least to claims from Cape Breton–based investors that *their* ideas and businesses should be the basis for economic renewal. It did, after all, make more sense to bet on an investor who lived in the com-munity and planned to stay there, than one who was parachuted in from southern Ontario, where he would quickly return when things went wrong. The problem was, politicians liked announcing multi-million-dollar initiatives that would employ hundreds; the media wouldn't listen to a government announcement of assistance to a company already operating—especially if the company only planned to hire two or three more people. Supporting small business might improve the economy in the long term, but it didn't generate votes. One of the local investors who did make it in Industrial Cape Breton is Lou Whalen of Glace Bay; he received government support for his plan to make pre-formed cultured-marble bathroom fixtures and counter-tops. His company, Marble-Waye, remains a successful business; it doesn't employ the hundreds of people promised jobs by some of the Ontario investors, but the jobs it created are still there.

The painful and often failed efforts to revive the island's slowly dying economy did have some positive effects on the people living there: the adversity drew them even more closely together. In Cape Breton the people and communities are closely knit, and Cape Bretoners have never been too busy to lend a helping hand when it is needed. There was also a renewed strength and pride born from continued hardship. Cape Bretoners have always been fiercely proud people, first because of the tough times they faced, working in coal mines or eking out a living from the sea, and later because of the struggle to find alternatives as the old jobs disappeared. For a whole generation growing up in Cape Breton, the future meant leaving home for more-prosperous regions, while those who did not want to leave took what jobs they could get. In a difficult economic environment, a fast-food chain offered a steady, reliable income—not a lot of money, but better than jumping from one government grant to another in the hope that a permanent job would materialize before you ran out of luck and unemployment insurance.

The employees working overnight at McDonald's in Sydney River had a variety of reasons for being there. For Arlene MacNeil, McDonald's was a place to earn enough money to go to university, where she hoped to get a degree, maybe in business administration. Donna Warren's job would eventually pay the tuition for law school in Halifax. Jimmy Fagan felt the restaurant was his best chance to keep working year-round in an area where many people couldn't even secure seasonal work. As for Neil Burroughs, he was probably going to be at the restaurant the longest. The twenty-nine-year-old relied on McDonald's to help support his wife and child. The pay at McDonald's didn't provide many luxuries for Neil, his wife, Julia, and their son, Justin; but his pay, combined with Julia's income from a hairdressing job, kept the family going. And they were living where they wanted to— at home, close to their parents, siblings, and friends.

Derek Wood, the new McDonald's employee, had also been raised in the economic disparity of Cape Breton, but he did not have the same kinds of long-term plans or goals. Wood spent the early years of his childhood in the Whitney Pier area of Sydney. His parents' marriage broke up, and his mother later moved to British Columbia, but Wood led a pretty normal childhood nevertheless. Derek's dad worked in the meat department at the Sobeys supermarket in the

Cape Breton Shopping Plaza, across Kings Road and down the hill from the Sydney River McDonald's, while Derek—like dozens of other kids—went to school and developed keen interests in computers, video games, and the latest in pop music.

"The Pier," as Derek's childhood community is known in Sydney, grew quickly at the turn of the century, as immigrant workers flocked there, drawn to jobs at the huge steel mill that dominated the neighbourhood's landscape. Most of the steel plant jobs are long gone; at one time, thousand workers at the plant, but by 1992 only about seven hundred people could call themselves steelworkers. Many of the descendants of those immigrant steelworkers still live in the Pier, which is also home to Atlantic Canada's largest Ukrainian community as well as large Polish and Black neighbourhoods.

The Pier is separated from the rest of Sydney by a small overpass that rises above the railway tracks linking the steel mill to the rich Cape Breton coalfields, once a ready supply of the raw material needed in the steel-making process. The tracks are usually empty now; modernization has moved the steel plant away from the old process, and scrap metal has replaced raw iron as the key ingredient, eliminating the need for coal. But the overpass remains—once a means to allow traffic to flow, uninterrupted by the flow of coal cars, it continues to provide a clear physical break between the Pier and the rest of Sydney. Kids growing up in the Pier often find themselves on the defensive when they head "over town" to high school, perhaps because of the perception of the area as the "wrong side of the tracks." For many Pier teens, the attitude that they are worth less than their counterparts from the "finer" neighbourhoods is a daunting, if ill-founded, reality. As an extension of this insecurity, many teens cling to the other Pier myth; that kids from there are tougher than kids from across the overpass.

The Whitney Pier stamp appeared to be part of Derek Wood's personality, even after he moved away, while he was still in elementary school. Classmates remember Wood as being quiet, sullen, and awkward in his new surroundings. They say he was quickly singled out by bullies looking for an easy target. This shy, self-deprecating awkwardness remained the prominent feature of Derek Wood's personality, even at the age of eighteen, when the high-school dropout began working at the Sydney River McDonald's. His co-workers there described him as nice enough, but too strange to fit in with the rest of the crowd. One time, when a fellow employee had his apartment robbed,

Wood piped up, claiming to have friends that could "take care" of those responsible. The other man laughed off the offer, dismissing it as an attempt to gain points for himself in his new environment.

His fellow workers couldn't have guessed that Wood, unlike the other McDonald's employees, might have felt his life was out of control. About a year before, while training with the Cape Breton Militia District, Wood became highly intoxicated on a weekend outing, and began talking about ending his life—there were lots of weapons around, and it would be easy. He was reported, and senior officers investigated. Wood dismissed the episode, saying he was just drunk and talking stupid; it didn't mean anything. Still, the militia commanders decided to send him home before his training was complete. On other occasions, in telephone conversations with girls from his school, the teenager often complained about his life and his general unhappiness. Like his co-worker at McDonald's, and like Wood himself, one of these friends dismissed his talk; it sounded to her like typical teenage angst. Another kid not happy with his lot.

Not that he seemed to have much reason for this attitude. Wood had strong family ties in Industrial Cape Breton. His father, who later remarried, lived near Sydney with his wife and daughter; Derek's brother had an apartment outside the city; and Mike Campbell, his cousin and close friend, lived with his parents on a small lane in the Hardwood Hill area. Derek often stayed at Mike's house, although he occasionally went to his brother's, or even his father's. He didn't particularly like his stepmother, but he adored his baby sister and welcomed any opportunity to spend time with her. Still, Derek Wood had not yet earned enough to provide his own private space—not an apartment, not even a small room he could call his own. Almost nineteen, he did have a job, but no real future. Perhaps if he worked a little longer, a little harder, he could make that happen.

Donna and Arlene were not thinking about why they were working at McDonald's, or what they planned for the future, as they walked out of the rear office that morning. They were just thinking about driving home. Both girls lived on the north side of Sydney harbour, Donna in the town of North Sydney and Arlene a little farther away, in the community of Bras d'Or. When they worked night shifts, the two young women liked to set out for home together. They did not share a car, but instead drove one behind the other until they reached the North Sydney turn-off, at which point Arlene would travel the rest of the way alone. They felt safer driving the dark highway that way, and their parents liked knowing that car trouble would not leave either of them stranded. Although Cape Breton was still considered a safe place, where people helped each other, this concern was natural for attractive young women like Donna and Arlene.

As the two friends were getting ready to go home, Derek Wood was still at McDonald's, making a call to the pay phone in front of the Tim Hortons in the shopping plaza across the street, the same plaza where his dad worked during the day. But nobody was answering. He knew his friends Darren Muise and Freeman MacNeil would be there, waiting in front of the phone booth, so he figured the problem had to be with the phone itself. Wood decided to head down to Tim Hortons to see what was going on.

TWO

NOTHING ABOUT DARREN MUISE or Freeman MacNeil suggested to their friends or family that they were capable of extreme violence. At eighteen, Muise had just dropped out of high school, in February. His thick, curly black hair, good looks, and athletic prowess made him popular with the young people he knew in Sydney. The problem was, he either didn't know he was well liked, or didn't feel it was enough. He craved attention and went out of his way to get it. The youngest of four boys, Muise always seemed to be trying to prove that he was as good as everyone else. He felt he came from a tough background, but while there was not a lot of money to go around at home, he had had a very fortunate upbringing; he was loved and supported by his parents and other relatives, who hoped he might return to school someday, or perhaps go into business with his dad, who had wanted for some time to work for himself and possibly with his sons.

Like Muise, and like many young adults with no special skills or education, MacNeil was still hanging around Sydney with no real direction in his life. It hadn't always been that way. MacNeil had finished high school, and even spent a year at the Nova Scotia Teachers College; he worked briefly at Malcolm Munroe Junior High as a student teacher, and the students and faculty liked him a great deal. But MacNeil had given up on that ambition, and worked for a while as a private security officer in Halifax and Sydney. The work was not steady enough to keep him from drifting into a new, dangerous friendship—with Muise and with Derek Wood. The youngest in his family, Freeman had been raised by his mother and sisters after his father committed suicide while Freeman was a child. Now, at twenty-three, instead of spending his time making the kinds of decisions that could guide him towards a secure future, he was living an aimless existence, hanging out late at night in coffee shops, talking with other young adults who, like him, were unsure of what they were going to do with their lives. Darren Muise was one of these young people; he and MacNeil had acquaintances in common, and they soon met. As for Derek Wood, he and Muise had known each other ever since Wood moved away from the Pier and ended up attending the same school as Muise, in the Hardwood Hill area of Sydney. Restless energy and late-night conversation brought the three together.

In part perhaps out of a sense that there was nothing to lose, and in part perhaps out of the gnawing knowledge that they were headed nowhere at a time in their lives when they should have been embarking on careers or at least working towards something, the three decided to shun convention and take what they could get without earning it. If the economy of Cape Breton stood in the way of getting what they wanted, then a life of crime might deliver it.

The idea of robbing the McDonald's restaurant had evolved over the winter and early spring. In early March, shortly after he started his job at McDonald's, Derek Wood was working the day shift when he made a discovery that would form an integral part of the plan to rob the restaurant. Deliveries to the restaurant are usually made at the employees' entrance, at the back of the building; the trucks are unloaded and cartons carried to a conveyor belt that runs from the kitchen to the basement, where the stock is stored until needed. One day, the conveyor system broke down, and Wood and a co-worker were asked to go down to the basement and open the black steel door outside the crew training room. It would be easier to carry the stock through that room and into the storage area than to lug it down the basement stairs. As Wood walked out that basement door for the first time, and found himself standing at the bottom of the driveway, the beginnings of a plan came to life.

Wood floated the idea of robbing McDonald's to MacNeil and Muise, and they seemed game. The three convinced themselves that as much as $200,000 could be sitting in the old black safe in the upstairs office. All they had to do was get inside the building, and Wood's discovery was the answer to that dilemma—he would just leave the basement door open, and they could slip inside, unnoticed by anyone in the kitchen. Nobody ever used that door unless the conveyor belt broke down. The door also presented a problem, however. If they could get in that way, then employees could run out the same way during the robbery. The trio decided they needed a fourth person in order to make the job foolproof. Freeman MacNeil would drive the car and be ready for a quick escape; Derek Wood was to be responsible for opening the basement door and letting Darren Muise inside. The fourth robber would remain at the door, and if people tried to escape, he could club them into unconsciousness.

It was strange that clubbing innocent people was seen as part of the initial plan. Wood, MacNeil, and Muise had not been particularly violent young adults, but now they were clearly willing to use force. Both Muise and MacNeil had considerable martial-arts skills; but only MacNeil had any history of physical confrontation. He had been convicted and given a discharge after charges were brought against him when he pushed another youth outside Riverview Rural High School. MacNeil had a reputation among some students as a bit of a bully. He was big and strong—over six feet tall and about two hundred pounds—and he liked to show it. But even the smaller students whom he would hang upside down by their ankles did not think he was anything more than a schoolyard bully with a stupid sense of humour.

As they drove around Sydney in late April 1992, the three hoped violence wouldn't be necessary but felt they'd better take precautions. MacNeil decided he would take a gun from his girlfriend Michelle's father—a .22-calibre pistol, kept in a top dresser drawer in his room. It wouldn't be missed. MacNeil had even practised with the gun one time, on a secluded beach. He and two friends were out on a Sunday afternoon, and Freeman took the gun from the trunk of the car and fired seven shots at some bottles he had placed a few metres away. He missed with all seven shots. But the gun wasn't going to be necessary, anyway. If the robbery went according to plan, the real weapons would be Darren Muise's fists and feet. Muise had a black belt in tae kwon do and had achieved notable success in tournaments; he even taught the sport to children. Freeman MacNeil also had more than modest skills as a martial artist—he claimed to have broken an opponent's arm during a judo tournament—but in the early planning he was going to be the wheel man. MacNeil's size probably made him a better choice as the "enforcer," but he was the only one with access to a car. Muise would wear a Hallowe'en mask, and once inside the basement he would subdue any employees up in the kitchen. Once they were out of the way, Derek Wood could run upstairs and open the safe. He thought he knew most of the combination, and if he didn't, well, Muise could always force the shift manager to open the safe.

The trio had set out to commit the robbery on April 30, but the fourth participant, whom they'd asked to guard the basement door, did not show up. They quickly retreated to the coffee shop where they'd done much of their planning, and MacNeil tried to recruit a potential replacement. But their candidate wasn't interested, so the job was postponed for a week. And they would go ahead with or without a guard at the outside entrance.

At about seven-thirty on the evening of May 6, Freeman MacNeil drove Derek Wood to work. Before he entered the restaurant, Wood took the tiny silver .22-calibre pistol from MacNeil and grabbed a handful of ammunition. He stuffed the bullets and the weapon into the black-leather pouch he wore around his waist, and went inside. Down in the crew changing-room in the basement, Wood took off his street clothes and pulled on his McDonald's uniform. Then he put his clothes and the leather pouch into his brown canvas knapsack and headed up to work.

A few hours later, MacNeil picked up Muise at a local pool hall. The two parked on a side street near Sydney harbour, where they put on a second set of clothing over their street clothes. These outer layers would later be discarded; that way, any fibres left behind at the scene—or anything their clothing picked up while they were in the restaurant—could not be traced back to them. The would-be robbers expected to find between $80,000 and $200,000 in the safe, and they knew there would be an intense investigation when the job was done. After changing, they drove to the Tim Hortons in the Sydney River shopping plaza. As they parked in front of the coffee shop, the two could see McDonald's, just up the hill.

In the basement of the restaurant, Derek Wood took his knapsack and jammed it against the frame of the door that led to the black steel door on the outside wall; if the inner door closed, it would lock. After helping Arlene MacNeil with the inventory, Wood had gone to the crew room and changed out of his McDonald's uniform, which he stuffed into the knapsack, retrieving his leather pouch. With the inner entrance safely propped open, Wood closed the outside door almost all the way, leaving just enough space to allow him to grab an edge and pull it open when he returned.

Then he headed over to Tim Hortons. He jumped into the brown-and beige Chevy Impala and confronted Muise and MacNeil; he had tried calling them—why hadn't they answered? Apparently they hadn't heard the pay phone ringing. Well, they would go ahead anyway; after all, Wood had left the door open, so they could still get inside. Freeman MacNeil would play a more active role; he would go inside

Derek Wood, Darren Muise, and Freeman MacNeil made their way to this basement door, stepped inside, and closed it behind them. [RCMP crime scene photo.]

and guard the basement door while Muise went up to the kitchen and Wood waited for the all-clear to try the safe. The young men drove away from Tim Hortons and onto Kings Road, past the front of McDonald's and underneath the Sydney bypass. On the other side of the bypass, they entered a residential area and turned onto a dirt road, following it almost to the end, where it intersected with a secluded gravel road. There, the robbers stepped out into the night; they were at the corner of Britannia Street and Sheridan Drive. In front of them, across the bypass, was their target. The three walked across the field beside the highway, aglow in deep yellow light, then hustled across the brightly illuminated four lanes to the field on the other side—the one bordering the McDonald's property. They moved quietly towards the building, approaching the side away from the driveway, then made their way down to the front corner, where the basement door, still slightly ajar, awaited them. They stepped into the building and pulled the door shut behind them.

Meanwhile, Arlene MacNeil and Donna Warren were getting ready to leave the basement office where Arlene had been sorting the children's party favours.

Once the robbers had closed the basement door, they found themselves in a dark, windowless little porch outside the crew training room. The cement floor was covered with dirt and leaves that had blown in beneath the door. They groped their way to the inner door, still propped open by Wood's knapsack. Before entering the training room with his accomplices, Wood took the small silver handgun out of the pouch around his waist. Muise pulled a rubber Hallowe'en mask over his head and took two knives from a sheath on his ankle.

The mask was in the likeness of a ghoulish, white-haired old man with horribly distorted features. Freeman MacNeil held a shovel handle, in case he had to knock anyone out, and there were ropes in his pockets to tie them up afterwards. All three wore dark clothing. They crept into the crew room, allowing the door to swing shut behind them but failing to notice that the door did not close fully. Instead, it came to rest again on the beige knapsack Wood had placed in the threshold. The pack had a label sewn into its seam: ESCAPE.

Donna and Arlene were on their way out when they stopped suddenly at the sight of the three men creeping towards them. The men, too, came to a standstill as they realized they were not alone. Donna's heart pounded when she saw the Hallowe'en mask; she was prepared to open and empty the safe if they asked. Long ago, she had promised her mother that if anyone tried to rob the restaurant while she was on shift, she would gladly cooperate in order to avoid any trouble. She used to joke that she'd even carry the safe out to the car for them. Donna knew that resisting a robber could cause problems, not only for her, but also for Arlene and Neil, and as the manager, she felt responsible. But her fear turned to confusion when she recognized the small, sullen-faced blond man. Derek Wood was making no attempt to hide himself; he just stood there, looking first at her and then at the two men he was with.

Arlene, like Donna, quickly ruled out robbery when she realized the man was Derek Wood. As for the idiot in the Hallowe'en mask, he was obviously someone who thought scaring people was a funny thing to do. Arlene was angry at having been frightened, but she didn't want to show these three jerks that they'd succeeded in making her heart pop out of her chest. Donna would have to do something, she thought; the restaurant was closed, and Derek had no right bringing people inside, joke or no joke. She decided to lighten the moment.

"Is this a joke or what?" And she laughed.

It was the last time Arlene MacNeil's agile young mind would so quickly assess a situation and draw a reasonable conclusion—a conclusion that in this case could not have been further from the terrifying reality of what was about to happen. This was no joke.

"What's going on?" Donna demanded.

Derek Wood exchanged a long look with his partners. During the countless hours of discussing their options, a certain amount of macho bravado had emerged: Darren Muise claimed he would use his share of the haul to fly to Vancouver, where he had lined up a job running drugs for the Hell's Angels motorcycle gang; Freeman MacNeil showed his seriousness about the plan by obtaining the gun. Although their talk may have been nothing more than bravado—three young men trying to outdo each other as they dug themselves deeper and deeper into a plot they were, in fact, ill-equipped to carry out—at the moment when Derek Wood looked at his partners, he decided he was involved in a big-time score with big-time criminals. And he would not be the weak link.

As his partners looked down, Wood turned to the young women and raised his arm. Arlene saw the arm come up and saw the bright flash, but she did not feel or hear anything. She knew Donna was still beside her; she could see her friend's shoes as the floor came rushing up in a crazy, tilting dream. Arlene had fallen face down, her hand still clasped around the sticks she had been counting for the child's birthday party that was supposed to be held later that day. Donna crouched on the floor beside her friend, confusion filling her mind. "My God, Arlene, we're going to die!" she screamed, putting her face close to her friend's ear. "They're going to kill us!" She could see blood beginning to pool on the floor near Arlene's face, but her friend was

Donna and Arlene came through the open door to face the killers. The colourful sticks
Arlene had been counting were still in her hand when she fell, face forward.
[RCMP crime scene photo,]

breathing; she was still alive. Donna looked up to see the masked man standing over her, gesturing with a knife and screaming at her to stay there. She wanted to help Arlene, but all she could do was cry. Donna wanted her mother, she wanted her bed, she wanted her cat; she did not want to be lying on the floor watching blood pour from a tiny hole beside her friend's nose. Donna Warren's mind went wild with panic, but she could not move.

"Hurry up!" Freeman Mac-Neil yelled at Wood.

Derek Wood ran upstairs.

Up in the kitchen, Neil Bur-roughs was scrubbing the sinks. Because the steel door at the bottom of the basement stairs was closed, and because there

The stairs up to the kitchen: the conveyor belt to the right is the one that broke down shortly after Derek Wood started his job, prompting the plan to rob McDonald's. [RCMP crime scene photo.]

was a lot of noise from the equipment in the restaurant, he couldn't have heard the shot, or the screams from the basement. Burroughs was down on one knee, wiping the stainless-steel skirt below the sinks, when he suddenly felt weak and fell to the floor. Something was wrong, but he could not figure out what had happened. Blood was coming from his ear, and there was a terrible taste in his mouth. He could see the blood beginning to pool on the floor, and knew he needed help.

As he began to push himself up from the floor, Neil realized someone was standing beside him: shocked and confused, he did not see the mask the man was wearing as a threat. Neil Burroughs wanted help—he *needed* help—and he hoped this stranger would de-liver it. He looked into Darren Muise's eyes, and Muise stared back at the helpless man in front of him. Burroughs sought sympathy, and help, but instead he saw, in those eyes, a frightening expression heightened by the ghoulish rubber mask that framed them. Muise took a brown-handled hunting knife and plunged it five centimetres into the soft tissue on the left side of Burroughs' neck, then pulled it back in a clumsy, failed attempt to severe the jugular vein.

Face down on the cold tile, blood streaming from his ear and neck, Neil Burroughs began to think of Justin, his three-year-old son, and Julia, his wife and best friend. He was going to teach Justin to play ball this summer; whatever was going on here would not prevent him from doing that. Once again, Burroughs pushed himself up from the floor. In the spinning confusion around him, he now saw two men. Maybe this new stranger would understand; maybe he would help.

"Help me! Please help me!" Burroughs could not be sure if the words were coming out, if the tall stranger could hear his plea. He could see his blood covering the arms of the masked man, who was still standing there; he could hear as the man shouted excitedly to the newcomer: "The guy won't die! Derek shot him, and I cut his throat, and he still won't die!" The masked man ran off, and Burroughs again begged: "Please, please help me!"

It made no sense. He could see that the stranger was listening, but why was he raising that shovel handle? The young father was kneeling now, looking into the face of the stranger, trying to understand what was happening to him. Why did someone he did not know want to hurt him? He was just cleaning the kitchen, doing his job, trying to support Justin and Julia. Why was this happening? Neil felt a crushing blow across his forehead and against his nose as the handle swung violently down. Freeman MacNeil looked on as Burroughs fell to the floor once again.

But his misery would not end with that vicious blow. Nor would the struggle. Unable to lift his head, Burroughs extended a pleading hand for help; he could feel the steel front of the sink, but it was too slippery for him to pull himself up. As the strength ebbed from his body, Burroughs felt something in his left hand, and he grabbed hold of it—something solid, something to cling to. It was one of the legs holding up the sink. He looked up to see a flash, then darkness, as a bullet entered his brain through a small hole just above his right eye. He did not feel the third and final shot, fired with the gun pressed firmly against the back of his head.

While Neil Burroughs was fighting in vain for his life, Donna Warren was experiencing a terrifying ordeal of her own. After shooting Burroughs in the ear, Derek Wood had returned downstairs to find the young manager. "C'mon, bitch, get up." Wood grabbed Donna, led her upstairs to the tiny office, and ordered her to open the safe.

Donna's hands shook, tears blurring her vision as she wrestled with the dial. "I'm going as fast as I can." She wept, gasping for air, trying to remember a combination that she knew perfectly well. Finally the last number clicked in, and the door swung open. Donna, who had been kneeling as she fought with her panic and the lock, rose to her feet, hoping that Derek would let her go back to help Arlene, and crying uncontrollably as she thought of her friend.

Suddenly she felt a terrible pain and a spinning in her mind; barely aware that she had collapsed, she found herself on the floor, the top of her shoulders against the wall, her legs folded beneath her, her head tilted forward as she watched Derek Wood rifle the safe. Everything around her began to close in, as though she were looking through a narrowing tunnel. The masked man came to the door and gave Wood a kitbag, then left. She saw Wood get to his feet. A flash— and then a bullet entered her right eye; Donna never realized she had already been shot in the back of the head.

The 1:00 a.m. news had just ended as Daniel MacVicar turned his cab into the driveway, drove up the ramp, and parked just past the drive-through window, where he knew the employees' entrance was

Neil Burroughs was cleaning the sinks at the back of the kitchen when he was attacked.
[RCMP crime scene photo.]

located. Jimmy Fagan grabbed his light blue Canada Games kitbag and opened the door. He handed MacVicar the fare and said goodnight, swinging the door behind him. As Jimmy turned to walk away, he realized the door had not shut properly, and it was not in his nature to ignore it. He stepped back to the car and closed the door properly, waving to MacVicar again as he turned towards the restaurant. McDonald's employees who arrive after the restaurant is closed can only gain entrance if someone inside opens the large brown door at the back corner of the building; like the black steel door at the front corner of the building, the rear door cannot be opened from the outside. Jimmy rang the buzzer and turned to watch the cab drive away, noticing that Arlene's and Donna's cars were still in the lot, along with Neil's. He'd have someone to chat with.

At that moment, Derek Wood came out of the upstairs office, carrying a kitbag, a plastic bag, and a metal cash box from the safe. He headed for the door, calling to Muise and MacNeil: "I'm gettin' outta here. Let's go." MacNeil wanted to go downstairs to check on Arlene—she might be alive; she had been breathing when he left her—but Wood argued that it was time to get out. He grabbed the door handle and swung open the door.

Jimmy Fagan turned as he heard the door open. At first he was startled—he'd expected to see Neil, Donna, or Arlene—but he relaxed when he recognized the new employee, whom he'd met a couple of times when Wood worked the morning shift.

"Hi, guys." Jimmy's smile turned to a puzzled frown as he heard someone say, "Shoot him!" Jimmy saw the muzzle flash after the bullet left the barrel. The bullet entered his brain through his forehead, and all his motor control ceased; there was not even enough reflex action left in his body for him to reach out and break his fall. Jimmy Fagan's face hit the tiled kitchen floor hard, and his legs remained outstretched in the doorway, preventing the big door from swinging shut. He did not feel the door hit him, nor did he see his attackers jump over his body and run into the darkness.

As Daniel MacVicar drove down the ramp to Kings Road, he heard what he thought was a firecracker. Glancing back at the restaurant as the car moved forward, he saw two figures run out of the restaurant, carrying kitbags. He wondered it they were workers leaving—maybe they needed a taxi—but instead they headed in the opposite direction, into the field at the edge of the parking lot. Before he could get a good look at them, the car rolled past the corner of the building, and they were gone from sight. On reflection, MacVicar felt something might be wrong, so he stopped the cab and, putting it in reverse, floored the accelerator in the hopes that the screeching tires would get someone's attention inside. He stopped as he cleared the side of the building, but no-one came to see what all the noise was about. Putting the car in drive, MacVicar turned back towards the drive-through service window and the employees' door. As he moved past the window, he saw Jimmy Fagan in the doorway.

MacVicar grabbed his radio mike. "Dispatch, I heard a shot and my passenger's hurt or something. You'd better get the RCMP and an ambulance out to the McDonald's in Sydney River." Another driver answered: "Is your passenger O.K.? Can you check him?" MacVicar was about to park when another voice came crackling over the radio: "Danny, don't get out of your car. Keep moving and don't let anyone in until we get there." It was one of several taxi drivers speeding towards Sydney River.

The taxi dispatcher quickly called the RCMP and then Curry's ambulance station, where attendants George Kolezar and Wayne Fitzgerald were relaxing and hoping for a quiet shift. When the call came in, the two rushed to their ambulance and sped to Sydney River; with the aid of their lights and the almost-empty roads, they made the trip in less than five minutes.

It may have seemed a quick run to the ambulance attendants, but time slowed and panic built as Daniel MacVicar circled around and around the McDonald's parking lot, the doors locked, praying that help would come soon. Little did he know how close he came to encountering the gunmen he feared.

About twenty metres away, panic was also building in the minds of Freeman MacNeil, Darren Muise, and Derek Wood as they ran blindly through the field beside the restaurant and towards the Sydney bypass. The three stopped at the edge of the highway, then darted across, into the safety of the darkness on the other side. They plunged into a field, crushing the ice that covered a small brook in the field as they ran uphill, towards the dirt road. The kitbag containing the money struck Derek Wood's leg as his feet pounded the gravel. Finally they could see the two-tone Chevy Impala parked in the darkness where they had left it only a short time before. The few homes in the area were still; the residents were fast asleep as the men ran to the car.

MacNeil decided to get rid of the bloodied shovel handle he had used to club Neil Burroughs, so he ran down into the ditch beside the car and hurled the handle lengthwise into the culvert that ran beneath the street. Then he clambered back up to the car and jumped in behind the wheel. Darren Muise was on the passenger's side in front; Derek Wood was in back with the bags. Through the windshield, they could see the top of the large golden *M* outside the restaurant.

three

MACNEIL STARTED the car and drove towards Highway 4, while Darren Muise crammed his mask and blood-soaked gloves into a duffel bag he grabbed from the floor behind the seat, then began taking off the extra set of clothing he had worn over his street clothes. "I finally got to slit someone's throat," Muise bragged, as though it had been a lifelong ambition. It was a

strange comment, coming from someone who had made it clear to his oldest friend only a few months before that he was not into violence. Muise and his friend were out on the town when they encountered a group of teens who had roughed up the friend a week earlier. The friend saw a chance to even the score, knowing Muise's martial-arts skills would give him the upper hand. But Muise declined, saying he preferred to do his fighting in a gym.

As the big Impala sped away from the dark gravel road, Derek Wood removed his gloves. It was less than an hour since Wood had volunteered to help Arlene with the inventory; now

The inner door to the basement storage area at McDonald's, with Derek Wood's backpack still propping it open. [RCMP crime scene photo.]

she lay on the floor in the restaurant basement, the victim of a bullet he had fired. A sudden sickening realization hit Wood, but it was not a sense of guilt or remorse. "My fuckin' bag! We left my fuckin' bag in the door downstairs—we gotta go back." Ironically, the backpack marked ESCAPE was now standing in the way of a clean getaway.

The three headed back to the restaurant; they could get the backpack and, at the same time, go back inside and see if Arlene MacNeil was still alive. Fortunately for Arlene, when the Impala came to a stop at the bottom of the restaurant driveway, the three killers saw the taxi circling above and drove away. MacNeil sped towards the intersection of Kings Road and Keltic Drive, swinging hard left through the intersection and driving down Keltic towards his home. Darren Muise lit a cigarette as the three men tried to figure out a way to explain the pack.

That gave Wood an idea. "Let me out. I gotta create an alibi," he demanded, digging through his pockets and emptying the contents onto the seat beside him. He wasn't sure what he had with him, but if he was going to talk to the police, he didn't want to be carrying anything that could tie him to the robbery. MacNeil pulled over just before he reached the Sydney River bridge, and Wood jumped out and disappeared into the darkness.

MacNeil pushed a cassette into the tape player in the dash. He needed to think, and Muise was beginning to ramble. The heavy bass lines filled the car as dance music shook the windows. Muise gulped the smoke deep into his lungs as the two raced towards MacNeil's home.

Behind the Impala, back at the intersection of Keltic Drive and Kings Road, another big car sped past, this one coming from Sydney and heading towards McDonald's, not away from it. It was a taxi driver, John MacInnis, rushing to help his friend Daniel MacVicar and see what was happening at the restaurant. He had not noticed the Impala racing in the other direction. MacInnis turned left and sped up the driveway, coming to a stop near his friend's cab as it too came to a stop after what, to MacVicar, had felt like an eternity of circling the lot.

Both drivers got out of their cars and ran to the doorway where Jimmy Fagan lay, face down. MacInnis gently turned Fagan over, noticing the blood running down his face. Fagan was alive, gasping and clenching his teeth in pain. MacInnis laid him on his back and ran to his car to get some paper towels. The stocky, dark-haired driver was surprisingly calm, moving quickly but without panic; he had seen bloodied people before, when he worked as a security guard in downtown Toronto. MacVicar also ran for his car, to radio that his fare been shot in the head and that somebody better get the Mounties over there fast. The calls for help would soon be answered: the ambulance dispatcher had received a second and third call reporting trouble at

McDonald's, and he decided to take a second ambulance and an employee who was working in the company garage, and go out there himself. The second call had come from Sydney police who, along with the RCMP, had been contacted by the taxi company; the third call from an unidentified man, who sounded panicked and would not identify himself.

At the scene, John MacInnis returned to the doorway and bent over Jimmy Fagan, gingerly pressing a wad of paper towel to the wounded man's forehead in an effort to stop the bleeding. As he knelt there, MacInnis could hear a telephone ringing inside the restaurant, and he decided to check it out. Following the noise to the manager's office in the kitchen, he saw Donna Warren slumped on the floor, her shoulders at an awkward angle against the wall. MacInnis reached for the phone on the counter above her head and lifted the receiver; he heard a beeping sound, but no-one was there. Hanging up the phone, he knelt down and tried to help Donna. He pulled her body away from the wall so her neck would not be bent at such a severe angle, hoping this would make it easier for her to breathe. Was that a look of thanks he saw in her eye? He didn't know.

Still not feeling any real panic, MacInnis decided to return to the door to tell MacVicar he had found another victim. On his way through the kitchen, he glanced to one side and saw Neil Burroughs lying face down, his head in a widening pool of blood that already extended more than a metre from his body. Burroughs's head was tilted to the right, his right arm reaching out from his body, his left hand clenched around the leg of one of the big steel sinks. MacInnis lifted Burroughs's right arm and felt at the wrist for a pulse. There was none. He lowered his ear close to the purple McDonald's T-shirt to listen for sounds of breathing. There were none.

MacInnis began to feel unnerved, and he slowly retreated from the restaurant towards the relative safety of the parking lot. As he walked past the stairway that led to the basement, he heard a gurgling sound—and he knew it was not a mechanical sound. The driver suddenly realized that the killers might still be in the building; he was not about to investigate any further.

Shortly before 1:00 a.m., RCMP Corporal Kevin Cleary finally finished his paperwork. The corporal was working the four-to-twelve shift as supervisor, and was determined to finish a report he'd been working on through the evening. Rather than take the work home, he stayed the extra hour after his shift ended.

Kevin Cleary, now a sergeant with the New Minas RCMP, joined the Mounties as a teenager, fulfilling a childhood dream. [RCMP photo.]

Kevin Cleary was six-foot-two and weighed 210 pounds. He was a policeman's policeman who, after almost twenty years of service, still walked with the erect posture of a cadet in training. Cleary had joined the Mounties at nineteen, fulfilling a childhood dream; by the time he started his training, in Regina, Saskatchewan, he knew the RCMP was for him. He thrilled at the physical challenges the training presented and truly enjoyed the mental discipline instructors demanded of cadets. Cleary, now a corporal and soon to become a sergeant, still loved his chosen career; he still felt he was providing a worthy service to the community.

As Cleary prepared to head home, something caught his attention. He heard communications officer Stan Jesty radioing a patrol car. Jesty had taken a report on a possible shooting near the Sydney River McDonald's from the taxi dispatcher and was asking Constable Henry Jantzen to check it out. Jantzen, who had been on patrol in Howie Centre, another bedroom community outside Sydney, turned around and headed for the restaurant—a five-minute drive on Highway 4. Cleary, as the senior officer on duty, would have to respond if the report was genuine, and he was even closer to the restaurant than Jantzen, so he ran out to his patrol car and set out for McDonald's.

Not that he believed there was anything to the call. Almost every police office can recall at least one incident of chasing down a report of a gunshot, only to find that a car was backfiring or someone was target-shooting in the middle of the night. Besides, Cleary thought, it would make sense that this was another case of a car backfiring. The Sydney bypass ran behind the restaurant, and Kings Road was in front of it; both major arteries would have some traffic, even at this hour. Still, Cleary drove quickly towards McDonald's. He would check out his theory in person.

"Detachment. Three-zero-seven." That number identified Cleary's car—307. He was radioing Stan Jesty.

"Three-zero. Go ahead, Kevin."

"Stan, could you phone that location and get someone on the line, please?"

"...four."

As he neared the end of Kings Road, Cleary could see McDonald's. He thought the place looked strangely dark but wrote the impression off to anxiety. Trying to put his mind at ease, the corporal radioed Jesty again

"Three-zero. Any response there, Stan?"

"No, no answer, Kevin." Jesty, busy with car-radio traffic, had not noticed that the line ringing through to McDonald's had finally been picked up. John MacInnis had tried to answer it when he discovered the body of Donna Warren, but no-one was on the other end.

For Kevin Cleary, the report that the call had gone unanswered set off a series of alarms. He lived near McDonald's; he had passed the building at all hours and was certain there was always someone working inside. Cleary pulled up the driveway to find Daniel MacVicar still in his car, where he'd remained after radioing to confirm that his passenger had been shot. MacVicar was staring at the back door, where his buddy John MacInnis had gone into the restaurant. A third cab driver, Cyril Gillespie, had arrived and was trying to help Jimmy Fagan.

Cleary pulled his car next to the taxi, and MacVicar quickly told his story—how he had heard the "firecracker" and seen two people run—and he pointed towards Fagan. Cleary ordered MacVicar to pull over to the back of the lot and wait until someone took his statement, then went to the door to investigate. He was approaching the building just as MacInnis came screaming out the back door, almost knocking over his fellow driver; Cyril Gillespie was still with the fallen Fagan. Gillespie backed away at the sight of MacInnis's terror-stricken face.

"They're still in there—I heard them!" MacInnis shouted. "There's bodies everywhere, and they're still in there!" MacInnis started away from the building, and the officer grabbed him, trying to calm the frightened driver and direct him to stay with Daniel MacVicar.

Then, Corporal Cleary pulled out his gun and made his way towards the door. He checked James Fagan and could hear him struggling for breath, and see the tiny bullet hole in his forehead. Cleary had to make a quick assessment of the situation. The excited driver had given him information to work with: there were other bodies, and although the driver had not seen an assailant—or assailants—he had heard sounds from the basement and was under the impression that somebody dangerous was still inside. He also knew, through Daniel MacVicar, that at least two people had run away, which could mean that the people left inside were all victims. Cleary radioed Stan Jesty to make certain that ambulances were on the way; MacVicar had said they'd been called by the taxi dispatcher, but Cleary wanted to be certain.

Next came the question of going inside. Henry Jantzen would be there any second, but Cleary still needed to decide whether or not they would go in. His first reaction was to call for Emergency Response Team backup, but that would take more than a hour—even if the team was able to fly from Halifax on a moment's notice. The Sydney RCMP subdivision once had its own ERT, but it had been disbanded; the Halifax-based squad now handled the entire province. ERT members were trained to deal with armed assailants inside a building, but Corporal Cleary knew his first duty as a policeman was the protection of life—and there were injured people inside. Cleary decided to sweep the building alone. Grabbing the portable radio he'd taken from his car, he reported his intention. "I'm going in to see what's in there. We have several injuries at least." Cleary's throat was dry as he released the transmit button and prepared to go in. Before he could move, his radio came to life with a response. "You want me in there with you?" It was Henry Jantzen. The burly, heavy-set constable was on portable radio as he ran across the parking lot to join Cleary. The corporal's "Yes" was the last radio transmission Stan Jesty would hear from the two officers for several agonizing minutes.

The first ambulance rolled into the parking lot behind McDonald's as Kevin Cleary and Henry Jantzen inched inside the restaurant with their guns drawn. At the same moment, Derek Wood ran out from between an Irving gas station and the Sydney Video Entertainment store on Kings Road, about a half-kilometre away from McDonald's. He ran across the road and headed for a tiny strip mall that housed a fried-chicken franchise, a submarine sandwich shop, and Kings Convenience, a twenty-four-hour variety store with video poker machines that Wood had played a few times before. On familiar ground now, he burst through the door of Kings and ran to the counter, demanding to use the phone. The startled clerk was irritated at first—Wood had interrupted a couple purchasing cigarettes—but when he recognized the young man and saw the state he was in, he left the other customers.

"There's been a shooting at McDonald's. Call the cops. I need to call the cops," Wood blurted as he reached the counter.

The clerk checked the list of emergency numbers next to the phone, dialled, and handed Wood the receiver. Wood thought the clerk had made a mistake—he didn't think he was talking to the police—but by then he was genuinely panicked and couldn't be sure. It sounded more like the guy said "Ambulance" when he answered, not "Police." Whoever it was, the guy said they had people on the way, so Wood hung up. He paced and lit a cigarette and worried, and finally decided he should call the police again. This time a second clerk dialled the RCMP number from memory. Whichever call connected Wood to police, it was Stan Jesty he reached. Jesty recorded the incoming call at 1:21 a.m.

"RCMP Sydney. Emergency." Jesty's voice was clipped; he was in the process of directing officers to the scene and was waiting to hear from Cleary and Jantzen.

Derek Wood quickly got Jesty's attention. "Hello, yes, I just called a…like, reported fellows shooting."

"Yes." Jesty was listening.

"I was wondering, like, I'm fuckin' scared shitless here, eh, 'cause I, like, fuckin' I was there."

"What's your name?"

"Ah, Derek Wood."

An officer stands guard outside the employees' entrance to the Sydney River McDonald's, where Jimmy Fagan's body was found. [RCMP crime scene photo.]

"Were you at McDonald's, Derek?"

Wood seized the opportunity he had hoped to create. "I don't know. I was, like, in back having a smoke, and I heard a shot."

"Were you inside the restaurant or outside?"

This was Wood's chance to explain the bag. "I was outside with the door, like, the doors are open, and the metal door there. All I heard was 'Bang!' and it was, like, from inside."

Jesty asked for Wood's address and phone number; he felt he had a witness on the line. Wood gave the officer the address and number of his brother's apartment in Sydney. The teenager was staying there, but would soon have to leave; like many other young Cape Bretoners, Derek's brother David had lost his job and decided to move away from the island in search of work. Just as Wood asked what he should do next, Jesty was interrupted by a call from Corporal John Trickett, whom he had phoned after hearing Kevin Cleary's transmission indicating several people were injured at the scene. Jesty knew Trickett and his police dog, Storm, would be needed, and now the dog master was en route to the restaurant, wanting to know what he was driving into—was there any danger, or could he take Storm directly to the building? Trickett usually had time to get such information earlier, but he lived only moments from the restaurant and knew he'd be there before he had a chance to gather his thoughts. As Jesty informed Trickett he was not yet certain of the situation, the radio came alive with other requests from the officers at McDonald's. Jesty had his hands full, so he told Derek Wood to go home, where officers would contact him in the morning. In fact, the police attempted to reach him within the hour, but Wood had not gone back to his brother's place.

While Derek Wood was reporting the shooting at McDonald's, Kevin Cleary and Henry Jantzen were discovering its horrifying aftermath. Once they had moved a few feet inside the doorway, the two officers parted. Jantzen headed down the stairs and slowly pushed the steel door open, looking to see if anyone was waiting for him on the other side. What he found was Arlene MacNeil, gasping for breath; she was inhaling blood from a puddle that had formed around her face on the floor. He rolled her over to ease her breathing, then notified Cleary by portable radio that he was standing guard over a victim who showed strong signs of life and needed medical attention, and fast. Upstairs, Kevin Cleary moved slowly, turning to the right around a corner near the entrance to the drive-through service area, his body in a crouched position as he proceeded. The restaurant had to be secured before he could let the ambulance attendants come in. First he saw blood on the floor, and then, as he inched closer, he saw Neil Burroughs.

The pool of blood was still widening around the fallen man's body, but there were no signs of life. Just then, Cleary noticed an unusually powerful odour, something he had never encountered in any of the murder investigations he had carried out in the past. Then he realized what it was—a smell of fresh blood and gunpowder, a sickening combination, which he would never forget. The realization reinforced his biggest fear, that he was at a crime scene so fresh that the criminal or criminals were still inside. After seeing Jimmy Fagan and Neil Burroughs, Kevin Cleary realized he was dealing with killers like none he'd ever contemplated. At any moment, he could join the victims on the floor with a bullet in his head: whoever was responsible would not stop at killing a cop.

Every nerve in Cleary's body tingled as he continued his crouched advance towards the front of the restaurant, sweeping his gun ahead of him at every step. He turned left and found himself inside the main service area of the restaurant; tucking his head down, below the counter that held the cash registers, he made his way to the other side of the kitchen. At the far end of the service counter he turned left again, heading back towards the basement stairs, where Jantzen had headed. On his right, through an open door, he saw a foot. Another victim. *My God,* he thought. *It's got to stop.* Cleary took a deep breath and moved forward again. There was an open safe door beside the foot, and then he could see two feet, and legs. It was a woman. Cleary put his back to the wall outside the tiny office and peered in through the door.

What Kevin Cleary saw inside that office continues to haunt him to this day—an image that clearly depicted the savage, senseless nature of the crime. There on the floor lay a pretty young woman with a hole in her right eye; a large black stain surrounded the eye, making it appear that she had been hit in a fight. But this was no bruise; it was gunpowder stippling and sooty discharge, telltale marks left on a victim when a gun is discharged at close range. Blood stained the wall behind Donna Warren's head, and her hair was matted with blood where her head had slipped closer to the floor. Then Kevin Cleary was shaken to his core. On the floor in a pool of Donna Warren's blood was a crumpled five-dollar bill and a mixture of change. *God, no! There was no way this could be about money. It had to be about more than money.* Cleary took another deep breath and got back to his job. This was no time to allow himself to feel anything—not sympathy and not anger. He had to think clearly.

The corporal's search had taken him to the doorway leading away from the kitchen and into the public area of the restaurant. He moved quickly, remaining quiet as he carefully searched the area. With the public area clear, there was only one more place to check. Kevin Cleary had taken his kids to this restaurant many times and knew that the only enclosed areas in the public portion of the building were the two washrooms at the back corner. He moved to the door of the first washroom and swore to himself as he realized that the door opened towards

The safe in the office where Donna Warren died. A stack of two-dollar bills was left behind in the till, and change was scattered on the tile floor. [RCMP crime scene photo.]

him. Pulling it open, he moved away from the line of fire, quickly stepped inside, and kicked open the door to the stall. It was empty. Cleary hoped the other washroom would be vacant as well; surely if there were anyone inside, they would have heard him kicking open that stall door. And he was right. Secure in the knowledge that the upstairs was clear, the officer rushed back to the entrance to get an ambulance attendant inside. The attendant confirmed the officer's first impression— Neil Burroughs and Donna Warren were beyond help—so the two returned to Jimmy Fagan. The second ambulance had arrived, and Cleary sent that attendant down to the basement to have a look at Arlene MacNeil, still being guarded by Henry Jantzen. The taxi drivers joined in the effort, and moments later Arlene and Jimmy were on the way to hospital.

Cleary pressed the transmit button on his radio. Nothing happened; it was dead. He moved quickly back to the door where another officer, Constable Dave Trickett, was now standing guard at the entrance. Seeing the problem the corporal was having, Trickett handed Cleary his portable radio. Cleary turned his attention to securing the scene and helping Henry Jantzen in the basement, where those responsible could still be hiding—or, God forbid, more victims were yet to be found. He needed more backup, and he had to deal with the strong possibility that those responsible had escaped. Before Cleary could call Stan Jesty and arrange to bring in every available officer, he heard someone else on the radio. It was Corporal John Trickett, asking Jesty what the situation was. Cleary quickly interrupted, not knowing that he and Trickett were forcing Jesty to cut short his conversation with Derek Wood: "Three-zero-six, come into McDonald's right away." Cleary wanted to use Storm to search the basement, so that officers would not be put at risk.

Other traffic on the radio kept Trickett from hearing Cleary's call. Jesty cleared the channel. "Go ahead, Kevin, give him a call again."

"Three-zero-six, do you copy? Come in as soon as you can. We want you to check out the inside. We got several down, and we need you to check inside and, ah, Stan, call other PDs." Cleary wanted roadblocks set up in the area, and the RCMP did not have enough officers for the job. Jesty called municipal police in Sydney, Glace Bay, Dominion, North Sydney, Sydney Mines, Louisbourg, New Waterford, and Eskasoni. Every available law-enforcement officer in the area would help in any way possible. Cleary instructed Jesty to call RCMP

The crew training room at McDonald's, where Henry Jantzen waited, sweating, for backup from fellow officers. [RCMP crime scene photo.]

in Port Hawkesbury, about 150 kilometres away; he wanted a road-block at the Canso Causeway, the man-made link that joins Cape Breton Island to mainland Nova Scotia. Cleary was going to take advantage of geography. No flights were leaving Cape Breton at that hour, and he would make sure that no-one responsible for the carnage in McDonald's would simply drive off the island into the night.

As Cleary made those arrangements, Corporal John Trickett arrived with Storm. Officers already at the scene were happy to see the big German shepherd; in the years since Storm had been posted to the Sydney subdivision, he had helped nearly all of them out of tough situations, his mighty bark prompting more than one criminal to call out from a building that he was prepared to surrender. Storm knew he was about to go to work, and was leaping back and forth in the back of the big four-wheel-drive truck as Trickett came to a stop in the parking lot. As the big truck shook under the dog's weight, the other officers thought about why Storm was there—that he was trained to take a bullet to protect any of them. A sickening feeling settled into their stomachs as they realized he might have to do just that in the moments ahead. But none of them said anything about it.

Corporal Trickett went over to Kevin Cleary and got a quick rundown on the situation. Henry Jantzen had already reported finding locked offices, and he had come across an open room where he saw a door held open by some kind of bag; he had backed away from the room but was keeping it in his sights. Jantzen enjoyed working out on the target range, and now he wondered if all that practice would prove useful. He knew he could empty, reload, and empty his gun again into a target in a matter of seconds, and drew some comfort from that knowledge as he watched the open door.

Comfort was just what the young constable needed. Sweat matted the burly officer's flyaway hair and rolled down his back, staining his uniform shirt. It seemed an eternity had passed since he pushed open that basement door to find Arlene MacNeil lying on the floor, inhaling her own blood. Every sound in the eerie atmosphere of the restaurant basement was amplified; compressors from the pop fountain and freezers clicked and hummed unexpectedly, heightening his anxiety. After Arlene was whisked away by the ambulance attendants, Jantzen moved gingerly through the basement, all too aware that a culprit, or culprits, could be in one of those rooms he passed. His pulse quickened as he tried the doors; they were all locked. But there were more doors ahead and, ready to react to any sound, he crept ahead, his gun held out in front of him. He hoped he would not have to test the skill he knew he had.

Outside, Corporal Trickett was expressing doubts that Storm could work inside the restaurant. The dog would become so agitated by the presence of the two bodies that Trickett felt he would not be able to accurately read Storm's reactions. Cleary decided he would use the officers on the scene to search the basement, and asked Trickett to use Storm to track the two people that cabby Daniel MacVicar had seen run off.

Trickett knew he would have to keep his eyes on Storm, so he wanted another officer with a shotgun to back him up; the dog could very quickly lead him into a deadly situation, if those responsible for shooting all these people were still hidden in one of the fields nearby. Kevin Cleary assigned an officer to cover Trickett, but Constable Dave Trickett stepped forward. "If anyone's gotta watch out for him, it's gonna be me." The other officers understood. The shotgun was handed to the younger brother as both Tricketts, donning bulletproof vests, set out to find the killers. The taxi driver had told police that he thought he saw two people running alongside the building, in the direction of Kings Road, so the officers led Storm across the road and down towards the Sydney River Shopping Plaza. It was the same route Derek Wood had taken after he left his kitbag in the door and went to meet his accomplices at the coffee shop.

"You remember when we used to walk along the shore back home with our pellet guns? Never thought we'd be doin' this." Dave Trickett was trying to relieve the intense strain he and his elder brother felt as they moved along, not knowing what was ahead of them. The older Trickett picked up the theme. "Yeah, well, as long as you don't decide it's time to get back at me for stealin' your pellet gun all those times you weren't around."

"Don't you worry. I'm watchin' your back, brother."

The brothers had grown up near Conception Bay, Newfoundland, where John had decided he wanted to be a Mountie after seeing officers in RCMP shore-patrol boats. The younger Trickett had followed his brother's lead a few years later.

• • •

AFTER FINISHING his conversation with Stan Jesty, Derek Wood was baffled. He didn't know what he should have expected when he called the police, but he didn't think he would be told to go home; he thought they would want to come and get him—to protect him as the lone survivor of a major crime. Instead, the officer on the phone had been in a hurry to get rid of him. Derek called his cousin Mike and asked him to come get him, but Mike Campbell was half-asleep, and Wood was not sure he understood what he'd been asked to do. Then he called Freeman MacNeil's house, but MacNeil's mother said he was not home. Where had MacNeil and Muise gone? Wood became frightened and confused, and found himself beginning to cry. He had to leave the store and go somewhere to clear his head.

Now that Wood had managed to break out of his image as an awkward loner and step into the role of a big-time criminal, he was not sure what to do. He figured he'd covered his tracks with the police, a clever move that made up for forgetting the kitbag in the door in the first place. (Of course, using his own bag to hold open the door, when there were any number of items readily available in the basement, showed how small-time Wood really was.) Wood decided he would walk to Freeman MacNeil's house—more than six kilometres away. Maybe he would find MacNeil and Muise parked somewhere along the way.

MacNeil and Muise *were* parked, at the side of Beaton Road, not far from MacNeil's house. They had decided to take the duffel bag containing their clothes and hide it in the woods, where they also disposed of the spent shell-casings. As they jumped back into the car and drove the short distance to the house, they did not notice several unused hollow-point bullets rolling around on the floor in the back of the car. Edith MacNeil heard them come in, and she got out of bed to find out what was going on. Freeman, who had a remarkable ability to create believable explanations for his actions, told his mother he'd driven out to the house to get an inhaler his girlfriend had left there. Edith knew that Michelle Sharp suffered from asthma, and Freeman added credence to his alibi by phoning Michelle to tell her he'd found her puffer. Then he told his mother he'd be staying at Michelle's for the night, and he and Darren left, taking some of their loot with them and leaving the rest in a dresser drawer in Freeman's bedroom. In all they had $2,017.27—tens of thousands less than they had expected to get.

AFTER LEAVING the MacNeil house, the two drove to a secluded brook, a few kilometres away. Grantmire Brook runs through a large culvert underneath Beachmont Road. The point where the road meets the brook is a deep valley, perfect for getting rid of evidence without being seen from any residence in the area—or from the road, empty of traffic at one-thirty in the morning. In the darkness of the secluded road, MacNeil and Muise emptied the car of everything they could think of that was connected to the crime. A tin cash box was thrown into the woods. More than a dozen tiny red change purses containing McDonald's gift certificates were tossed into the fast-running brook. Also discarded was a sheaf of papers Derek Wood had grabbed from the safe—everything from a petty-cash expense sheet, to a paycheque being held for a vacationing employee. Muise then tried to rinse blood from the blade of the larger of the two knives he carried, and MacNeil threw both weapons into the brook, one at a time, on either side of the road. Muise also threw his deck shoes in the brook. The two had chosen a great location to get rid of these items; the fast-running brook quickly carried them out of sight into the dark, wooded areas of the Coxheath hills.

There was more evidence to dispose of, but the branches hanging over the brook made throwing clothing in there a bit too risky. Mac-Neil and Muise decided to drive towards North Sydney, taking Keltic Drive, which runs along the inner harbour, to a one-lane bridge. They got out there with some clothing they had not put in the duffel bag they'd left in the woods near MacNeil's house, threw the clothing into the tidal waters of the Sydney harbour, and headed back to Sydney. But first they had to get back up on the bypass. Staying on Keltic Drive would be too dangerous; that cab driver must have phoned police, and Keltic would take them back to Kings Road, only a block from McDonald's. Driving past the restaurant on the bypass did not concern them; Muise, glancing over, noticed an ATV News truck parked at the side of the highway behind the restaurant—just where he, Mac-Neil, and Wood had run out of the field a short time before. The ATV truck had arrived at the scene at 2:15 a.m., only moments before the killers casually drove past. In it were cameraman Bruce Hennessey and I. We had no idea how close we were to the killers; we were too preoccupied with what was happening around us, and, of course, we wouldn't have known who they were.

MacNeil drove to Muise's home, on Patnic Avenue, just outside Sydney. Muise realized he didn't have his keys, so he asked MacNeil to take him to the Sanitary Dairy, a twenty-four-hour convenience store on George Street in Sydney. Muise wanted to try his luck at the Mega Double poker machines; he loved the game but usually didn't have enough money to play. But tonight he could pop quarters into the machines and kill a few hours. He'd head home later, when his father would be awake for work. Less than two hours after cutting an innocent man's throat, Darren Muise was feeding a video-gambling machine with money taken in the commission of that grisly act.

MacNeil left the store and drove to his girlfriend's place. Michelle Sharp lived with her mother and stepfather in a trailer on East Broadway in Whitney Pier, not far from Derek Wood's former home. Michelle's mother, who was on the couch watching TV, noticed nothing unusual about Freeman as he said goodnight and headed to bed. As he drifted off to sleep, the big-time criminal was unaware that he had left a critical piece of evidence in the back of the car. The tiny silver handgun had been thrust down behind the seat cushion in the confusion of the getaway.

While MacNeil and Muise were carefully discarding evidence and police were beginning their search for clues at McDonald's, Derek Wood continued looking for his accomplices. Wood walked from Kings Road up Keltic Drive to Coxheath Road, passing Riverview Rural High School, where he and Muise had both dropped out and where MacNeil had graduated. From there he climbed Mountain Road, descending to the intersection with Beaton Road. There was no sign of the Impala; maybe MacNeil and Muise had not gone to MacNeil's after all. It had taken Wood an hour to cover the distance to Beaton Road, and now he decided to walk back. The night was raw, with temperatures running below the freezing mark, but Wood was too preoccupied to feel the cold. He still did not know what to do; he still felt uncertain about what had happened in the restaurant. He knew he

THE KILLERS NEXT DOOR

THE KILLERS NEXT DOOR •

had shot Arlene, Donna, and Neil, but he had heard other shots after Darren took the gun from him while he rifled the safe. He tried to re-play the whole crime in his mind, in slow motion, but the pieces weren't fitting. Where had Donna and Arlene come from? What were they doing in the basement? He couldn't understand it. Had they been in the manager's office downstairs? Why was Arlene even there? Her shift had ended with the inventory, hadn't it? And what should he do now? As Wood continued to sort through the events, and his options, he found himself back at Kings Convenience, but now the store was locked. That made no sense, either. That store was always open, and there were two clerks inside; he could see them. Wood pounded on the window—he wanted to call his cousin Mike again—and one of the clerks came over but would not open the door.

By the time Wood was walking down Mountain Road, police had already visited all the twenty-four-hour businesses in the area and told employees not to allow anyone inside until they were informed that the situation was safe. Then they blocked off a section of Kings Road, from the Sydney bypass, back about a kilometre and a half to-wards Sydney, to the intersection of Kings Road and Kenwood Drive. There were several all-night or late-night establishments in that corri-dor, and police were afraid a cornered suspect could turn one of them into another blood bath.

The roadblocks created an eerie effect in the area, and the yellow glow of street lights added to the ghost-town atmosphere. The area was well lit, but nothing was moving; it was as though all the people had disappeared—except for John and Dave Trickett, who, with Storm, were still trying to find out where the culprits had gone.

After failing to pick up a trail in the area of the Sydney River Shopping Plaza, the officers returned to McDonald's. At Kings Road, an excited motorist stopped and told them he had seen someone running up behind Jasper's restaurant, one of the few all-night busi-nesses that had not yet been ordered closed. The motorist, who had driven down from a side street inside the cordoned-off area, gladly agreed to allow Storm to jump in the back of his small white truck while he drove the officers to the restaurant. What they found was a group of teenagers in the middle of a drinking party; what they lost was precious time. John Trickett knew very well that every second away from a fresh trail was a second in which it could be contami-nated. Dave Trickett ordered the kids to leave, and the brothers re-turned to McDonald's.

Kevin Cleary had finally managed to secure the crime scene, and officers were being detailed to take footwear from the taxi drivers and ambulance attendants who had tramped all over the floors. Footprints were now a crucial concern: Henry Jantzen had discovered a trail of prints, leading from the door where he'd found the kitbag, to the inside of the building. The leaves and dirt in the small porch between the outer and inner steel doors had covered two sets of footprints, only to be pulled off by the tacky, freshly waxed tile floor in the crew training room. For some reason, Muise's deck shoes did not pick up grit or leave prints.

Cleary knew the footprints were a start, but he also knew a crime scene could hold a variety of more-telling clues, some as minute as a hair or fibre. This was a large scene, and one that had to be examined carefully by experts trained in evidence collection. The first to enter was the medical examiner, Dr. Murdock Smith, who officially pronounced Donna Warren and Neil Burroughs dead at the scene. The bodies would later become evidence to be handled by a pathologist, but first, Corporal James Leadbetter of the Sydney Identification section had to catalogue the crime scene.

• • •

AN "IDENT" OFFICER approaches a crime scene the way a storyteller does, and Leadbetter knew that eventually he would have to tell all the stories revealed by this scene to a judge and jury. The first step towards preparing a scene in a murder investigation is a walk-through with the chief investigating officer: the two carefully examine—without touching—everything at the scene, and detailed notes are taken. Then the Ident officer takes an extensive series of photos that will give jurors a complete picture of the crime.

After finishing his photography, Corporal Leadbetter went out to his station wagon and opened a case containing a video camera. He wanted the horror of this crime scene brought home to any judge, prosecutor, defence lawyer, or juror to become involved in the case; he wanted each of them to see the senseless brutality that had so deeply moved him and the other officers present. Leadbetter began by sweeping the camera slowly over the bloodstained floor where James Fagan had fallen. He walked the camera over to the body of Neil Burroughs, slowly zooming in to capture the grisly nature of the wounds he had suffered. Then he turned the camera towards Donna Warren, whose body had been pulled from the tiny office by ambulance attendants hoping to revive her. They had left her on the floor, her skirt spread neatly down past her knees, her legs together, almost as though she had been laid out by a mortician. Downstairs, Leadbetter filled his viewfinder with the coloured sticks, now clustered in a pool of blood where Arlene MacNeil had fallen.

While Corporal Leadbetter captured the disturbing images inside the restaurant, other cameras were causing problems for investigators outside. Upon returning to the restaurant, John and Dave Trickett began a new search with Storm; the dog quickly picked up a trail at the back of the building, leading to the field behind the building and towards the highway, then veering to the left and back to a garage at the corner of the parking lot. What the officers found there was not a suspect hidden in the bushes, but a television cameraman and a newspaper photographer, who had walked down from the highway to get closer shots of the action behind the restaurant. The brothers

The kitchen at McDonald's hours after the crime. The bloodstained paper towels were used by cabbies trying to help Jimmy Fagan; the marks on the door are fingerprinting dust.
[RCMP crime scene photo.]

guided the big dog away and moved farther into the field. Suddenly they froze; night had turned to day. The sight of the dog master searching the field, protected by an officer carrying a shotgun, was too much for veteran CBC cameraman Frank King to resist. King flipped on the bright light on top of his camera, illuminated the field, and began recording; the photographer, Ray Fahey of the *Cape Breton Post,* was busy taking his own shots. Within seconds, the Trickett brothers recovered from their shock and ordered King away from the crime scene—but it made for a powerful image. Within hours, the tape was picked up by CNN and broadcast around the world as reports of the multiple murder at the Sydney River McDonald's filtered out. In Newfoundland, the mother of John and Dave Trickett was among the thousands in Atlantic Canada riveted by reports of the hideous crime. She was left speechless when she turned on the television, only to see her sons wearing bulletproof vests and searching the woods in the darkness.

• • •

BY THE TIME the camera had captured the search behind the restaurant, Kevin Cleary was already being distracted by the media. His early transmissions on open radio to Stan Jesty, which made it clear there were several victims, were monitored in the local newsrooms in Sydney. Initial reports filed by a radio reporter had been fed to the international wire services, and a sergeant arriving on the scene informed Cleary that the detachment had already received calls from news organizations as far away as California. Reports of an unknown number of people gunned down inside a McDonald's restaurant made for the kind of news that travels fast. Cleary had more pressing things to do and could not afford the time to deal with reporters, but he knew that in a few hours, Cape Breton residents would awaken wanting to know what had happened to their community overnight. A controlled flow of information could prevent panic and might even help the investigation. He called media liaison officer Dave Roper.

Constable Roper was asleep at home when his phone rang at about 3:00 a.m. His crime-prevention and media-information duties meant that calls in the middle of the night were no longer supposed to be a part of his routine, so he and his wife were startled by the ringing. When he hung up, Roper was more than a little confused; he pulled himself out of bed and told his wife there had been a shooting at McDonald's, with several people involved, and he was needed at the scene. Roper dressed quickly and got in his car. As he drove towards Sydney River, Dave Roper began to wonder whether this was some kind of prank; or worse, whether someone was trying to get him out of the house in the middle of the night for some nefarious purpose. But his doubts evaporated as he approached Sydney River; the flashing lights up ahead were all he needed to see. It was a Louisbourg police car, guarding a roadblock that had been set up in the area where Highway 4 runs beneath the Sydney bypass and merges with Kings Road, near McDonald's.

When Roper arrived at the scene, Kevin Cleary was assigning duties to the large group of men and women who had been called out to work on the McDonald's case. Roper stood by while Corporal Brian Stoyek was asked to visit the late-night businesses and interview the workers—find out what the people behind those now-locked doors had seen. Other officers were sent to the address Derek Wood had given them, to find the potential witness. Still others secured the building and property, placing yellow plastic ribbons—POLICE LINE: DO NOT CROSS—around the perimeter. Because his forays with Storm were coming up empty, Corporal Trickett was sent back to the detachment for a briefing. His brother would not be so lucky: Dave Trickett was one of the officers who would be informing the families of Donna Warren and Neil Burroughs that their loved ones would not be coming home. Positive identification of the slain McDonald's employees had been provided by a badly shaken Garfield Lewis; it was an experience the restaurant owner would never forget.

Finally Dave Roper had a chance to talk with Cleary. He wanted to walk through the crime scene, but Cleary said no; enough people had already been inside, and so far no real evidence, except the footprints, had been uncovered. Cleary wanted the scene protected from further contamination. Roper was adamant; he knew the Cape Breton rumour mill would run wild, and he would be the one asked to quell the panic it would undoubtedly spawn. He knew he would not be allowed to tell reporters exactly what he saw inside, but he had to be ready to face questions from reporters who'd had calls claiming the killings were ritualistic slayings, or proposing some other wild theory. If he hesitated or did not comment because he did not know, Roper knew full well that reporters would run with a phrase like "RCMP have not ruled out—," filling in the blank with the latest rumour. If he saw what was inside, he would be able to respond without telling reporters too much about what had happened. He finally convinced Cleary and was taken inside the restaurant.

For the few reporters who'd been called out that night—myself included—the rumour mill was already providing more information than we could ever responsibly use, but there was also relatively reliable information coming out. A curious motorist, who had stopped on the Sydney bypass when he saw police lights down at McDonald's, walked down to the building and almost entered the rear door before he was noticed by an officer and sent away. The motorist described the scene for me but did not want to appear on camera. Instead, cameraman Bruce Hennessey recorded the interview without lights—all that viewers would see was a silhouetted image of the motorist as he talked about seeing blood all over the restaurant, and at least one body. In fact, what the "eyewitness" had seen was a small patch of blood in the doorway where Jimmy Fagan had fallen. The stain seemed much larger because a taxi driver had slipped in the blood while running to help an ambulance attendant, causing the blood to spatter on the wall. Still, his description was more accurate than he knew: just out of his sight, inside the kitchen, many litres of blood had been spilled on the floor.

Most of the information coming out had to be confirmed by the Mounties, but the incident at McDonald's had already been discussed by taxi drivers and their fares throughout the area. It was the subject of intense talk in all-night coffee shops in and around Sydney, and people were phoning newsrooms with tidbits of information, hoping to get more from journalists. Even at the side of the road, people stopped us to ask questions and offer what they'd gathered from the firestorm of speculation sweeping the city. But that kind of information is problematic. A taxi driver may tell his fare that there were people shot at McDonald's, and that his buddy was there; by the time the story reaches a reporter, it may have been passed on by three or four people, each adding a bit in the telling, until the story has seven or eight people killed at McDonald's, including a taxi driver, or even *by* a taxi driver.

Because Sydney is a relatively small community, there is none of the bitter competition between reporters that is common in larger urban centres. Some information is kept under wraps, but journalists with the two TV stations, three radio stations, and one daily newspaper run into each other frequently, and often exchange favours. In fact, there is an informal agreement between the CJCB Radio and ATV newsrooms that dates back to a time when both stations were owned by the same family. On the night of the McDonald's murders, it was veteran CJCB reporter Russ White who called me at home to say something big had happened in Sydney River.

A benefit of the positive working relationship among local reporters is a tendency to question some of the wilder rumours that get started. While an anxious young reporter may want to go with information picked up in a coffee shop, to the effect that seven or eight people are dead, a seasoned journalist will advise caution. On this occasion, for example, a few of us noted that only two ambulances were parked behind McDonald's, and only two gurneys were sitting behind the drive-through window. Flashes from inside indicated an Indent team was at work photographing bodies before they were taken to the morgue. The evidence suggested two fatalities, not the numbers being circulated in the rumour mill. A call to Sydney City Hospital might determine the number of people killed or injured; the exact condition of the victims might not be available, but a harried nursing supervisor would probably tell a persistent reporter how many people had been hospitalized.

Our real challenge was to get good pictures. The RCMP had decided that television cameras were creating a hazard by attracting the attention of passing motorists—not that there were that many people driving the Sydney bypass in the middle of the night, but as usual our presence had stimulated curiosity. Fortunately, the cameras had already captured images that would be replayed many times in the weeks and months ahead: the open back door of the restaurant, police crowding in and out of the door, and the waiting ambulances. There was even a telling shot of Corporal Leadbetter standing outside the door with his video camera, turning on his light, and slowly walking inside.

As long as the ambulances were there, it was unlikely that the cameras would leave. We had a job to do, and there was a way around the dilemma the RCMP had presented. Bruce Hennessey and I decided to get closer to the restaurant, but away from the motorists who were still out that morning. CBC cameraman Frank King decided he'd come with us around the other side of the building. What we ended up doing, without knowing it, was to retrace the steps of Darren Muise and Freeman MacNeil. We drove out the Sydney bypass and doubled back onto the old North Sydney highway, only a few kilometres from the bridge where the killers had disposed of their soiled clothing. While Muise and MacNeil had turned onto the bypass to avoid coming too close to McDonald's, we wanted to do the opposite.

We took Keltic Drive to the shopping plaza, skirting the police road-block at Keltic and Kings Road by cutting across the plaza parking lot, our trucks luckily unnoticed by the officer at the roadblock. We parked at the Tim Hortons where, a few hours earlier, Muise and Mac-Neil had waited for Wood. It was more than a bit disappointing to discover that the two young women inside had locked the shop. A coffee would have been nice; it was nearly 4:00 a.m. and it was very cold. We walked away from Tim Hortons and went back up the hill to-wards McDonald's, where the cameramen began recording without lights. Kings Road was well lit, and red-and-blue police lights were streaking the building with waves of colour.

A Sydney police constable was standing guard outside the black steel door at the front corner of the building. He'd been there since Kevin Cleary had determined that the knapsack inside was holding open a door located just behind the big black door. Two other Sydney policemen were talking to the guard when one noticed the cameras. Hoping to delay the order for us to leave, I walked out to meet the of-ficer as he came across the street towards us.

Another good thing about a small community is that reporters and police officers generally get to know each other fairly well and can develop a good working relationship. This officer and I had known each other ever since I had covered a police strike, years be-fore. "How the hell did you guys end up over here?" he asked. Appar-ently he didn't want to order us away just yet. "We circled around the Sydport road. What's going on in there?" The officer did not want questions; this was an RCMP case, and he was there simply to provide any assistance he could. "You'll have to talk to them; I don't know anything. Listen, you guys can't stay here. This is all a secured area."

Time to negotiate. "Look, they asked us to leave the bypass be-cause we were drawing a crowd. Let us stay here, and we won't move around. We just want to get a few shots of the cars coming and going, and the ambulances when they leave." The officer wanted to agree, but wasn't sure. "They want the area kept clear for the dog," he said.

"Well, if we walk back to the cars now, we'll be leaving more tracks than if we just stay. Who's in charge over there, anyway?"

"I don't know. Staff Davies was around—probably him." (That would be Staff Sergeant Herb Davies.)

"Could you go tell him we're here, then, and we won't move, and maybe ask him when they'll be making a statement?"

"O.K., don't move any further than you are, and I'll see where he is." I went back to the roadside opposite the restaurant to tell the cameramen they had to work from that spot. That was fine by them. They could see officers using flashlights to search the restaurant lawn; there were several squad cars in the lot; and by panning left they could also get the roadblock at Keltic Drive. I knew we were doing all right when I saw the Sydney policeman drive away in his squad car.

While Bruce and Frank essentially mimicked each other's actions, pointing their cameras at anything that moved, I began to wonder how bad the situation inside really was. I had waited outside crime scenes many times while police completed their work before releasing a body to the coroner. While the area around the murder scene is always cordoned off, police do not usually broaden the barricades to include roadblocks, and then close businesses in such a large area. I hoped Dave Roper was over there but figured that wasn't likely. He had come to a few crime scenes in the past, but normally he met with us later, back at the detachment. I had a feeling we might have to wait a while.

Five

WHEN DEREK WOOD was turned away by the clerk inside the locked convenience store, he decided to walk towards the flashing police lights at Kenwood Drive, about a half a block away. If he told them who he was, they would at least drive him home. As he approached the roadblock, an RCMP cruiser pulled into the lot behind him; Wood did not notice it, nor did Corporal Brian Stoyek notice him. Stoyek was following Kevin Cleary's instructions, interviewing people working in the area. He knocked on the window at Kings so he could question the two young men inside, when one of them ran to the door. "He was just here. The guy you're looking for—he was just here. I wouldn't let him in; he looked too spooky."

"Who? Who are you talking about?"

"The Wood guy, the guy who phoned to report the shooting." The clerk knew the surname because he knew Wood's elder brother. Stoyek had been told that officers were out looking for a Derek Wood, who had been working at McDonald's overnight but had disappeared after phoning Stan Jesty.

"Where is he now? Which way did he go?" The clerk pointed towards the roadblock, and Stoyek jumped back in his car.

Derek Wood approached the officer guarding the roadblock; it was Constable John MacLeod of the Sydney police. The officer had noticed Wood a few minutes earlier, when he appeared out of nowhere inside the cordoned-off area. He watched the young man walk over to the convenience store, where he stood in apparent confusion for a few minutes before making his way to the roadblock. Wood began talking when he was still about two metres away. "I was at McDonald's when the shooting happened. I ran."

The officer was taken aback and looked again at Wood, this time more closely, noting that the young man was pale and shaken and appeared to be reacting slowly. Before MacLeod could decide what to do, Brian Stoyek pulled up. The husky, imposing-looking corporal introduced himself to Wood, then started asking questions.

"Are you the guy who phoned to report the shooting at McDonald's?"

"Yeah, the guy told me to go home."

"Would you mind coming with me now?"

"No." The two got in Stoyek's car, and the corporal asked Wood to spell his full name. He then asked what had happened. Wood appeared calm at first, but Stoyek watched the young man closely for any signs that might suggest a problem. The first thing he noticed was a cut on the knuckle of Wood's right hand. "How'd you hurt that hand?"

"Oh, I cut it a couple of days ago, opening a can." The answer didn't satisfy the officer; there was fresh blood on that hand. Something else caused Stoyek to become concerned: when he asked Wood where he had gone after running away from the restaurant, Wood blurted out the answer very quickly—too quickly. Stoyek got the impression that Wood had been drinking, although he could not smell alcohol. He did not understand why the young man had suddenly become excited and then settled down. He was quite calm when they met and then relaxed again after blurting out his version of the route he'd taken. The response didn't feel right to the experienced officer. And there was another problem. The route itself made no sense. "I don't know where I went first," Wood tried to explain. "I just ran, but I ended up by the Sydney River bridge. Then I ran along the harbour and came out over there and ran across the road to Kings, where I called you guys."

"What did you do after that call?"

"I went for a walk. I'm not sure where I was going. I went down by Keltic Drive and then over by Riverview and up the road by the Lands and Forests office, and I came back and the store was locked." That route made no more sense to Brian Stoyek than the other one. He decided to take Wood to McDonald's, but saw that the young man was reluctant to go anywhere near the restaurant. "You don't have to get out of the car, Derek. I just have to let them know I found you, and then we can retrace your route. O.K.?"

Back at the restaurant, Stoyek pulled up the ramp to the parking lot and got out of the car to have a word with Kevin Cleary and Staff Sergeant Herb Davies, now the senior officer on the scene. While Stoyek told Davies about his concerns, Cleary approached the patrol car—not to talk to Wood but to observe him and make a note of his condition. Wood was pale and seemed very nervous, his head twitching occasionally. Cleary found this suspicious, but he realized Wood's behaviour could have been caused by the shock of hearing what had happened inside the restaurant.

The three officers regrouped and agreed that Wood should be taken out and asked to retrace his steps; then Corporal Trickett and Storm could go over the route and check for evidence. After Wood finished showing Stoyek where he had gone, he should be taken to the detachment for questioning; Cleary would meet Stoyek there later. Corporal Stoyek got back in his car, started down the ramp, then came to a stop and asked Wood to concentrate on how he had gotten from the restaurant to the bridge. "Well, if I was doin' it now, I'd run back and forth to keep anyone from followin' me," the young man replied. "I learned that in my military training." This puzzled Stoyek and added to his growing sense of unease, because his experience told him that a person fleeing the scene of a shooting tends to run in a straight line, not back and forth in a manner designed to throw off tracking dogs. The corporal pulled ahead a few more metres, then stopped again, this time beside the big black basement door.

As the two discussed the best route to the bridge, Bruce, still filming the crime scene, decided to take a shot of the car leaving the restaurant—just another in a growing collection of similar images that would be broadcasted and rebroadcasted in the coming days. Many months later, after Stoyek testified in court that he and Wood had begun their drive at 4:15 a.m., I realized we must have been there, so I reviewed the tape and found the shot—there was the husky Stoyek behind the wheel, and a small, sandy-haired figure beside him: Wood.

It took Stoyek and Wood a half-hour to retrace the route and then drive to the Sydney RCMP detachment, where, at 4:45 a.m., Derek Wood was taken to an interrogation room and left alone.

Wood found himself in a cramped space about three metres square. The walls, bare except for a light switch, were covered in perforated white acoustic tile, which extended up the door to a square area near the top where a mirrored glass window allowed observers to look in but prevented those inside from seeing out. The floor was carpeted, and the only furnishings were a rectangular table and three uncomfortable chairs. Wood sat down in one of them and tried to get his bearings. He did not know that he would be in this room for a very long time.

• • •

BY 5:00 A.M., an eerie calm had settled over the crime scene. Kevin Cleary and the other investigators had either returned to the Sydney detachment building or headed out to conduct the tasks that had been assigned to them. Inside the restaurant, Henry Jantzen stood guard in the basement as James Leadbetter continued his documentation of the scene. Leadbetter marked, photographed, and catalogued the footprints in the training room, and began a search of the upstairs floors, looking for matching prints. He found only one full print, just outside the manager's office; there was a partial print beside the safe, but it was so faint that it could not be photographed. The sticky wax surface on the training-room floor, which had fortuitously stripped debris from the sneaker bottoms to clearly show the tread patterns leading into the restaurant, had also stripped the footwear clean. It was impossible to determine where the killers had walked after leaving the room. Leadbetter began the painstaking job of dusting surfaces throughout the building in the hopes of finding fingerprints that might later help convict those responsible. Trouble was, the killers had worn gloves, and none of the many fingerprints in the restaurant would link them to the scene.

Outside, the officers left guarding the doors stood in silence as ambulance attendants removed the bodies of Neil Burroughs and Donna Warren. For the three of us still waiting in front of the building, there was a haunting calm as the cameras recorded the silent procession. Two ambulances rolled slowly down the driveway and turned onto Kings Road; the normally busy street was empty of traffic. The police roadblocks remained in place as the ambulances drove past Kings Convenience and headed to the Sydney City Hospital, where doctors were frantically working to save Arlene MacNeil. They had already determined that Jimmy Fagan would not survive.

The parents of Jimmy and Arlene had gathered at the hospital hours before, summoned just after the two young people were wheeled into the emergency room. The families of Donna Warren and Neil Burroughs were still fast asleep; the job of notifying the families of the slain victims fell to police, who had been busy at the crime scene and would shortly be making the painful journey to the Warren and Burroughs homes.

The doctor who called the Fagans and the MacNeils had told them only that their children had been shot, and that they were needed to consent to surgical procedures. Theresa and Al Fagan were the first to arrive; they lived only a few blocks from the hospital. Al attempted to calm his wife by suggesting that there must have been some kind of an accident and that Jimmy had probably just been hit in the arm or leg. It was nothing serious, he kept telling his wife—and himself. But that hope faded quickly as the couple rushed into the emergency room to find an ambulance gurney abandoned in the hallway. Theresa Fagan put her hand over her mouth as tears welled in her eyes. The pillow on the gurney was covered in blood, and there was no staining anywhere else.

"Oh my God, Al, he's been shot in the head." Al Fagan grabbed his wife to comfort her as he looked for someone—anyone—who could tell them about Jimmy. As they ventured farther into the emergency ward they were pushed aside by an emergency medical team rushing past with a body on a stretcher. They saw Arlene MacNeil, her face caked in blood. "My God! What's going on here?" Al Fagan's deep, booming voice filled the narrow hallway as a doctor rushed up.

"Who are you? You shouldn't be here now."

"Our son Jimmy…He was shot! Where is he?" Theresa Fagan pleaded for an answer; she just wanted to be with her son. Realizing who the couple were, the doctor took them to a "quiet room," saying he'd be back when he had information for them. There, the Fagans sat agonizing over what they had just seen in the hall. They decided they should phone Jimmy's brothers and sisters in Halifax. But what could they tell them? Al knew his boys would be filled with questions, and he had no answers. Within an hour, a big car left Halifax, bound for Cape Breton: Jimmy's family was coming home.

As Al and Theresa Fagan sat alone in the hospital, at the beginning of what would be a long and harrowing vigil, Germaine MacNeil was speeding towards Sydney. Arlene's mother was trying to understand the call she'd received a few moments earlier. Arlene had been shot…How could that be? Germaine glanced at the speedometer and realized she had to slow down; Arlene needed her, and she could not afford to have an accident. The fastest route to City Hospital was via Kings Road, but as Germaine pointed the car down the exit ramp, she saw the flashing lights of a Louisbourg police car: the entrance to Kings Road was blocked. Germaine shifted back into the lane that continued along the bypass and to the next exit into Sydney, her heart pounding at the sight of more flashing lights around McDonald's. The rest of the drive to the hospital was a blur of intersections and anxi-ety—a blur that would hang over Germaine MacNeil's life for months to come, as she and her family struggled to understand how their lives could have been changed irrevocably while they slept at home.

At five that morning, Olive Warren was awakened by her husband. She generally rose early to get ready for work at a nearby motel, but this morning Olive would not go to work. "There was a report on the radio about a shooting at McDonald's," said Donald Warren. "It says people were killed."

Olive looked at her husband. "What? Where's Donna; is she home?"

"No."

She ran to the kitchen, grabbed the phone, and quickly dialled the restaurant. Donna was the manager; if something had happened, she would have to stay, but surely she'd answer the phone. It seemed an eternity before the frantic mother accepted that no-one was going to answer. She quickly looked up the number for the RCMP in Syd-ney, but instead of calling the emergency number, she dialled infor-mation—and the Mounties had stopped answering that line as they began the initial coordination of the biggest investigation the de-tachment had ever handled.

Olive Warren's son was just coming into the kitchen as she slammed the phone down, then looked for the number of the Sydney police and debated going to the restaurant to see what was happening. No. She would call the Sydney police first. The night duty sergeant at Sydney police headquarters told Olive he was not sure what had hap-pened at the restaurant, and that the RCMP were handling it. Olive explained why she was calling. "My daughter was working there last night, and she's not home. Who can tell me if she's all right?"

"If you hang up, I'll call back in one minute, ma'am. I'll find out for you." She must be O.K., the family agreed, sitting in the dark kitchen and waiting anxiously for the sergeant in Sydney to phone again. When he did, the officer gave Olive Warren a new number to dial and told her someone was waiting for her call. That someone was Dave Roper; the information officer had been told that Mrs. Warren was trying to find out about her daughter. Roper did not want to take the call; there was no way he wanted to break news like this to some-one over the phone, and he had no idea what to expect as he picked up the phone. Olive quickly identified herself and explained that she was trying to find out what was happening at McDonald's.

Roper stalled. "Has your daughter arrived home yet, Mrs. Warren?"

"No, that's why I'm calling."

"Do you still live at the same address in North Sydney?"

"Yes, yes, I do—now can you tell me anything about what happened at McDonald's?"

"Mrs. Warren, an officer has been sent to your home to explain the entire situation to you. He should be there any moment now."

"Someone's coming here?"

"Yes, ma'am, and he can answer all your questions if you could just wait a few more moments."

"Thank you, thank you very much." Olive Warren hung up, and as she turned from the phone, her son noticed two cars pulling into the driveway. It was the RCMP and a North Sydney police car. Olive Warren knew at that moment that Donna was not coming home. Outside, Constable David Trickett braced himself for the job every policeman hates.

While Dave Trickett was steeling himself to knock on the door of the Warren home, Constable Darryl Aucoine was standing in front of the home of Neil and Carmel Burroughs, in the small community of Dominion, just outside Glace Bay. Aucoine had enlisted the help of the town police department; a constable from the Dominion force stood uncomfortably beside the Mountie as he knocked hard on the front door.

Upstairs, Carmel Burroughs awoke with a start. "Neil! Neil, wake up, there's someone at the door." Neil Burroughs, Sr., rolled over and said to his wife: "It's probably Neil. Go let him in." Their son often stopped on his way home from the back shift, to see if there was anything he could do to help his parents before going home to see Justin and Julia. Carmel Burroughs jumped out of bed and grabbed her robe. Surely that couldn't be Neil, she thought. It was too early. When she got downstairs, she realized the knock was at the front door; now that was *not* Neil. Carmel was confused as Darryl Aucoine identified himself; she vaguely recognized the other officer.

"Ma'am, is there anyone else at home?"

"Yes. My husband."

"Could you wake him please, Mrs. Burroughs?" Carmel was too confused to wonder about the request; she went to get her husband. The Burroughs had raised seven children, and they knew a visit from the police in the middle of the night meant something was wrong.

"Is it Neil?" Carmel asked when they came back downstairs; her son was still on her mind. There was no easy way to say what had to be said. Darryl Aucoine had a reputation at work as an officer with a keen sense of humour, who loved to make people laugh. But now, it was as if his cheerfulness had been drained right out of him, and all he felt was sick at heart.

"I'm afraid your son Neil has been brutally murdered." The words came out almost on their own. They hit Carmel Burroughs hard and fast. Panic and blackness engulfed her as she dropped to the kitchen floor. Her husband and Corporal Aucoine quickly picked her up and eased her into a chair as the other officer grabbed a glass of water. Carmel slowly came around, but she never fully recovered from the words she had just heard. Her little boy, her helper, her friend—*my God, Neil was gone.*

Once he had helped to comfort Carmel Burroughs as best he could, Darryl Aucoine faced yet another painful duty—informing Neil Burroughs's young wife that she was now a widow. He could see Julia Burroughs fighting for control as he spoke with her, but the shock in her eyes told another story. *Please, Lord, this can't be happening. Justin loves his daddy. Don't take his daddy away.*

In North Sydney, Dave Trickett tried to console Olive Warren as she reached for the telephone. There were people to call, things to arrange. Olive was acting out of reflex, trying to busy herself, and the young officer knew her state of mind could change at any second. He offered to wait with the family until the calls were made and relatives came to the house. Olive declined, and Dave Trickett headed back to his car, leaving a tearful and shocked family behind him. He was not sure what role he would play in this investigation, but the young constable wanted to help find those responsible for making him the bearer of such emotionally shattering news. Olive Warren's life had been changed forever when a bombshell was dropped by a policeman she did not know and whose name she quickly forgot as he drove away in silence.

● ● ●

WITH THE PAINFUL job of notifying the families completed, it was time to tell the public what had happened at McDonald's. Dave Roper had been busy writing a statement for reporters, who stood huddled in the cold outside the Sydney detachment, but he could not read it until he got clearance from Kevin Cleary and Herb Davies, the two officers in charge of the case. They were both busy debriefing officers who had been at the scene and formulating a plan for the next few hours. The first twenty-four hours are the most critical in any major investigation, and the RCMP were determined not to let this trail grow cold. Roadblocks had been set up in several key areas on the island; John Trickett was preparing to take his dog Storm on a daytime search of the area around McDonald's; and the restaurant owner and managers were being questioned about any possible motive for the shooting, other than robbery. Police wondered, for example, whether only one of the four victims was the target of the attack, and whether the others had just gotten in the way. There was also the question of the possible eyewitness, Derek Wood, still squirming in his uncomfortable chair in the interrogation room, elsewhere in the building.

Finally, Dave Roper came outside and invited the reporters into the building. The briefing was held in the reception area of the detachment, with Constable Roper standing behind the counter and reporters on the other side, reaching towards him with their outstretched microphones.

"Shortly after 1:00 a.m., RCMP received a report of gunshots fired at the McDonald's restaurant in Sydney River....Investigation at the scene revealed that as a result of an apparent armed robbery, two persons were killed and two other persons were shot and are in critical condition....All four victims are employees of the restaurant. Sydney detachment of the RCMP is requesting the assistance of the general public. Anyone who may have been in the area...is asked to call." The call for public assistance became Roper's signature in the days ahead, and it paid off; the phones began to ring steadily and continued to do so for days. At the end of the prepared statement, the questions began.

"Was the restaurant open at the time of the shootings?"

"No, and we want to make it very clear that all of the victims were employees of McDonald's. This is not a case of someone walking into an open restaurant and shooting people."

"Can you tell us the type of weapon or weapons used?"

"We believe at this time it was not a rifle."

"So it was a handgun?"

"We believe so, yes."

"Do you have any suspects at this time?"

"No, at this time we are pursuing a number of avenues." Roper knew that Derek Wood was being questioned, but the young man was still being considered a witness, despite the growing belief within the detachment that he was in some way involved in the tragedy. Besides, even if he was involved in the crime, two other people had been seen running away, and there was no point letting them know that Wood was already in custody. Roper cut off the questioning by inviting the reporters to come back at 3:00 p.m. for another briefing. At that time, Roper would face tougher questions and a group of unfamiliar faces; the reporters attending the first briefing knew Roper, and he knew them. In the months since he had become the media officer, he had met with all of them on stories ranging from crime-prevention initiatives to safe-driving campaigns. The reporters from the *Cape Breton Post,* CBC Radio and TV, CJCB Radio, and ATV had enough for now, but we'd be back.

With the information from Roper and the crime scene description from the motorist who had seen where Jimmy Fagan's body had fallen outside McDonald's, I headed to the ATV newsroom to file the first in a series of reports on the crime. The most powerful image we had was the tape that showed the ambulances leaving the restaurant, and it figured prominently in the first reports. Within hours, the procession that had been witnessed by only the three of us was seen by millions, as stations across Canada and the U.S. picked up the video. Local Crown prosecutor Ken Haley saw the report at home, on an American network; at first he thought the incident had occurred in some crime-ridden city in the States. When the news anchor reported that the shootings had occurred in the small Nova Scotia community of Sydney, Haley's heart skipped a beat. He dressed quickly and left for work, knowing he could get more information at the Crown office. Little did he realize how involved he would become in this case in the months ahead.

Just before 6:00 a.m., Corporal Brian Stoyek returned to the interrogation room at the Sydney RCMP detachment, where he found Derek Wood using the phone that was sitting in the middle of the table. "Who are you talking to?" Stoyek asked. "My cousin Mike," the young man replied. Wood had no idea that by making this second call to his cousin, he was also making Mike Campbell a potential suspect. He also had no idea what a complex chain of events was unfolding outside the small room. But he would soon discover that he was by no means home free.

"You'll have to hang it up," Stoyek said. "You can't talk to him until we finish asking you a few questions, Derek." Wood hung up, and Stoyek unplugged the phone and took it out of the interview room. When he came back, he was carrying a note pad; he told Wood he wanted to get a detailed written statement. In that statement, the young man told the officer he had finished his shift at McDonald's but stayed behind when Arlene MacNeil asked him to help with the inventory; they did that work in the lobby, and then he went downstairs to change. After that, he decided to have a cigarette, so he went out through the basement door, propping the inner door open with his knapsack and standing outside the big outer door to smoke. The outer door could only be closed and latched from the inside, so he didn't have to worry about holding it open while he enjoyed his cigarette. Wood said he was smoking at about one o'clock in the morning when he heard two shots that sounded like a C-7 or an American M-16; he recognized the sound of these high-powered rifles because of his training with the Cape Breton Militia District. The two shots came real fast, he said—real close together—and they were followed by a single scream, which sounded like Donna's voice. After hearing that scream, Wood said, he took off along the route he had shown Stoyek.

A short time later, Kevin Cleary joined Stoyek in the interview room; the corporal had convinced the investigating officer that something was not right with Derek Wood. The young man was unaware that he was becoming a focus of the just-developing case, but he was beginning to realize that his first impression—that it would be easy to fool the police—was far from accurate. At least, this big Stoyek guy and the Cleary fellow were obviously not ready to accept what he had to say at face value. But he wasn't particularly worried when officers came in to check his sneakers; if his footprints were by the basement door, it only supported his story.

The two officers kept pressing for details and pointing out things they said didn't make sense. Wood tried to buy time, filling in blanks with facts he was sure of, things that had happened before and after the shootings. He told them that he made two calls from Kings Convenience, but that he was pretty sure the first call was to an ambulance company. He told them that he phoned Mike from the same store; he told them that he went for a walk. He talked about helping Arlene with the inventory and then having a cigarette with another cash worker before she left. But then they would do something like ask him how it was he could smoke inside after working with her, and then have to light up outside the back door later.

Wood was relieved when Kevin Cleary left, at about 8:00 a.m. Maybe he would get a break. Cleary had decided to check on a few points in Wood's story; he was not comfortable with what Wood was telling him, and he wanted to see how the evidence at the scene fit into the picture. Back at McDonald's, the corporal talked with Ident officer James Leadbetter, who was still working inside. Leadbetter showed Cleary where he had marked the footprints on the blue tile floor in the crew training room—the faint set of prints leading to the basement door, and the more clearly defined ones, extending from the back door into the restaurant; one of the stronger prints lay directly across one of the prints headed out of the basement. Clearly, the people coming in were the last ones to walk in that room, which did not fit with Derek Wood's story about having a smoke, then running away after hearing shots. Wood must have let them in, at least.

Then, Cleary and Leadbetter tested the big black steel door, which had been locked when officers arrived on the scene. Wood's explanation was that he slammed it when he ran away. Corporal Leadbetter slammed the door; it did not lock. Again and again it did not lock. Leadbetter must have slammed that door twenty times, and only twice did the steel lever fall into the bolt. It was highly unlikely that anyone running away could get that door to lock by slamming it. Finally, the two officers searched around the door and the driveway for fresh cigarette butts; Derek Wood said he had smoked two. There were none.

The evidence at the scene; the cut hand; the phone call to his cousin from Kings, looking for a drive home; his decision to walk away from the store and not wait for the lift. This was all very disturbing—and Cleary had a new concern about Wood. He learned that Wood had phoned Freeman MacNeil's house from Kings—and that the young man had neglected to tell police about this. Wood had told Stoyek that Freeman drove him to work that night, but he hadn't mentioned the phone call he made later. Police found out about that call early in the morning, after Corporal Trickett visited the MacNeil home to ask Freeman a few questions. The young man wasn't there when Trickett arrived at the MacNeil home on Beaton Road, so Trickett spoke to his mother.

The corporal really liked Edith MacNeil; the slight, friendly woman reminded him of his own mother, and he repeatedly assured her she had nothing to worry about—he just wanted to ask Freeman about a friend he had driven to McDonald's. Edith asked if that friend was Derek and told Trickett he had called there looking for Freeman at around one in the morning. Derek had missed Freeman by only a few minutes, she said; her son and a friend had left after picking up an asthma inhaler that Freeman's girlfriend needed. That was probably where Freeman would be now, she said. As the officer was about to leave, she wished him luck, saying: "We'll be thinking of you. I hope you catch the people who are responsible." Trickett would have liked to stay and chat with her a while longer, but he couldn't afford the time; there was too much to do. He told her he appreciated her good wishes, and turned to go, noting, as he drove down the long driveway, that the old white house needed a paint job.

In the small interview room, Cleary began to confront Derek Wood with some of the inconsistencies in his story. Wood had no explanation, and as Cleary talked, he began to fold himself into a fetal position in the chair—a posture that suggests to police that a person has something to hide, something to protect. By noon, it became clear to the officers that they were not making a lot of progress; they left the room to plan a new approach.

It had been a very frustrating morning for Brian Stoyek, who occasionally left Wood alone so he could clear his head and try to figure out how to get through to the small blond teenager who sat in the room, fidgeting but showing no signs of panic, or any other emotion, for that matter. Stoyek was certain Derek Wood knew something—at least who he had kept that basement door open for—and he could not understand how this apparently normal young man could sit in the interrogation room and protect killers, instead of helping police avenge the deaths of his co-workers.

After the two officers talked, Cleary decided it was time to let Derek Wood know he was no longer being considered a witness. At 1:07 p.m. on May 7, Derek Wood was told he was under arrest on two charges of murder, two of attempted murder, and one of robbery. This was really just an attempt by the police to show Wood just how serious the situation was. They did not arraign the eighteen-year-old or even consider taking him before a judge to be formally charged; they knew there was no evidence to support such charges—but maybe he would decide to hand over those who were responsible. After all, during the interrogation they had continually told Wood they did not believe he was responsible for the shootings but that they did feel he knew more than he was admitting.

Wood could see that the situation was deteriorating, but he held onto the comforting knowledge that police still felt he was not the killer.

SIX

THE NAME Industrial Cape Breton is a throwback to the days when coal mines and the steel mill thrived, employing thousands. By 1992 the steel mill had been modernized and downsized, and the Nova Scotia government, the owner for more than twenty years, had decided to sell the money-losing enterprise. The coal mines, too, had seen more-prosperous days; coal was developing a reputation as a dirty fuel, as communities and regions became more environmentally responsible. Yet the industry-town attitude remained a strong part of the Cape Breton identity: people knew their neighbours and cared about what happened to em. Community spirit had grown strong in the 1920s, when over-worked and underpaid coal miners fought for their rights. The bond, created during that struggle and strengthened when mining tragedies struck, remained an important component in the fabric of the industrial area. On May 7, 1992, it did not take long for word of the shootings at McDonald's to spread throughout these communities and shake them to the core. Cape Breton was changing; in fact, it had changed. Violent crime, once something read about or seen on TV, was hitting much too close to home.

Cape Breton had not been immune to murders; it was just that this one was different. For the most part, murders on the island involved people who knew one another—friends or lovers, who, for some reason—usually one intensified by alcohol—reached an impasse that ended in a moment of violent passion. That was part of the reason the RCMP were looking closely at the victims in this crime; people were usually killed by someone they knew. But for Cape Bretoners, the McDonald's murders represented a turning point: it was the second time in only a few months that random violent crime was dominating their conversation. On a stormy March night, convenience store clerk Marie Lorraine Dupe was stabbed to death during an apparent robbery. Sydney police still had not solved that case, and people in Cape Breton, the police included, began to wonder if there could be a connection between the two crimes; thus police were especially motivated to move quickly to find those responsible. The idea of a crazed killer or killers on the loose changed the way many people saw themselves and their neighbours. The island was a place where people felt comfortable sleeping with unlocked doors, but for many that sense of security disappeared as word of the McDonald's murders spread.

In the newsrooms on the island, we were trying to tell two stories on Thursday, May 7. We wanted to convey what had happened in Sydney River—a story I told by using Dave Roper's news briefing and the interview with the motorist on the highway behind the restaurant—and we wanted to describe the community's reaction to the crime. The second story was an easy one to tell, because very few people we encountered did not have something to say about what had happened and what it meant to them. The mayor of Sydney said that Cape Breton had changed overnight, that violence was becoming a daily occurrence. Church leaders cited chronic unemployment as a contributing factor, saying that people without work and without hope could resort to desperate acts. Many business owners immediately began taking action to protect their employees; video surveillance systems became a hot seller, and the area's security-system companies were quickly tasked with installing new alarms and monitors. And some business people concluded that late-night operating hours were simply no longer worth the risk.

Teenagers in the area seemed particularly overwhelmed by what had happened. The Sydney River McDonald's is only a short walk from Riverview Rural High School; students frequented the restaurant daily, and many had found part-time employment there. On the morning of the murders, small groups of teens gathered around the school property, whispering and wondering about what had happened. Word spread quickly that a former student, Derek Wood, had been the one to call police—that he was lucky to have escaped alive. Other employees who had worked the night shift spoke about police coming to their homes to take their sneakers and ask who was left in the restaurant when they had finished work. The murders became the prime topic of conversation among the student population, as it did in almost every sector of the Cape Breton community.

Those of us covering the story quickly realized the scope of the tragedy as we were swamped with requests from media outlets outside the region. For me, it was very difficult to grasp what was happening in the community, although in the days ahead I would get a better understanding of how the people I had grown up with felt our island had changed. I had covered many murders in my thirteen years as a reporter in Cape Breton, including a triple murder just off the island, in Antigonish County; but nothing prepared me for the intense demands for information that came with this crime. While I desperately tried to fill the demands of the assignment desk in Halifax with live updates throughout the day, I also had to attempt to track down whatever details I could, and at the same time field an endless stream of calls from viewers and friends who just wanted to talk to someone connected to the crime. It seemed that every time I stepped in front of the camera to deliver another brief update, the phones would start ringing off the hook again.

The reaction to the murders was not confined to Cape Breton. As reports spread across North America, reporters and camera crews came pouring in from everywhere. And those of us who covered Cape Breton daily pulled out all stops. Both ATV and the regional CBC decided to host their evening news programs from the island; news anchors were rushed from Halifax to Sydney. Dave Wright, who delivered the evening news to Maritime audiences every day, decided to host his newscast in front of the restaurant, and the ATV satellite truck was sent from Halifax, marking the first time live satellite technology had been used to cover a crime on the island.

• • •

FREEMAN MACNEIL was having no problems convincing officers he was not involved in what happened at McDonald's. Shortly after 1:00 p.m., Constable Glen Lambe and Sergeant Phil Eagan arrived at the tiny trailer on East Broadway in Whitney Pier—Freeman's girlfriend Michelle's place. When the young man answered the door, the constable found himself looking up. MacNeil was just over six feet tall, heavy-set but not overweight, and exceptionally clean-cut compared to many young people of his age. Lambe liked MacNeil right away, because he appeared to be a clean-living young man and because he was at ease and cooperative with the police.

Lambe explained that he was investigating the McDonald's murders—a statement that must have sent a spear of anxiety through Freeman MacNeil's heart, although it drew no visible response. The constable said he wanted to ask MacNeil a few questions about Derek Wood. "No problem," MacNeil said, throwing on a pair of slippers and following the officers out to the unmarked police car. Sergeant Eagan, an experienced investigator, knew very well that you cannot judge a person by appearances, and he wanted to make sure this interview elicited facts about Freeman MacNeil's knowledge of, and involvement with, Derek Wood. Eagan had been lied to many times in his years as a narcotics control officer; he knew what to look for. The sergeant relaxed slightly when he saw how comfortable the young man was in the company of police, which stood to reason when MacNeil said he had worked as a security guard in Halifax and Sydney. Still, Eagan watched closely as Glen Lambe began taking a statement, looking at MacNeil's hands and the colour of his face, and even trying to detect any change in his pulse by watching the vein in the side of MacNeil's neck.

MacNeil told the officers he knew Derek Wood because Wood used to date a friend of his girlfriend's. Wood had called the night before and asked him for a drive to McDonald's, and MacNeil took him there at around eight o'clock, telling him to call if he needed a ride home; he did not see Wood again. MacNeil went out again later, he said, but not until after 1:30 a.m., when he went to get an asthma inhaler for Michelle. Near Tim Hortons, he saw another friend, Darren Muise, so he picked Muise up and took him along for the drive. MacNeil added that he'd noticed police around McDonald's and thought there must have been a bad accident, but that he did not stop to look because he wanted to get the puffer back to Michelle. Constable Lambe wrote down MacNeil's story, and Eagan noted that the young man had easily passed his unofficial lie-detector test.

After the two Mounties left, Freeman MacNeil decided to head out to Beaton Road. His mother would be at work, and he had some work of his own to do. He had already talked with Darren on the phone, and he knew "Woody" was in custody; that was a problem, but as long as Woody stuck to his smoking story, they would be all right. In meantime, there was a kitbag, containing some bloody clothes and a mask, to be burned. As he drove out of the Pier, Freeman blasted the car stereo. He loved loud music; now that he had money, he would have to get some better-sounding speakers for the car.

As MacNeil headed home, another young man was contemplating the events of the night before. Greg Lawrence, who had an apartment in South Bar—on the outskirts of Sydney at the end of the Pier—was relieved that he had not gotten involved in the scheme that his buddy Freeman and a couple of other guys had planned at McDonald's. But he was also worried. He knew something had gone terribly wrong. Lawrence had been listening to his police scanner overnight and heard reports of a gunshot at McDonald's. He also heard an officer saying there were several injured at the scene. Then the radio traffic got busier and busier, and Lawrence couldn't believe his ears. Jesus, these guys had talked about the robbery right here in his apartment! And he had seen the gun in Freeman's trunk; hell, they asked him to join them on the job. Lawrence didn't know what to do. He couldn't call the cops on his friends, and even if he could bring himself to do that, Kristine would be put at risk. Lawrence was worried about what MacNeil, Muise, and Wood might do to his girlfriend if they thought he was going to turn them in; Kristine had been there when the robbery was being discussed.

Lawrence thought back to the day MacNeil and Muise approached him outside the Tim Hortons coffee shop on Townsend Street in Sydney. He barely knew the two guys—they had only met a month or so before—but they seemed O.K. He was only a little surprised when they invited him to take part in a robbery they were planning. It was no real big deal; lots of people were involved in minor crimes, and stealing stuff from parked cars was a popular means of getting quick cash for some of the young people hanging around in downtown Sydney. Lawrence listened while Freeman explained the plan, and then declined. He wasn't interested. Later that night, Darren Muise came into the same Tim Hortons and asked Lawrence to talk to him outside. They walked to the car: Freeman MacNeil was in the driver's seat, and a blond guy they called Woody sat in the back. Freeman explained that the three of them had been set to rob McDonald's that night, with the help of Woody, who worked there, but that another guy who was supposed to help them did not show up. They quickly explained their plan to Lawrence and again asked him to participate. Lawrence was sceptical, but Freeman persisted, offering him twenty thousand dollars for his role. All he would have to do was stand outside a door with a stick and knock out any employees who could not be subdued and who managed to make it to the door. Lawrence said no again, and maintains to this day that he did not take the offer seriously either time it was made. At the time, Lawrence thought the three guys had a plan, but did not have the guts to see it through. He did not want to get involved with them.

Now, a week later, Greg Lawrence was wondering what would happen next. Freeman had called him early that morning and said that someone else had beat them to the restaurant. Lawrence had his doubts about MacNeil's story that the three robbers drove to McDonald's to find it surrounded by police, but he didn't express them. Still, what would they do if they thought he didn't believe their story? And what would he do? More to the point, what *should* he do?

Derek Wood had more important things on his mind than Greg Lawrence. Within an hour of being placed under arrest, Wood decided to take the officers up on one of the options they'd offered. He wanted to talk to a lawyer. Corporal Stoyek provided a telephone and the number of the local Nova Scotia Legal Aid office; Wood could not afford to hire his own lawyer.

In his years as a Legal Aid attorney, Art Mollon had defended his share of people accused of murder, but he'd never been involved in a case as big as this one. Mollon was not really surprised when he was called by the young man being questioned by RCMP; lawyers around the Legal Aid office half-expected to be called whenever there was a murder in the area. Legal Aid ended up handling most murder cases in Cape Breton, and the big ones usually found their way to Art Mollon. As he drove the short distance from his office to the RCMP detachment, Mollon wondered what he was up against this time. He knew from radio reports that the shootings had occurred around one in the morning, and that meant his new client had probably spent the past thirteen hours telling police more than he should have.

The first meeting between lawyer and client was a short one. After the introductions, Wood explained his dilemma: the police were not believing him and had arrested him. Mollon was in the habit of advising clients of the importance of adhering to their right to remain silent. The police had a job to do, but convincing someone to incriminate himself—although a popular tactic with veteran investigators—did not have to be a part of the process. Police could ask all the questions they wanted, but Mollon made it clear to his client that he did not have to answer. If there was going to be a charge laid, both Mollon and Wood would be given copies of any evidence the police had in the case; then a decision could be made on what he should say in his own defence. The meeting lasted less than fifteen minutes, but Derek Wood was now ready to deal with the police.

When the lawyer left the building, Corporals Stoyek and Cleary returned to their suspect. Cleary controlled much of the conversation, trying to appeal to Wood's conscience. "Look, Derek, we don't think you're the trigger man. You're involved in something here that you've got to deal with; it's important now that you tell us the truth. We don't think you wanted to see anybody killed, but if someone convinced you to leave that door open, we have to know who it is before someone else gets hurt. Whoever did that, Derek, whoever did that could do it again. Who was it, Derek? How did you get involved in this?"

"I have no comment." It was an answer Cleary would hear repeatedly in the hours that followed. However, when they broached the subject of Arlene MacNeil, both Cleary and Stoyek thought they had found a way to reach Wood. "Derek, you have to understand the seriousness of this matter. That gun is still out there, and we have to find it. I was in that restaurant. I saw poor Arlene lying there in her own blood." Cleary's words brought an immediate response: Derek Wood's eyes filled, and although he did not start crying, both officers felt he was on the verge of breaking down. They pursued their line of questioning with some success. Finally, at 6:20 p.m., the officers believed they had reached Wood. "I don't know as much as you think I know," he said. "I don't know where the gun is. Let me call my lawyer, and I'll talk." The officers had already told him that they would be happy to take his statement while his lawyer was present, and now they were convinced he was going to accept the offer.

While Wood was debating whether or not to cooperate with police, most Maritimers were getting their first full reports of what had occurred. The McDonald's murders dominated the supper-hour newscasts. At six o'clock, Dave Wright stood across the street from the restaurant and faced the cameras, speaking to ATV viewers in Nova Scotia, New Brunswick, and Prince Edward Island. "I am standing here outside the McDonald's restaurant in Sydney River. The restaurant was the scene of a grisly multiple murder and robbery early today." Wright paused, communicating to his audience that he did not like telling them that such a horrible thing had occurred in what he commonly referred to as "the Maritime neighbourhood." Wright then introduced me, and I began the first full-length report on the murders. TV screens throughout the region were filled with foreboding images. Darkness surrounded McDonald's, the only light coming from an open rear door where a group of police officers stood looking inside. The scene changed as the ambulances were shown leaving, carrying the victims, who had been identified and who we were now able to name.

Then, the face of Dave Roper appeared on the screen; during his three o'clock press briefing, the information officer had delivered unsettling news, which would convey to the public that the Mounties didn't yet have much to go on. "RCMP have removed the roadblocks that had been set up around the island because of the limited information we have. At this time, we know two subjects were seen fleeing the building shortly after the last shot was fired. We do not know if these subjects were male or female." The report also contained the first information on an unknown employee who had been outside having a cigarette when the shots were fired. So far, reporters had been unable to track down this man—Derek Wood. They did not know that he was in a room a short distance from where they had been briefed by Dave Roper.

As the newscast ended and Maritimers began talking about the horrifying events in Cape Breton, Darren Muise was getting ready for a night out with friends. It was a quiet, casual evening of joking and talking, the conversation occasionally shifting to the McDonald's murders. Muise voiced his concern for the victims and for his friend Derek Wood. The police shouldn't keep on questioning Woody, he said; the guy had been through enough. It did not appear to bother Muise to express sympathy for the victims and concern for one of their killers in the same breath. The friends with him that night said later that he was acting the way he usually did; in fact, the only unusual behaviour they noted in the days following the McDonald's murders was Muise's tendency to spend money, something he usually had very little of.

While Muise was telling his friends how concerned he was about Derek Wood, Wood himself was in the middle of a second, longer meeting with his lawyer. If Derek Wood began that meeting intending to give police a statement, he ended it with a different agenda. At 8:40 p.m., Art Mollon emerged and told Brian Stoyek that his client would not be making a statement; he then asked Kevin Cleary if charges were to be laid. Cleary and Stoyek were puzzled and disappointed. "We're still investigating at this point," said Cleary. "We're not certain what charges will be brought forward."

"Fine, but my client will be observing his right to silence, gentlemen. Good night." Mollon left, and the officers returned to Derek Wood, who had resumed his protective posture and was once again responding to questions with "No comment" or "I wish to remain silent." After twenty minutes, Kevin Cleary decided to leave the interrogation room and follow up a lead that was developing on a new front. Stoyek was asked to continue to work on Derek Wood.

The promising avenue Kevin Cleary had decided to pursue came from a young woman who had contacted the RCMP earlier in the afternoon. Police were cautious with her at first; she seemed too good to be true. Not only did this cooperative citizen, Cynthia Long, claim to have information on the crime, but she also claimed to know who had committed it, and even where the weapon was. According to Long, she had been with her brother and two other men the night before, and they were the ones responsible. "We parked at the bottom of the driveway, and they went in to rob the place," she told police. "I stayed in the car, and when they came out, we went to the government wharf, and they threw the gun in the harbour."

Cynthia Long told a compelling tale, and despite their concerns about her nervous demeanour, the officers in the Sydney detachment began to believe her. She seemed to feel that what she was saying was true, and it made no sense for someone to try to falsely accuse their own brother of such a horrible crime. The police knew that if the story was accurate, they had to protect this witness and move in on her brother and his friends.

Her account gained more credibility as officers realized it fit with other information they had. John Trickett and Storm had found a trail along the dark side of the restaurant, opposite the driveway. The trail led to the corner of the building, near the black steel basement door but also near the place Cynthia Long claimed the car was parked. If she was telling the truth, this was the trail left by the people Daniel MacVicar had seen running from the restaurant; they had gone around the building and back to their car. Police also had a witness—a worker from a nearby restaurant—who reported seeing a car, fitting the description Long had given and parked where Long said the killers had parked. The clincher for police came when a caller to the Crime Stoppers police information line identified the same three suspects as possibly being involved. This was an odd coincidence—one possibly generated by Long herself, if she told others her story before going to police, thus unintentionally starting a rumour that helped verify her statement to police. What officers did not know was that Cynthia Long was a disturbed young woman who warranted further checking. For Cleary and the other investigators, there was not a second to waste in the effort to get the killers and their weapons off the street.

While time was a critical factor, this time Kevin Cleary was not facing the pressure of wounded victims in need of hospitalization; he would call in the Emergency Response Team from Halifax. Anticipation filled the briefing room at the RCMP detachment—they had names, they had a witness, and they were certain they had an accomplice already in custody. The RCMP were going to get their men and do it quickly. The anticipation of a successful bust eliminated any fatigue that officers might otherwise have felt; no-one had been able to get any rest for the past twenty-four hours. The plan was worked out through the night; heavily armed ERT members would sweep down in the early hours of the morning and take the suspects into custody. But, while there was excitement among the officers, there was also concern—it was very possible this could turn into a shoot-out or a hostage-taking situation. The condition of the crime scene at McDonald's had made it clear to the police that they were dealing with dangerous people. ERT training involves hostage-taking scenarios, and members discussed possible options and complications.

As the Mounties prepared for their morning operation, the relatives of Jimmy Fagan prepared to say goodbye. Jimmy was hooked up to life-support systems, but his family knew he was already dead. The bullet that hit him cut a path through the right hemisphere of his brain, coming to rest against the inner wall of the skull, at the back of his head. The severity of the trauma to the brain caused a swelling that could not be stopped; his brain literally crushed itself under the pressure. Meanwhile, his head, face, and hands also swelled, to a degree that frightened his family as they stood helplessly by, knowing that Jimmy would never awaken.

After being told that their son, was clinically brain-dead, his parents had made the decision to donate his organs so that a part of their son would continue to live. It was something they knew Jimmy would want. Organ donation had been discussed by many Cape Breton families in the weeks before the McDonald's murders. Carmen Young, a teenager from North Sydney, had become the champion of a campaign aimed at having everyone sign an organ donor card; Young was in an Ontario Hospital awaiting a lung transplant. The decision to donate Jimmy's organs meant that his body would continue to be kept alive until an organ retrieval team flew in the following day. This prolonged the agony for the Fagan family; they could not leave Jimmy, even though they knew he would never awaken. A vigil was kept at his bedside, where a family's tears were often the only sound. It was difficult to stay, but impossible to leave.

For Germaine and Howard MacNeil, the prognosis wasn't much better. Their only child was still alive, but doctors didn't hold out much hope for Arlene. The bullet fired by Derek Wood had fragmented when it hit her face, and part of the slug was deflected by a piece of bone and travelled up into the frontal lobe of her brain. Doctors had operated to relieve the pressure, but their view was that the young woman would remain in a coma indefinitely. Germaine Mac-Neil wanted another opinion, though; she was not going to give up on Arlene. She insisted her daughter be transferred to a hospital in Halifax, but doctors said it couldn't be done—at least not yet. It would be too risky to move her at this stage, they said.

As the Fagan family spent their final hours with Jimmy, and the MacNeils prayed for their daughter, Derek Wood began to falter under Brian Stoyek's relentless questioning. Shortly after 10:00 p.m., Wood hinted that he had more information than he had given. "I don't know everything you want," he said.

"Maybe not, Derek, but you do know some things, and it is important that you get them out here and now."

"I might know some things, but not everything you think I know."

"Look, Derek, if you know anything, you've got to tell me. If you lied before, it's time to come clean now. Tell me why did you lie."

"Because I ran away."

"What do you mean? Tell me what really happened."

Wood changed his story, but still kept himself away from any involvement in the crime; however, he did point police towards Freeman MacNeil once again. "I propped open the door and walked down to Tim Hortons, I wanted to see if Freeman was there. I needed a drive. He wasn't, so I headed back."

The version Derek proceeded to tell answered the questions Stoyek had been pressing him on. The black steel door had been locked from the inside because Wood had gone back into the basement after returning from the coffee shop. He said he was inside the basement when he heard a shot—just one—and a scream; when he went to investigate, he saw Arlene lying in a pool of blood near the basement stairs. Wood looked up the stairs to the kitchen and saw two men running out the back door. He did not know who they were, but one was wearing a mask, while the other was carrying a kitbag. Then he ran upstairs and out the back door, where he saw a second body in the entrance. Strangely enough, he did not identify Jimmy Fagan, a fellow worker, a man he knew. Upon realizing that he was following hard on the heels of the two men, who were headed towards the highway, he turned and ran to Kings Convenience. His excuse for lying the first time? He did not want to get involved.

Derek Wood may well have had a degree of confidence as he wove this new tale. Cleary and Stoyek had already told him they knew who he was involved with, that they knew who he let in the restaurant. But the names they gave him—those provided by Cynthia Long—did not have the desired effect of convincing him that police were on the verge of breaking the case—and, of course, there's no reason they should have.

With his new statement in hand, Brian Stoyek left the interview room to confer again with Kevin Cleary. The officers did not sense that they were getting the truth yet, but at least Wood was admitting that he had been inside the restaurant after the shots were fired. At least he was beginning to change his story. While the officers discussed their options and continued planning for the morning raids, Derek Wood curled up on the floor of the interview room and went to sleep. The interview room remained quiet for hours, but a short distance down the hall, the building hummed with activity as dozens of police officers prepared to capture some cold-blooded killers.

• Seven •

FRIDAY, MAY 8, started out as a glorious day in Cape Breton. The sun shone brightly, and forecasters were promising unseasonably high temperatures by midday—the RCMP would be basking in the glow of that sun in a matter of hours. The ERT team was in position in Glace Bay, ready to make the first arrest. While the squad got ready, Kevin Cleary maintained radio contact; he wanted to be certain that everything went according to plan. As Corporal Cleary focused his attention on the pending arrests, Derek Wood was told he could go home. He refused to change his new story, and he could not be held indefinitely. Cleary had told officers he wanted Wood's clothing taken before he was released, but unfortunately the request was overlooked. The young man did not go back to his brother's apartment after being set free. Instead, he went to his cousin Mike Campbell's place; the two would be almost inseparable in the week ahead.

Kevin Cleary was not the only one in the Sydney detachment keeping a close eye on things in Glace Bay. Sergeant Gary Grant, the RCMP media liaison officer for Nova Scotia, had arrived from Halifax. Although Grant outranked Roper, he decided to let the constable conduct all news conferences. Roper had handled himself admirably under extreme pressure the day before, and Grant figured it would be better to let the local boy keep a high degree of visibility. Both Roper and Grant knew they would have big news to release in the next few hours, so they began to plan a formal news conference. This time, the media would be asked to go to the Cambridge Suites Hotel in Sydney, where ERT members and other out-of-town Mounties were staying. The decision to move away from the detachment was an effort to make a tough job a little easier for the team investigating the case. The size of the regular complement of officers at the Sydney detachment had swelled, due to the magnitude of the case;

more than forty officers were taking part in the investigation. Most were working wherever they could find space in the main office area of the detachment. A media circus in the foyer was just too much of a distraction; besides, the reception area was simply too small. The entrance lobby had barely held the throng of reporters who gathered for the three o'clock briefing the day before, and Roper and Grant expected an even bigger crowd today. Reporters had started calling first thing in the morning, most wanting to know if any arrests had been made overnight. Some had heard about unusual police activity in the Glace Bay area and were asking if it was connected to the McDonald's case.

John Trickett had been assigned to back up the ERT team; he and Storm were being held back in a staging area as the team prepared to move in on the first suspect's home. The big dog was eager to get back to work, and Trickett hoped the two of them would be able to uncover some evidence in the house as soon as the arrest was made. Just before the team got into position, there was a radio message from the special observation unit, also called the "O team." They had the suspect "on the move," meaning he was outside the house; that complicated things a bit, but the team was still ready to roll. The ERT van, loaded with heavily armed RCMP specialists, got started. Shortly after it did, police were forced to circle behind a credit-union building in an effort to intercept a rusting hulk of a van—driven by one of the most-wanted men in Canada.

Gary McIssac was happy to see the sun. The van's heater wasn't working very well, and it would be good to be able to drive around without freezing. He reached for the radio, figuring he'd catch a newscast and see what was going on with that McDonald's case. Gary knew some bad guys and had been in a few scrapes himself—but, man, whoever was responsible for that mess was in need of some serious help. Suddenly the big van rocked as a loud bang startled McIssac. Well, shit, he had hit something. He turned to get out and see what had happened, when suddenly he was looking down the barrel of a gun. There were cops everywhere, and they were looking very serious. Gary looked from one officer to the next; they looked like something out of a movie, complete with bulletproof vests. One of the cops pulled open the door and ordered Gary to step out with his hands in plain sight. Gary wasn't sure what was going on, but he knew he wasn't going to argue with these guys; he'd go wherever they wanted to take him. As he stepped out, he found himself flung to the ground, chest down, his arms pulled behind his back and secured with plastic police ties. Gary McIssac had no idea what was happening.

John Trickett watched the arrest from his truck, about half a block away. Aside from the collision between the two vans, everything appeared to have gone well. One down, two to go. The second suspect lived in Sydney, near the Hardwood Hill home of Mike Campbell, where police knew Derek Wood was staying. That made sense to police; he could be the connection with Wood. Like Gary McIssac, Bill O'Handley had no desire to argue with the heavily armed police officers he suddenly found himself facing.

In typical small-town fashion, word of the movie-style arrest of Gary McIssac spread through Glace Bay in a matter of minutes. Telephones in newsrooms back in Sydney began ringing; the Mounties were "all over" Glace Bay; one "witness" was certain that shots had been fired—and had even seen the broken window in the suspect's van. (The glass broke on impact; no shots were fired.) The sudden rush of public interest complicated matters for police as they began searching the home where the third suspect was expected to be. Hundreds of people gathered across the street and watched as officers came and went, some with shotguns in hand. An amateur video photographer was recording an officer standing by a squad car, when suddenly a young man came walking up to him, wanting to know why all these cops were at his place. Glen Delaney had been across the street with friends when they heard the commotion outside. As Delaney talked with the officer in the car, a second officer ran from the house and grabbed him; he was quickly taken into custody and whisked away, in a police cruiser. All three suspects were now in custody; interrogations would begin within the hour. And the video tape of that arrest would play prominently on the evening news.

Veteran RCMP officer Sylvan Arsenault was one of the first to suspect that the Mounties had been duped. He watched carefully as the suspects were questioned at the Reserve Mines detachment building, near Glace Bay. These guys were just too cool, Staff Sergeant Arsenault thought; either they were the most cold-blooded and heartless killers imaginable, or they were innocent. The three men repeatedly insisted on having their alibis checked and kept telling investigators they were wasting their time. The sick feeling Arsenault had in his stomach quickly spread to the other members of the investigating team; by late afternoon, officers assigned to check on the suspects' stories came back to report that the alibis were indeed checking out. Searches of their homes had turned up nothing; nor had a diving team combing the bottom of Sydney harbour, near the government wharf, looking for the gun.

Rumblings that these arrests might not hold up were on Dave Roper's mind as he prepared to walk into a news conference at 2:00 p.m. Roper was uneasy, but the news conference had already been delayed twice, and the reporters and camera people were getting restless. He hoped that some of the officers were simply expressing nervousness, but he knew he had to somehow explain the Glace Bay arrests and the presence of the diving team; the reporters knew about both operations, and wanted answers. This briefing would be carried live on radio and TV, and Dave Roper had to figure out a way to hedge his bets. He decided he would not come right out and say the three men had been arrested for the McDonald's murders.

The banquet room in the hotel basement had been transformed into a formal briefing room. Microphone cables snaked along the length of the floor, reaching up from the podium to a cluster of plastic cubes, adorned by radio and TV station logos. Each cube surrounded a mike, and had been put there by a reporter ready with questions. Larger video cables ran from the room down a hallway to a fire exit, and from there to a big satellite truck parked outside, powered by gas generators that hummed beside the vehicle. Powerful lights had been placed at the back and sides of the room, and smaller lights shone on top of the cameras crowded into the centre aisle. As Dave Roper walked into the room, he was startled by the crowd of reporters and array of equipment, and dazzled by the burst of artificial light.

For me, Dave Roper's entrance marked a debut. The satellite truck outside was for my broadcast; anchor Dave Wright had returned to Halifax, and I had been asked to introduce the briefing and conduct a question-and-answer session with Wright afterwards. It was the first time I had reported live from an event. As Dave Roper approached the podium, I stood to one side of the room and informed ATV viewers that we were coming to them live from Sydney, where the RCMP was about to release new information on the McDonald's murders. I quickly directed the camera to the podium, and Roper began with a prepared statement. "Police acting on investigative information detained three male adults in Glace Bay and Sydney earlier today," he said. "The detention of the three persons went without incident....It is confirmed that a third victim has died as a result of wounds suffered during this incident. Mr. James Fagan of Sydney passed away at approximately eleven-thirty this morning....There is obviously a sense of fear and emotional trauma within the area. It is the wish of the RCMP to instil in the public that an intensive investigation is being carried out to apprehend the people responsible."

With that final sentence, Roper was planting the seeds for the explanation he would be forced to give in a few hours. As he finished, the provincial RCMP press officer, Sergeant Gary Grant, stepped forward to choose which reporters would be invited to ask questions; the RCMP wanted to control this news conference. Roper made it clear he could not comment on what evidence had been collected in searches in Glace Bay or by the diving team. (As far as he knew, nothing of note had been found anywhere, but that was not something he would say here.)

I was able to ask a couple of questions before a voice in the earphone I was wearing told me to break away and direct the camera back on myself so that I could begin the question-and-answer session with the anchor in Halifax. As I began to answer Wright's question, which only I could hear (in my earphone), there was a sudden and very awkward pause. Dave Rope just stared at me, bewildered, as I spoke to a camera only a few metres away from the podium. He then looked from me to Gary Grant, who was also rather unclear as to exactly what I was doing and how they should react to it. Finally, to my relief, another reporter brought the officers back to their briefing. "Just ignore him, Dave." Roper did just that—and turned his attention to the other reporters' questions. And there were many of them.

To begin with, reporters wanted to know when the three suspects would appear in court. That was a tricky one. Roper, like many other members of the investigation team, was not certain these suspects would ever appear in court. He skirted the question, saying it was too early to determine what, if any, changes they might face. Then Roper told reporters that Garfield Lewis had asked to speak to them. That was fine, because they had a few questions for the owner of the McDonald's in Sydney River. They wanted to know if there was an alarm system at his restaurant, if he had fired anyone recently, or if a former or current employee could have been involved. They also wanted more information about the victims. How long had they worked at the restaurant? What were they like? Was McDonald's preparing to do anything to honour them? By the time Roper introduced Lewis, the live portion of our coverage had concluded and I took my seat with the other reporters, hoping that Lewis would be able to fill in some of the blanks for us. As the restaurant owner stepped up to the podium, he too said he had a prepared statement. We waited anxiously to hear what he had to say and then get to the questions.

Heavy-set and tall, with thinning, sandy hair, Garfield Lewis seemed shy in front of the cameras. He quietly thanked the RCMP for the tremendous job they had done, and then began talking about the slain employees and their families. It was when he uttered the word *sympathy* that Garfield Lewis began to cry. His family, standing behind him, moved in closer as he struggled to continue. His voice cracking, tears filling his eyes, Lewis offered his condolences to the families of the victims, naming each in turn. The picture of Donna and Neil on the floor at the restaurant rushed back to him, and the images he had tried to suppress after identifying the victims for police could no longer be contained. "Thank you. I'm sorry." Lewis moved away from the podium, his shoulders shaking as his wife reached around to hold him and his son moved quickly to his side. The Lewis family walked out. There had been no questions.

The live broadcast of the news conference assured quick circulation of the good news that the RCMP had arrested the men responsible. Within an hour, a crowd began to gather at the Cape Breton County Courthouse. Sheriffs' duties said they have never seen anything like it—hundreds of people gathered on the courthouse lawn and in the parking lot. Many people gladly agreed to explain in front of the TV cameras why they were there. "I want to see the animals that did it," one said. Another offered: "We want to know who could do a thing like that." These comments were typical of the mixture of anger and curiosity that characterized the mood of the crowd, and the immediate and intense public reaction led to a second night of live TV from Cape Breton. We moved our satellite truck to the courthouse in the hopes that the suspects would either be there by news time— or, even better, arrive during the six o'clock news broadcast.

I returned to the station to assemble a report, then went back to the courthouse. But the building was locked. That was not a good sign; if suspects were to be arraigned that day, court staff would have had to be there. The prosecutor's office is located next to the courthouse, and I noticed a lone car in the parking lot, so I went to the door. Inside, Ken Haley was awaiting a call from police; a prosecutor also would be needed for any arraignment. I asked Ken if the police might just bring the three before a justice of the peace and have them remanded to the correctional centre for a day or so, until things outside calmed down.

Haley conceded that would be the most likely approach, if anyone was to be charged that night, but added that he didn't know whether or not a JP would be called. He would be standing by until the RCMP contacted him. It wasn't much, but at least I would inform viewers of how any charges were likely to proceed, and let them know that we might have more to tell on the late-news broadcast.

The news of the arrests had not gone unnoticed by those responsible for the murders. As Derek Wood slept after his ordeal with the RCMP, Darren Muise began to believe that things might return to normal. Muise decided to call a childhood friend, Kris Granchelli, whom he had not seen much over the past few months. Granchelli didn't think Muise's renewed attention was surprising; he knew his old friend wanted to talk and figured they would find the time to get together soon enough. Granchelli later said he felt Muise may have been trying to return to the life he'd led before he decided crime was an appropriate career choice. Unfortunately, it was too late to turn back.

Freeman MacNeil used word of the arrests as an opportunity to shore up the story he had given to Greg Lawrence. MacNeil drove to Lawrence's South Bar apartment with his girlfriend, Michelle—just a regular visit among friends, nothing out of the ordinary. That might have been what MacNeil wanted, but his friends were not so sure things were normal. Kristine Borden, Greg Lawrence's girlfriend, watched Freeman closely that afternoon. She thought he seemed very pale and wondered why he continually rocked back and forth in the rocking chair. His appearance and actions spooked her. Greg Lawrence was not ready to openly accept that MacNeil, Muise, and Wood had headed out to rob McDonald's only to discover that someone got there ahead of them. Still, if the RCMP had made arrests, maybe the incredible story was true. Lawrence thought Freeman looked quite normal as he commented that he was glad the RCMP had gotten the people responsible, and wondered aloud what kind of bastards could do such a thing. While Michelle and Kristine visited inside, Greg and Freeman went out to do some work on the stereo in Lawrence's car. MacNeil was good with that sort of thing and soon would turn his skills to the stereo in the car he drove.

By late that evening, high-ranking Mounties had accepted the mistake they had made and were beginning to rethink the investigation. Corporal Cleary would remain as chief investigator, but Staff Sergeant Sylvan Arsenault would take over as coordinator. Arsenault had a way with people, and he knew his first job was going to be to help the officers get over the emotional defeat they felt upon learning they had arrested the wrong people. For Kevin Cleary, the emotional blow was the realization that he had been chasing ghosts while Derek Wood was allowed to go free. Cleary was convinced that a guilty man had walked out of the building while innocent people were being arrested. But he recovered quickly and began to concentrate on Derek Wood.

Gary Grant felt he should be the one to inform the media that the three men were being released: Dave Roper could be the good-news man; let the "Halifax heavy" take responsibility for the mistake. Earlier in the evening, Grant had told reporters he might have more information before the night was over. Some expected a late-night arraignment that would avoid the kind of crowds gathered at the courthouse earlier. Instead, Grant told reporters that the investigation was continuing but that the men detained earlier in the day had been freed; there was insufficient evidence to hold them. The RCMP would later release a detailed statement explaining that they had operated on incorrect information provided to them by a member of the public. Cynthia Long was later charged with mischief, but after months of delay due to psychiatric issues involved in the prosecution, the charge was dropped. A civil suit against the RCMP was later filed on behalf of at least one of the men arrested that day.

For the family of Neil Burroughs, it had been a tough day of making funeral arrangements; the only good thing they could talk about was the arrests of those responsible. Neil's brothers, who had heard a couple of names mentioned in connection with the case, sat down with other family members to watch the late news on ATV. Maybe the people who killed Neil would be identified. But their anticipation quickly turned to shocked disbelief, then anger. As they sat watching, I was standing in the parking lot outside the ATV station on George Street in Sydney, the camera trained on me as the late-night anchor asked if there was any danger of reprisal against those arrested. Did people in Cape Breton believe they were responsible but had been released on a technicality? In retrospect, it was a question loaded with irony. Not five hundred metres away was the house where one of the real killers, Derek Wood, was living. But it was perfectly understandable at the time that the focus of the community—and especially the victims' families—should be on the people arrested and then released. The Burroughs boys continued to fume, their anger growing and spreading through the family until someone decided to call the RCMP. Staff Sergeant Arsenault tired to calm the caller, saying he

RCMP press liaison officer Dave Roper talks to the author the day after the false arrests. [Print from ATV video tape.]

would send an officer to the house if they could just hang on.

At two in the morning, Dave Roper's phone rang, once again waking him from a sound sleep. This public relations job was not what it used to be. Staff Arsenault explained the problem: the Burroughs family wanted to know why they had not been informed about the decision to release the suspects, and they wanted to talk to someone about it. Arsenault asked Roper to try to settle things down with the Burroughs.

On his way over, Roper tried to figure out what he would say. The damage had been done, and there wasn't much he could do to change it. Roper tried to be a diplomat, not so much defending the RCMP as explaining what had happened. The family convinced Roper that victims should be given a higher priority in investigations like this; it was not enough to drive to their house and inform them that someone they loved was dead. They wanted more from the police; they wanted to be kept informed as the investigation proceeded. Roper promised the family this would be the last time the family learned of a major development from a news report. Now all Dave Roper had to do was convince his superiors, and he was pleasantly surprised by the response from Sylvan Arsenault. Not only would the force agree to inform the Burroughs family before releasing information, but special constables would be assigned to the families of all four victims. These officers would be available to answer any questions they had, not only during the investigation, but also in the months between the arrests and the first court proceedings. It was the beginning of a practice that has since become standard procedure for many police forces. Victims' rights were beginning to take on a higher priority.

• • •

MAY 9 MARKED the point in the RCMP investigation when officers began to recover from the false lead and begin a new, highly focused probe aimed at uncovering the mystery presented by McDonald's employee Derek Wood. Investigators would find out everything they could about Wood, and the next time they sat down face-to-face with the teenager, they would be ready. In the days ahead, almost all the officers involved in the investigation would be told time and time again to go home at the end of the shift, only to be found back at work long before their next shift began.

Many of the investigators credit Sylvan Arsenault with fostering the team atmosphere that developed at the Sydney detachment that week. As coordinator of the probe, Arsenault divided the team into two twelve-hour shifts, so the investigation could continue twenty-four hours a day. He held briefings early every morning, as the night shift finished and the day shift prepared to pick up the thread of the investigation once again. Arsenault's main point was that there were no menial tasks here; every assignment was a critical component of the case the RCMP would build against the killers. In the first day of the investigation, rookies and senior officers alike found themselves collecting and examining the contents of the garbage receptacles in and around the Sydney River McDonald's. It was not a pleasant job, but it was one that could produce results. Criminals have been known to discard evidence carelessly in the panic of escaping the scene. That would not prove to be the case in Sydney River, but the police officers gladly rolled up their sleeves and sorted through the assortment of burger, French-fry, and soft-drink containers that filled the bags they had taken from the restaurant.

Corporal John Trickett, who had worked with all the veteran officers and knew the young ones as well, was surprised at the way personality conflicts that had surfaced during other investigations simply disappeared after the McDonald's murders. People who only days before had felt animosity towards one another became partners committed to working together on a case that consumed them. Detachment commanders marvelled at how quickly and intensely the team came together. Many of the officers caught up in the investigation later pointed to the early-morning briefings as a source of the cohesiveness that developed. Sylvan Arsenault did not simply assign officers to tasks; he explained where the investigation was headed and why a particular job was important. He let everyone know what had been uncovered or ruled out by the previous shift, and what new questions had to be addressed by those coming in.

An investigation with the high profile of this one was not without its drawbacks—the Cynthia Long experience had shown them that—and Arsenault made it clear they could expect other false leads. Any information had to be treated as the key to solving the case. Arsenault and other senior investigators knew only too well that ignoring an apparently ridiculous piece of information could come back to haunt them; if the information found its way to a defence lawyer, the investigating officer had to be able to deal with it in court.

Cleary and Arsenault set up the nucleus of the inquiry in a small office—a room not much bigger than the one in which Derek Wood spent twenty-six hours, and one in which Sylvan Arsenault and Kevin Cleary would spend many, many more. A long table and a set of metal file cabinets dominated the room. On a wall behind the table, a flow chart resembling a family tree plotted the progress of the Mc-Donald's investigation. Derek Wood's name on the chart had a number of lines leading away from it, one of them connected to the name Freeman MacNeil. His name, in turn, pointed to others on the chart: during the interview with MacNeil, police learned that his actions on the night of the crime could easily be verified by the people he was with, such as Michelle Sharp and Darren Muise. Those interviews were believed to be formalities, since Sergeant Eagan and Constable Lambe were certain that young MacNeil had told them all he knew about Derek Wood and his actions on the night of May 6–7.

It was becoming clear that solving this case would take good, old-fashioned police legwork. The forensics experts had had two full days at the crime scene, and it was not telling them enough. Patrick Laturness, an expert in the examination and interpretation of blood patterns, had been flown in from the RCMP Regional Forensic Identification Support Lab in Ottawa. The amount of blood in the restaurant had convinced investigators that Laturness would be able to help them piece together exactly what had occurred. Unfortunately, the large pool of blood around Neil Burroughs had spread away from the body after the killers left, erasing any patterning that could have told Laturness something about the attack. Blood-spatter experts examine the shape of bloodstains to determine whether they are passive or active, and Laturness did discover some active, or cast-off, stains near the garbage can by the rear door where Jimmy had been killed. A cast-off stain shows where blood has made contact after being flung from a moving object, such as a knife or club swung through the air. But the stains on the inside wall by the door at McDonald's were attributed to the slip and fall of the taxi driver who had run into the restaurant to help ambulance attendants.

Laturness also noted a trail of passive bloodstains (left when blood drips from a static object) leading to the front service counter from the area where Neil Burroughs died. However, it was impossible to determine whether one of the killers had walked down the corridor, or whether the blood had dripped from Kevin Cleary, a taxi driver, an ambulance attendant, or even the medical examiner, all of whom had come in contact with Burroughs.

Laturness was only able to tell officers what they already suspected—that the bloodied fingerprints trailing down the front of the sink were most likely left by the victim, who had been struggling to get up; and that the bloodstains on the basement floor showed a pattern consistent with someone inhaling and regurgitating blood, which Henry Jantzen had seen Arlene MacNeil doing. The expert from Ottawa was not able to tell investigators anything about the people responsible for the murders, even whether they were covered in blood when they left the restaurant. Much of the blood at the scene could have been left behind, because the victims bled slowly after their assailants fled. As difficult as it was for officers who had been at the scene to accept, it was more than possible that the attackers escaped without so much as a drop of blood on their clothes; in fact, the small calibre of the weapon made this almost certain. Although all four victims had been shot in the head at close range, there were no exit wounds. All the bullets had stayed in the bodies of the victims, reducing the amount of blood-spattering that occurred during the shootings. There was some small consolation in this evidence; it relieved some of the sting Kevin Cleary felt about Derek Wood leaving the detachment before anyone bothered to ask him for his clothing. Cleary still would have preferred to have those clothes, but he knew it was too late now.

So it was hard slogging that would solve the case. The job of keeping track of Derek Wood was handed to the special observation unit of the RCMP, whose members had been brought in from Halifax for the first arrests. The unit was trained in following and observing suspects in major crime cases, but they were having their problems here. The McDonald's murders had people in the Sydney area jumpy, and a number of occasions helpful citizens phoned the RCMP to report suspicious cars parked at all hours of the night in the Hardwood Hill area. Mounties took the calls, then informed the observers they'd been "made" by the neighbours! Time to find a new place to wait and watch. The ATV parking lot turned out to be a good place for the unit, just up the road from the place where Wood was staying, and almost always full of cars. The arrangement also proved valuable for me. It didn't take a rocket scientist to recognize the guys parked discreetly in the corner of the lot as police officers. Maybe I could develop a relationship with them and learn something new. At first, the officers were reluctant to do more than confirm they were police and ask if it was all right for them to remain parked in the lot. Later, one of them, who was getting bored sitting in the car for hours while Wood watched movies at Mike Campbell's, began to open up. We would chat late at night about the duties of the observation unit and how they were kept separate from the main investigative team's assignments. The officer would not confirm who he was watching, but as I continued to spend time crouched beside the driver's window talking to him, I found myself picking up other tidbits of information—especially when the officer's radio squawked an order to move or a report from another observer.

While the observers kept track of Wood, Constable Pat Murphy worked frantically with prosecutor Brian Williston. The RCMP wanted wiretaps on phones at Mike Campbell's home and Derek's brother's apartment, and on two pay phones he was known to use. Because of the reluctance of courts to tap public telephones, police had been forced to set up surveillance at both pay phones so that Pat Murphy could convince a judge that Wood was using them regularly. Obtaining a wiretap is nothing like the process portrayed in TV crime shows. It is an intricate legal process involving sworn depositions prepared by officers familiar with a case, and requires that officers explain to the court why more-traditional means of investigating a case are insufficient. The courts are not inclined to invade people's privacy, even if they are suspect in major crimes.

Williston, like prosecutors Ken Haley and Frank Edwards, had offered his assistance to police. Prosecutors in Cape Breton usually allow police to conduct their own investigations, stepping in only when the file is ready for them to examine. But this time the prosecutors wanted to be involved from the outset—not that they were afraid the RCMP would bungle the investigation, but they simply wanted to be making a contribution to the effort. Williston and Murphy were well-matched for the job they faced: both were sticklers for detail and were more than willing to put in twelve- and fourteen-hour days.

Pat Murphy had prepared wiretap depositions for drug cases, so he was selected to prepare the court documents for this case. The constable looked more like an NFL linebacker than a police paper-shuffler, however. Light-haired and fair-skinned, he had the kind of physique that would have made him a natural choice to play a cop in a movie. His regular features were creased with worry, as he focused on the toughest job he'd ever faced. Williston's almost boyish enthusiasm for his job belied his years of experience. Only his greying hair was a testament to the strain of hard work. The prosecutor's light, almost comical air disguised a sharp litigator's mind, as those who had crossed him in court well knew.

It would take five days for Murphy to complete interviews of all the officers involved in the investigations and provide detailed explanations of police suspicions about Derek Wood, and for Williston to complete the necessary documents. Finally, the wiretap request was granted, and would later be extended to other suspects.

For Brian Williston, being at the centre of such an intense investigation was an eye-opening and unnerving experience. One evening, Sylvan Arsenault pulled him aside to tell him that a squad car had been sent to his home after one of the neighbours reported seeing a prowler in the woods nearby. Williston was the longest-serving prosecutor in the Sydney office, and he was well aware that in such a small community, many of the people he put behind bars knew where he lived. The report turned out to be a false alarm—the "prowler" was a patient who had wandered away from a nearby mental hospital, and there was no threat to the prosecutor or anyone else—but the fact that RCMP reacted by sending a car to Williston's home reminded him that the officers really were nervous. As long as those responsible for the shootings were still out there, anything could happen.

Dave Roper knew his role in the investigation was to try to ease the anxiety in the community after word of the release of the three suspects. Roper met with reporters on May 9 to explain that even while the raids on the first suspects were being contemplated, officers were pursuing other avenues. He was stretching the truth a bit: investigators later admitted that virtually all their energies were directed towards the false lead and the fruitless arrests. Roper conceded that the arrests had been unfortunate, but insisted that they in no way impeded the flow of the continuing investigator; they were just one part of a much bigger picture.

Roper's job was about to be made easier by a terrible tragedy elsewhere in Nova Scotia. Roper preferred to deal with local reporters, whom he knew and trusted; he was not so sure about some of the national reporters who had flown in to cover the story. He and other officers were afraid that all the media attention would end with someone uncovering a critical piece of information and running it on the news before the police could track it down. Reporters were already pestering the City Wide cab company for an interview with the driver who had reported the shootings, and the Mounties knew those same reporters would eventually find their way to Derek Wood. By noon on May 9, however, the attention of the national and international media was drawn away from Cape Breton.

About three hundred kilometres southwest of the Sydney River McDonald's, an explosion had ripped through the underground workings of the Westray coal mine. Twenty-six miners were trapped underground, and despite days of searching by some of Canada's best mine-rescue teams, all the men died. The Westray disaster became the top story in the country, and Dave Roper was left to work with the handful of reporters who had been covering the McDonald's murders since the early morning of May 7.

For Freeman MacNeil, the evening of May 9, a Saturday, passed uneventfully—a quiet evening spent drinking beer with a few friends at the Cossitt Heights Industrial Park in Sydney. The industrial park was home to a couple of businesses, but mostly it was a deserted array of gravel roads and tree-filled lots where municipal planners hoped small businesses would someday locate. The quiet, secluded area made it perfect for late-night drinking parties, and MacNeil and his friends often went there to light small fires, tell stories, and enjoy one another's company. Those present on May 9 were interested in MacNeil's story about his friend Derek Wood, who had been working at McDonald's on the night of the murders but who had run away at the sound of gunfire. When the topic of the McDonald's murders was raised, another friend offered what he felt was a reasonable punishment for those responsible: "Whoever did that should be hung by the balls, have his legs cut off, and be left to bleed to death."

Like the others around the fire, Freeman MacNeil agreed this was an appropriate response, then continued to talk about his pal Derek as the conversation turned to the RCMP foul-up in Glace Bay. MacNeil told the others that Wood had been questioned by the Mounties—that they had even taken his sneakers for comparison with prints at the restaurant. MacNeil said he was afraid Wood might commit suicide; he was all alone, and the RCMP were ganging up on him. Those at the gathering saw nothing unusual in their friend's behaviour;

Freeman was his usual laid-back self that night. Earlier that day, another acquaintance had gotten a similar impression when Freeman came to pick up a used car-stereo amplifier and a set of speakers on which he had put a down payment a few weeks earlier. The only unusual thing Paul MacKinnon noticed about the business deal was the method of payment. Freeman MacNeil used five-dollar bills to pay MacKinnon the seventy-five dollars he owed him. When MacKinnon gave him a puzzled look, MacNeil quickly explained: "Don't cash your pogey cheque at Woolco." Another friend of MacNeil's also took note of his use of five-dollar bills when he put about fifty dollars down on another car-stereo component at a local shop—to which he would return on Monday.

Darren Muise and Derek Wood also spent an uneventful Saturday evening. They were together at Pockets Pool Room in Sydney, a regular haunt for Muise in the months since he had dropped out of school. Pockets doesn't fit the grungy pool-hall stereotype of the movies. Located on a downtown street, between an automotive supply store and a dental clinic, the spacious, fairly bright room features six pool tables, each lit by fixtures hung from the ceiling. Pockets also offers a number of video arcade games, pinball machines, and video-gambling machines, for patrons not inclined to try the tables. A classic Wurlitzer jukebox offers an assortment of country and rock-and-roll favourites; next to it sits a vintage Coke machine. People who work at Pockets feel confident enough about their regulars to openly count and roll the quarters from the various games on the same serving counter where they hand pool balls to the players. The money is easily within reach of anyone interested in trying a grab-and-run robbery. All told, Pockets is the kind of place where it is not uncommon to see a father and a son together, enjoying a game. Members of the Sydney Police street crimes unit say drugs could be obtained from some of the regulars there, but quickly add that the same can be said of almost any business catering to young people—or any high school, for that matter. Sydney police did not have any problems with the pool hall.

Regulars at Pockets were used to seeing Muise, and they knew Wood as well, so they thought nothing of seeing the two there a few times in the week after the McDonald's murders, although one patron was taking more careful note of Darren Muise. He had suspicions about the young man, which would intensify as time went on. The only other unusual thing anyone can remember was that Muise was spending money, which he didn't often have. In fact, he was buying ten-dollar rolls of quarters for the gambling machines. But Derek Wood didn't seem to be spending any more than he normally would.

Late Saturday evening, Sylvan Arsenault realized it would be Mother's Day in a few hours, and he asked the officers working that night if they had remembered to pick up cards for their wives and mothers. It turned out that the officers who had not purchased a card or gift before the crime took place had entirely forgotten about Mother's Day. Cards were picked up at the last minute and handed out for officers to sign—not a very personal approach, but then, there would be plenty of time for that after the case was solved—something the wives and mothers of dedicated police officers understand. A few days later, Neil Burroughs's sister would deliver the Mother's Day gift Neil had bought for Julia before he was killed. It was one of the many painful moments Julia Burroughs would experience in the months ahead, as she tried to adjust to life without her husband.

For the mothers of the victims, there would be no celebrating. Mother's Day would be spent in funeral homes in Sydney, North Sydney, and Glace Bay by Theresa Fagan, Olive Warren, and Carmel Burroughs. Germaine MacNeil would spend the day in an ambulance with her only child; Arlene was going to be moved to a hospital in Halifax, where she would undergo more brain surgery.

Eight

THE FAMILIES of Donna Warren, Jimmy Fagan, and Neil Burroughs attended crowded funeral services in churches near their homes on Monday, May 11. People who had never met the victims also went to the services, trying to show support for the grief-stricken families. For the relatives, the proceedings were a blur of words and condolences in a world gone crazy. An emotional numbness had taken hold. Eventually the numbness would be replaced by anger, but in the days following the murders, the deep sense of loss and the persistent, unanswered question—Why?—left the mourners exhausted and confused. For many, the reality of what had happened had yet to take hold.

Inside the large white wooden church in Dominion, thoughts of Neil Burroughs filled the minds of his wife, his parents, his brothers, and his sisters. Neil meant something different to each of them, but loosing him was difficult for everyone to accept. The words, the music, and the heat in the church swirled in the minds of the mourners, occasionally replaced by powerful memories. The image of a mischievous brother, for example, who would jump out of a closet just to watch his sister scream with sudden fright and then as quickly win her forgiveness with a silly grin and a teasing laugh. For Julia Burroughs, the memories were of a devoted young father who spent every spare moment with his son; when Justin was born, it was as though her husband had grown another limb. It was difficult to think of Neil without thinking of Justin, and that made this day even more painful, because from now on Justin was going to be without Neil. Helping her son adjust to that reality would be the first thing the new widow would have to do as she tried to build a normal life for their child. Neil's brother Joey was also thinking about Justin and trying not to shake with the anger building inside, as the memories of father and son flooded his mind. Someone would have to pay for this, and

Joey promised Neil he would see it through. This vow was silently being repeated by others in the packed church, as they watched Carmel
Burroughs grieve for her son. The family would make damn sure
those responsible paid the price.

Reporters were also at the three services, discreetly writing down
the words of ministers trying to comfort people in their loss and bring
a rational perspective to a senseless tragedy. I was sent to the funeral
of Donna Warren in North Sydney, but decided to remain outside
with the camera operators. I had covered enough funerals to know
that quotations from the minister would ring hollow on television or
the radio. There was no way to ease the pain being felt by Donna's
friends and relatives, and the presence of an unwanted stranger at the
back of the church was an unnecessary intrusion. The camera could
dramatically demonstrate the loss by recording the emotional procession from a distance as it left the church.

Video-taping a funeral procession is always a difficult assignment.
In most cases, funerals warranting coverage are those of celebrities or
others who have served the community in such a capacity as to make
their passing a matter of public concern. On such occasions, the relatives of the deceased often feel the intrusion of television cameras, but
media attention is something they have dealt with throughout their
relative's life. The same cannot be said for the parents of a young
woman gunned down while she worked. While public attention was
certainly to be expected, Donna Warren's family did not need to be
subjected to the spectacle of photographers waiting on the church
steps as they followed her coffin to the hearse. In a larger community,
I may not have been allowed to mix compassion with editorial judgment. If there were a number of other news teams camped outside the
church door, we would have been forced to look for a comparable camera position. However, in Cape Breton, I knew compassion would be
expected and felt that ATV, as a member of the community, should
show the same respect its viewers demonstrated for the families affected by this tragedy. I was happy and surprised when senior producers in
Halifax accepted my recommendation that they not send a camera to
the funeral of Jimmy Fagan; the Fagan family had asked that they be
allowed to say goodbye to Jimmy privately. There were cameras located across the street from the church when Jimmy's casket was walked
out into the sun, but ATV had stayed away.

George Reeves was the cameraman sent to Donna Warren's funeral
with me, and we both decided that if we had to show the community

the terrible loss being experienced by the Warren family, we'd do it from a distance. We parked the news truck on a side street not far from the church and walked to an area where we could see the steps but not easily be seen by those leaving. George flipped the extender switch on his camera, which made the lens more sensitive and allowed him to push the viewers' perspective much closer to what he was recording. As we stood there, a few people walking in the warm spring sun stopped to reflect on what was happening. Although we felt awkward, the residents of Donna's home town were, in a strange way, happy to see us. It was as though they felt our presence confirmed what they felt inside—this was somehow much bigger than the loss of a local girl. The tragedy reached well beyond the borders of their small town.

As the rear doors of the church opened, an honour guard of uniformed McDonald's employees walked out. The young adults hugged and comforted one another as they cried. The funeral director positioned Donna's co-workers on each side of the church steps as he prepared to lead the pallbearers past them to the waiting hearse. The camera recorded the emotional group and Donna's casket as it was taken from the church. It was the first time I had seen Donna's mother, and it was difficult to watch as Olive Warren hugged her mother and walked slowly out into the sun: the pain was evident in every movement of the two women. As George and I watched in North Sydney, another camera operator was doing the same thing outside the church in Dominion, where Neil Burroughs's coffin was being followed by his grieving relatives.

I had managed to find out that Donna Warren would be laid to rest in the large Lakeside Cemetery on Johnson Road, a little more than one kilometre from the McDonald's in North Sydney. Donna had left her job at the Sydney River restaurant to work closer to home when the North Sydney location opened, but after a short time she returned to Sydney River. Like all McDonald's restaurants in Cape Breton, the one in North Sydney was closed for the day of the funerals, and, as at all McDonald's restaurants in Canada, the flags outside flew at half-mast. As the casket was placed in the hearse, I tapped George on the shoulder and asked him to break down the gear. If we hurried, we could reposition ourselves across from the restaurant and record the funeral procession as it passed—a very telling shot, and one I felt would open our report that evening.

But the shot would never be recorded; someone had decided to spare the Warren family the pain of driving past McDonald's, and the funeral procession followed another route. We headed back to Sydney to call on Dave Roper.

• • •

AS THE TURNOUT for the funerals suggested, the people of Cape Breton were having a tough time adjusting to what had happened in Sydney River. Employees of the three other McDonald's restaurants in Cape Breton were particularly anxious, and executives with the fast-food chain took steps to address that problem. Peter Beresford, the vice president of McDonald's of Canada, released a statement that the hearts and prayers of his company were with the victims' families, employees of McDonald's, and the community. Beresford called the killings a senseless, isolated incident: the company was aware of the impact such a tragedy could have in a small community, but its executives were also sensitive about McDonald's image as a friendly family restaurant. Considering the size of the international restaurant chain, McDonald's had been the target of relatively few violent crimes; but when one did occur, the popularity of the restaurants made the incident big news. Perhaps the most notorious of these crimes occurred in San Ysidro, California, in July 1984, when a gunman opened fire inside a McDonald's restaurant, killing twenty-one people and injuring thirteen others before killing himself. McDonald's acted quickly, razing the building within days. Also in 1984, six people in a McDonald's in Detroit were shot to death by a youth who returned to the restaurant with a gun, after an argument there. In 1990 a gunman took his own life in a Hamilton McDonald's, after taking thirteen hostages. A little over a week before the Sydney River killings, three McDonald's outlets in the Far East were rocked by bombs.

While these incidents were isolated tragedies, as Beresford had said, McDonald's International had learned the importance of helping its staff through the emotional trauma associated with violent crime. McDonald's sent its head of security to Cape Breton to coordinate efforts aimed at assisting police and helping employees deal with the loss. Two psychologists set up a trauma clinic in the Cambridge Suites Hotel and offered counselling to all McDonald's employees and to relatives of the victims. Many teenagers and young adults arrived at the hotel to consult them. The young employees of the Sydney River restaurant were struggling to cope with the particularly powerful, horrific images of what had happened in a place they knew so well, and they wanted someone to explain where and how their co-workers had died. The workers had heard the rumours of ritualistic slayings, of execution-style murders, of torture. Many feared the day they would return to work. No arrests had been made; what if the killers came back? To address that concern, McDonald's initiated new security measures in Sydney River, and psychologists assured the workers that it was extremely unlikely the killers would return. The issue of the rumours, and the images of torture and a blood-soaked restaurant, were tougher to dispel. The company and the psychologists agreed it would be in the best interest of the employees to get the restaurant back to business as soon as police were finished with the part of their investigation involving the crime scene itself. This happened within days, and with Dave Roper's assistance, company representatives took employees through the building, hoping that by showing workers where the deaths had occurred and answering as many of their questions as possible, the young workers' anxieties would be eased.

The day the slain McDonald's employees were being buried, Freeman MacNeil was driving through Sydney with an old friend when he saw Darren Muise and Derek Wood walking along the road in the Hardwood Hill area. MacNeil pulled over and offered them a lift. The four drove quietly down George Street to Pockets, where Muise and Wood got out and said goodbye. It was the first time the three men had been together after the crime, but nothing said during the short drive suggested they had any involvement. While Wood and Muise played pool, MacNeil and his friend went shopping. They headed to Car Audio Plus, on Welton Street, where MacNeil had made the down payment on a pair of speakers for his car on Saturday. He was ready to settle up—the balance owing was just under eleven dollars—paying, once again, with five-dollar bills (and a loonie). Then he noticed a good deal on an amplifier, so he made another down payment, handing the clerk two more five-dollar bills.

MacNeil left the stereo store, but he wanted that amplifier, so he told his friend he would go borrow the money from his mother. The two chatted as they headed to Beaton Road, where the friend waited in the car while Freeman went inside. Back at the store, he handed the clerk ten more five-dollar bills and left with his amplifier. Since the night of the murders, Freeman MacNeil had purchased two sets of speakers and two amplifiers, and used thirty-nine five-dollar bills in the process. And his shopping spree would continue later.

While other McDonald's employees dealt with their grief by talking with counsellors, Derek Wood was finding a different way to cope with his. Wood had experimented once or twice with mild recreational drugs, but in the week after the murders he found getting high a great way to get away from the pressures he was feeling. On Tuesday, May 12, Wood got together again briefly with Darren Muise and Freeman MacNeil—this time they were alone in MacNeil's car and could talk. MacNeil and Muise assured Wood that everything was back in place and that the other evidence had been disposed of. Wood had contacted MacNeil over the weekend and told him about the gun; after three days of driving around with the weapon still in the car, MacNeil finally went out to retrieve it from behind the back seat. He washed the gun and returned it to the box in Michelle's stepfather's dresser. MacNeil and Muise felt secure; Wood did not.

After they had talked for a while, MacNeil threw a bag of money to Muise, who asked what it was and was told it was his share. Wood was not given any money, and he didn't ask for any. The robbery had been his idea, but now he didn't want the money, nor was he surprised that it had not been offered to him. He figured MacNeil and Muise were upset about the knapsack he had left behind. In the group, Wood was the weaker personality, neither prone to the grandiose schemes and claims of Darren Muise, nor as self-assured as Freeman MacNeil, whose size, age, and access to a car put him a little ahead of the others.

Surprisingly, the three did not talk much about the crime. The money was handed out, Wood was assured the evidence had been taken care of while he was in custody, and that was that. MacNeil left, and Wood and Muise headed to a secluded pond to smoke hashish and relax. Muise had tried the drug two years before and now used it occasionally. Whether it was due to the paranoia brought on by the drug, or because of the barrage of news reports on the extensive RCMP investigation, Darren Muise decided it would be a good idea to hide his take. The plastic grocery-store bag MacNeil had given him contained a wad of two-dollar bills. Muise grabbed some, leaving more than sixty of the crumpled bills in the bag, which he sealed tightly. Wood offered to help hide the money: he crawled out on a fallen tree trunk jutting out of the pond, reached into the water, and forced the bag down to the muddy bottom. Then he crawled back to shore and dried himself off.

A couple of hours later, someone else would be trying to stay dry beside a body of water in another part of Industrial Cape Breton—a person who would give police the break they'd been waiting for. As the late spring temperatures continued to climb, sports fishermen had started their annual migration to snow-swollen brooks and streams in search of trout. Mike Yurczyszyn, like many recreational fisherman, had his favourite haunts, and after work on May 12, he tried out one of them. The Grantmire Brook was as a good a place as any, he figured, as he parked by the road and made his way down to the fast-running brook. As he walked along the edge of the water, the high-school teacher noticed a grey metal container about the size of a tackle box. He went over to have a look. Yurczysyn realized very quickly that he was not looking at a discarded tackle box. The metal container was a cash box, and when he looked inside, the fisherman saw a faded yellow sticker bearing the slogan "Have A McHappy Day" and showing the familiar image of Ronald McDonald. Yurczysyn headed for a telephone and called the RCMP.

By midweek, John Trickett and Storm had begun retracing their own steps in the area around the Sydney River McDonald's. He and another dog master, Truro-based RCMP Corporal Kim Baldwin, had been conducting pattern searches of the wooded areas and fields in Sydney River since May 7; Baldwin had been called in because the case was too demanding for one team. If investigators did not yet have any assignments for the teams elsewhere, Trickett and Baldwin were content to continue to scour that area in case they found something that would lead to those responsible for the crime. But the dog masters were beginning to worry about their canine partners. Hours of searching without any results were not good for the dogs, who were motivated by the rewards they received from the trainers after finding something.

For several days, the dog teams had been the most visible part of the RCMP investigations, as TV cameras captured their searches and news reports replayed those images for the viewing public. All the attention gave Trickett and Baldwin a high profile in the community. Each morning before heading out with the dogs, officers would stop at a busy Tim Hortons in the day's search area, and several times, customers ahead of them in line insisted that the Mounties move to the front. People might be in a hurry to get to their own jobs, but they did not want to delay the men working on the McDonald's murders. Other officers were having similar experiences as they went about the business of interviewing people and checking on leads phoned into the detachment. Every day, there were reminders that the residents of

Industrial Cape Breton supported their efforts; even Mounties working on unrelated cases were told that the people were behind them. And all the encouragement spurred their determination to win this one.

At the Sydney detachment office, news of a McDonald's cash box found lying near a secluded brook sent renewed energy through the investigators. They knew that a grey metal cash box was missing from the safe at the Sydney River restaurant. Henry Jantzen, who had been named exhibit man for the case, was sent to Grantmire Brook; it was his responsibility to collect evidence and be prepared to explain in court how he had obtained each item. John Trickett and Storm were also sent along: if there was one item connected to the crime, there could be more. Unfortunately, it was getting dark by the time they arrived, so Trickett took Storm in the woods for a quick look around, then decided he should wait for daylight before conducting a full search. An RCMP officer was placed on guard for the night to protect the search area.

Back at the detachment, Kevin Cleary and other investigators were wondering about the location where the new evidence had been uncovered. A map confirmed that Grantmire Brook was near the end of Mountain Road, and police knew Wood had walked up that road after the killings; but could he have carried evidence that far and then returned? The investigators also knew that Freeman MacNeil lived on Beaton Road, which wasn't far from the end of Mountain and the brook. Suddenly, checking out the details of MacNeil's statement to Glen Lambe and Phil Eagan became a priority. Maybe MacNeil was telling the truth, but police generally don't believe in coincidence. They knew MacNeil had driven Derek Wood to work that night and that Wood had tried to phone him after the shootings, neglecting to mention that phone call to police. Now evidence had been uncovered near MacNeil's home. Adrenaline flowed freely again; the investigators felt very positive about the discovery at the brook and hopeful about the next day's search. Someone was also going to have to talk with Darren Muise, whose name was connected to Freeman MacNeil's on the flow chart in the investigator's office. Muise would either confirm the belief of Glen Lambe and Phil Eagan that MacNeil was not involved, or he would add weight to the growing belief among other investigators that Freeman MacNeil warranted a much closer look. Kevin Cleary sat back in his chair and stared at his flow chart. For the first time, he connected the names Wood, MacNeil, and Muise in his mind. The names would become inseparable in a matter of days.

• • •

As KEVIN CLEARY sat reflecting over his flow chart, the names MacNeil and Muise were being offered to another member of the investigative team. The daily television appearances had made Dave Roper the most-recognized member of the Sydney RCMP. Public perception might have been that Roper was at the centre of the investigation, but in reality his duties were confined to keeping the public informed. He was not conducting interviews or following the leads other investigators were. Still, Roper knew what the others were working on and he attended the daily briefings with Sylvan Arsenault.

Roper had been stationed in the Ingonish area of Cape Breton before coming to Sydney, and Freeman MacNeil's friend Greg Lawrence was then living near Ingonish. Lawrence recognized Roper on TV and remembered the officer as a friendly guy who was easy to talk to. He decided to give him a call. Lawrence told the officer who took the call that he wanted to talk with Dave Roper. No, he wouldn't give his name, and he would talk only with Roper about the information he had—information about the McDonald's case. When he was told Roper had gone home for the evening, Lawrence left a number where the officer could phone him in the next few minutes. There was some confusion at the detachment: Dave Roper had been receiving a constant flow of phone calls at home from residents who simply wanted to encourage him to keep up the good work. The volume of calls had forced Roper to change his home phone number the day before, and officers now scrambled to find out who had the new number. When he was contacted, Roper decided not to call this mysterious source from home; he was concerned about his wife and children. He drove to Sheldon's Kwik Way, a convenience store less than a kilometre from his home. There was a pay phone in the lot about thirty metres from the store, and Roper could talk without being overhead. Roper did not recognize the voice on the other end of the line, but the man said he knew Roper. He also claimed he knew who had committed the McDonald's murders. Greg Lawrence gave Roper the names of Freeman MacNeil and Darren Muise, and claimed he had heard them planning the robbery. Roper knew that the names were being circulated at the office and wondered if his caller was someone connected to MacNeil and Muise; maybe he wanted to find out how much police knew, or maybe he was trying to lead police in the wrong direction. Lawrence could tell from the officer's tone that Roper did not believe him, so he ended the conversation, refusing to give his name. Lawrence was angry, and a little disappointed in Dave Roper—maybe insisting on talking to him might have been a mistake. He would call back another time, and when he did, he wouldn't demand to talk to Roper. No, next time he would speak to someone who would believe him.

Wednesday, May 13, was another warm, sunny spring day, and the sun was indeed shining on the RCMP and their investigation. Soon after officers arrived at the Grantmire Brook, they uncovered more evidence. Along both sides of the brook, branches from fallen trees reached down into the water, creating natural nets for debris floating along the surface. Digging through the debris, officers found some clumps of paper and several red plastic McDonald's change pouches. Back at the detachment, investigators decided they would scrape the bottom of the brook if that's what it took to find every scrap of evidence at that site. Most of all, they wanted the gun. They had to recover the weapon; it was a nagging worry they had been dealing with since the morning of May 7. Kevin Cleary and Sylvan Arsenault knew that whoever was responsible for the murders might still have the gun, and might be willing to use it again. They needed to find that gun because it was evidence in their case, but, more importantly, because they wanted to get the thing off the street.

The RCMP diving team was sent to Beachmont Road; their daily dives into Sydney harbour had turned up nothing, and now they would have the chance to search an area known to contain evidence. The Grantmire Brook is not deep enough for divers to submerge themselves completely, but in places there are pools too deep to be examined by someone walking along the sides of the brook, or even down the middle. Two divers donned masks, snorkels, and wet suits, then settled themselves face down in the brook, reaching out to the sides to grab rocks or other protruding objects that would stop them from being pulled along too quickly by the rushing water. They inched their way along the brook, examining the deep holes and paying close attention to the fallen trees and their branches. As the divers found anything they considered worthy of a closer look, they would stand and take the item or items to another member of the team who was slowly walking along beside the brook with a kitbag. The bag bore a remarkable resemblance to the one used to take the clothing and other items away from McDonald's almost a week before—Freeman MacNeil had hidden it in the woods near his home and later burned it, along with the clothing he and Darren Muise had worn.

Police might now have that bag, too—but for circumstance. The morning of May 7, Corporal Baldwin and his dog were exploring Mountain Road to see if Derek Wood might have disposed of any evidence there, during his late-night walk. The team started just a little farther than Wood said he had walked—down the other side of Mountain Road, at the intersection with Beaton Road. There, Baldwin pulled his big truck over and let the dog run down Beaton Road for a few metres and relieve himself in the ditch. The tracking dog was within two hundred metres of the kitbag filled with MacNeil's and Muise's bloodstained clothing, but Baldwin had no reason to begin his search on Beaton Road. He was already past the point where Wood was believed to have ended his walk, and it would be a few hours before police learned that Wood had phoned Freeman MacNeil from Kings, and that MacNeil lived on Beaton, only a short distance away. By the time that information was available, the dog teams were concentrating their efforts closer to the crime scene—and MacNeil had burned the evidence. Kim Baldwin has repeatedly asked himself a painful question since that morning: "What if I'd let the dog run a little farther up that road?" There was no question that the dog would have detected the kitbag; blood has a strong odour, and the dog would have reacted very quickly to that familiar scent. Had that bag been found that morning, the investigation might not have gone as far off the rails as it did.

But Baldwin would soon turn up some very significant evidence, and the Grantmire search had proved fruitful. The change pouches, marked with a golden *M, had* to be from the Sydney River restaurant; the divers felt certain of it, and they were equally sure that the clumped papers, bearing numbers and codes, were somehow connected to the crime. Before long they recovered an object they were not so certain about. A dark deck-shoe was stuck at the side of the brook, and this, along with the other objects, was handed to Henry Jantzen.

George Reeves and I arrived at the brook just as Constable Jantzen was working his way through the dense underbrush beside the water toward the Ident station wagon with Corporal Leadbetter. Jantzen wore heavy black rubber boots to keep his pants dry as he moved around the brook, and was carrying a green plastic garbage bag. As soon as I saw the bag, I asked George to film the officers as they came out of the woods. The two of us had headed for the Grantmire Brook after getting a tip that the diving team was working in that area; neither of us knew where it was, but the caller named Beachmont Road, so we located it on a map and found our way there. When the officer who had been guarding the brook for the night saw us pull up, he radioed the Sydney detachment building and told Dave Roper that he should come out to the search scene; the media were beginning to arrive.

When Henry Jantzen noticed the camera, he just smiled and said good morning, casually placing the evidence bag in a large cardboard box in the rear of the police car. Jantzen had no time for me as I approached to ask what the divers had found and what he had in the bag. "I have what they uncovered, and that's all I can tell you."

"Is what they uncovered connected to the McDonald's murders?"

"That's why we're all here." Jantzen smiled, and made it clear he would not answer any questions. The burly young man was friendly enough, but it quickly became evident that he was one of those police officers who prefer their TV reporters safely on the screen, where they can be controlled with the remote. The other officer at the scene flagged me over; he didn't want me bothering Jantzen, either, but he also didn't want to ask us to leave the area. "Look, guys, Dave Roper is headed out here to talk to you, so if you could just stay up here on the road and wait for him, that would be great."

"Sure," I said. "We'll just get a few shots of the guys searching while we wait."

"Yeah, just make sure you don't step off the pavement. The dogs are searching the grass, and no-one is allowed down there."

"Thanks."

John Trickett and Storm were working in another area that morning, so the ground search was being handled by Baldwin and a third dog master assigned to the team. Baldwin and his dog found something that added to the mounting belief that the gun could have disposed of near here. It was a small black throwing knife with a dragon carved into its black plastic handle. There was no sign of blood on the knife, but investigators felt it might be the weapon that had been used on Neil Burroughs. The search was expanded, and officers were told to search the sides of the road where the steep bank descended into the thick underbrush that surrounded the brook. Reporters weren't the only ones restricted to the pavement; no-one wanted to step on evidence or contaminate a scent that might lead one of the dogs to the gun. A utility truck arrived, equipped with a long, telescoping boom that had a Fibreglas basket at the end—the kind of truck frequently used by telephone, power, or cable television companies. A young constable was placed in the basket, and the boom was moved out over the roadside as the truck slowly moved forward. When the constable spotted something, other officers walked in to examine or collect the item without destroying any trail the dogs might find nearby. Beer bottles, cigarette packages, and all kinds of other things foreign to Mother Nature—everything was checked.

When Trickett and Storm arrived, they were assigned to search an area on the opposite side of Beachmont Road, away from the section of the brook that had proved to be so rich in evidence. Trickett shrugged; he was last on the scene, so the others had already been given the most promising areas to examine. Still, he hoped *something* was left for Storm to find; Trickette remained worried about the hours the dog had been working without praise he could only receive when he found something. Storm knew he was going back to work, and as always the dog became excited; he wanted to find something—anything—that would please his master. The dog headed down into the ditch along the side of the road and began his search, while Trickett watched carefully for signs that he was on to a scent. It wasn't a long wait. Storm perked up at the sight of an object in the tall grass, and stood above it, waiting for his master. Trickett rushed over to see what the dog had found. It was a knife, a brown-handled hunting knife with what appeared to be a rusty blade. The sight of the rust diminished Trickett's initial excitement, but he hid this from the dog. Kneeling down, the officer affectionately rewarded the powerful police dog; it was time for Storm to get some much-deserved compensation. With the congratulations completed, Corporal Trickett took a closer look at the knife, moving the grass away from the blade and looking at the rust. His heart skipped a beat as he realized the blade was not rusty at all. It was bloodstained.

"Atta boy, Storm. Good work, partner." Trickett again heaped praise on the dog, patting his head and roughhousing a little. This time, the officer was as excited as the dog; and afterwards, Storm was happy and eager to return to work. "Hang on, buddy. Let's look after this first." Trickett grabbed the cellular phone he was carrying and dialled the detachment. Most of the other officers had already left the area, and Trickett needed Henry Jantzen and James Leadbetter. The Ident man would photograph and bag the knife, then turn it over to the exhibit officer. The RCMP were working under the assumption that their cellular phone conversations were being monitored, so Trickett told Kevin Cleary he had found the object the officer wanted, but did not identify the object. He did not want to say it was a knife. Cleary hung up the phone, a new rush of adrenaline surging through his veins, and sent Henry Jantzen back to Beachmont Road, where he believed Storm had located the gun.

As he waited for the recovery team, Trickett took a closer look at the blade. The thick metal was not only bloodstained, it was bent. When Jantzen arrived and asked where the gun was, Trickett looked puzzled but then realized Cleary had misunderstood him. He showed the young officer what Storm had found, and after Jantzen left, the team went deeper into the woods, the dog looking for anything that would make his trainer excited and happy again. As he walked behind Storm, John Trickett was anything but excited. In the quiet hours spent following the dog, Trickett often found his mind wandering, and he did not like where it was headed now. One of the advantages investigators have when working on a particularly gruesome case is the company of a partner—someone to talk things out with. When your partner is a dog, and you spend your time tramping around isolated fields and wooded areas you hope were frequented by killers, there isn't much to stop you from getting spooked. For Trickett, the bloodstained and bent knife blade kept returning to his mind, along with the grisly image of Neil Burroughs in a wide pool of blood. The hair of the back of Trickett's neck stood on end, and he moved a little closer to his partner. The image of weapon and victim became imprinted in his mind, and he would not soon banish it.

As John Trickett tried to shake the haunting image, his younger brother, Dave, was spending the day with the man who had used that knife to stab Neil Burroughs. Shortly after ten that morning, Dave Trickett and Glen Lambe were sent to the residence of Darren Muise. Lambe had taken Freeman MacNeil's statement, which he expected Muise to verify; the trip was not exactly a waste of time, but Lambe was confident he was just tying up a loose end. Still, you never know what might come up in an interview. Trickett drove the car as the two headed out to Patnic Avenue, off Mira Road. Muise's house was not far from where Derek Wood was staying, they noted as they pulled off the Sydney bypass.

Typical of most hard-working adults, the Muises wanted an easier life for their children. Darren was the youngest boy, and they hoped he would follow through on his latest stated ambition, to become a social worker. It certainly appealed to them more than his earlier plans to be a professional athlete, but now, three months after Darren had dropped out of school, his parents could see his chances of finding a truly rewarding career slipping past. Convincing an eighteen-year-old that he doesn't have all the answers is almost impossible. Sandy Muise was working as a cab driver in Sydney, and he wanted more for himself and for his boys, as he frequently reminded Darren. But that just created tension, and so far Sandy's efforts had not succeeded in getting a commitment that the boy would return to school. Sandy even tried telling Darren that he himself would like to go back to school, maybe get a trade in computer repair or something that could help him set up his own business. He had worked for many years running a men's clothing store for his brother, and wanted the chance to work for himself and maybe employ one or two of his sons.

With no school to get up for, Muise spent much of the day asleep in bed and then headed out to the pool hall for the evening. When Pockets closed, he would often go to Tim Hortons for a coffee and some conversation with friends, or go over to Sanitary Dairy and play the video poker machines, if he had the money. Muise stayed out most of the night, then went home to sleep all day again. The multiple murders at Sydney River McDonald's had not even put a brief dent in the daily routine; Muise was still sleeping until about three in the afternoon and then going down to the pool hall. On Wednesday, May 13, Darren Muise would not get to sleep in. Glen Lambe knocked on the door at Darren's house and was greeted by Gail Muise. Darren's mother, a warm and friendly woman, was a senior sales clerk at a local women's clothing store and was accustomed to dealing with strangers—but a police officer arriving at her door to see her youngest child was a little unnerving. It was especially unnerving in light of what the officer said he was investigating—in the past six days, people at the mall had talked of little else.

Gail had told her friends at work how she had been called at three in the morning the night of the McDonald's murders. It was Mike Campbell, a friend of Darren's, asking if Darren knew what had happened at McDonald's. Gail checked but Darren wasn't home, so she told Mike she'd have him call when he got in. Gail explained to her friends that Mike wanted to know if Darren had seen Derek—he was the one who ran from the restaurant and called police. Yes, Darren knew the poor boy who was working with those people before they were killed. Like most people in Sydney, Gail's friends at the store were anxious to hear anything about the case. They were fascinated by her story; the next time they saw Darren in the mall, they'd have to ask him about his friend.

Now Gail was worried. It was O.K. for Darren to know someone who was innocently involved, but why did the police want to see him? Constable Lambe reassured the worried mother. It was just a routine interview; her son's name had come up in connection with Derek Wood, and they just wanted to see if he could help them in any way. Well, that was fine. Gail wanted Darren to help the police if he could. Darren followed the officer outside and jumped in the back of the car. Lambe and Trickett introduced themselves and explained why they were there. They had talked with Freeman MacNeil, and he mentioned that he was with Darren on the night of the murders. They just wanted to know what Darren had to say about that night. No problem; Muise agree to help the officers. After all, answering questions hadn't hurt Freeman, and Derek had survived a prolonged interrogation, even though he hadn't quite been himself since.

"O.K., Darren, on the evening of May sixth and the morning of May seventh, where were you?"

"I was at Pockets Pool Hall on George Street until about one-fifteen that morning. I left alone and walked towards Tim Hortons. I saw Freeman MacNeil, he picked me up, and we went towards my place on Hardwood Hill. He was talking about going up to his place to pick up his puffer. I went for the drive 'cause I was bored."

"What route did you take when you went to Freeman's?" After less then ten minutes with police, Darren Muise was already wishing he were somewhere else. He was not sure what route he should describe; Freeman hadn't told him what he'd said to police, and Darren knew he was supposed to be confirming Freeman's story. Well, when in doubt make up a lie—but not one that can be easily detected. Muise told the officers he wasn't paying attention during the drive because he was fooling with the stereo and looking at some books in the car. Trickett and Lambe both thought it was odd that a young man who'd spent his entire life in the Sydney area did not know what route he'd taken to a friend's house, particularly a trip that took place on a night when most local residents could recall what they were doing simply because of the magnitude of the incident—sort of like people knowing what they were doing when John Kennedy was assassinated. Driving to the MacNeil residence was not like heading to a home in a crowded residential area, where one block looks pretty much like the others. It was a drive out in the country, and each of the three possible routes leading from Sydney to Beaton Road takes you through vastly different areas. For someone familiar with the region, even a brief glance out the window at any time during the drive would immediately confirm which highway you were on.

But no matter how they pressed, or which of the routes they discussed, Darren Muise would not be pinned to one or another. He suggested at one point that they had passed his school, but later took that back; he and Freeman could not have passed Riverview without driving past McDonald's, and he did not want to say they had done that. The officers finally decided to invite Darren to come to the detachment to look at some maps, and he agreed. Glen Lambe got out of the car and returned to the house, telling Gail Muise her son had agreed to help them look at some maps. Nothing for her to worry about.

Darren remained quiet on the way to the detachment, and Dave Trickett began to get an uneasy feeling about the young man in the back seat. At the detachment, Muise was placed in the same interview room where Derek Wood had been the week before. He had a cigarette and waited while the officers went to look for their maps. Didn't matter to him how many maps they got; he wasn't going to commit himself to a route. It became a sticking point throughout the afternoon, as Trickett and Lambe attempted to get a written statement from Muise. The officers noted that Muise was calm and laid-back as they discussed the issue, even laughing at himself and saying he had the worst memory in the world. Still, they were a little concerned, and noted that his voice sounded high, and a little strained, when he answered yes to the question: "Do you know Derek Wood?" Trickett continued the questioning:

"How do you know him?"

"From school. Elementary."

"Have you talked to him since the shootings?" Trickett was wondering how close the two were.

"Yes."

"When?"

"Yesterday I was talking to him, and the day before. The day before, he showed up with Mike Campbell at Pockets."

"What did you talk about?"

"I asked him how he was doing. He sounded really depressed, though. I asked him about McDonald's, but he said he's not allowed to talk about it. Me, him, and Mike played a game of pool to try to cheer him up."

"Who won the game?" Glen Lambe wanted to know more about what Derek Wood was doing at Pockets. The special observation team knew Wood had been in the pool hall, but it was difficult for them to see what he was up to inside.

"Me and Mike—we played a few games."

"How well do you know Mike?"

"Pretty well."

"Have you known Mike Campbell…Derek Wood to use or be fond of handguns?"

"No." Muise couldn't figure out why the police were interested in Derek's cousin, but since Mike wasn't involved, it couldn't hurt his friend to talk about him to police—or so Muise believed. Anyway, answering questions about Mike kept them away from the stupid route he and Freeman were supposed to have taken.

"What can you tell me about Derek Wood telling you things about the McDonald's shootings?" Muise decided to move away from Wood and into safer territory: "He didn't mention anything about it. It was Mike. Mike told me that Derek went to Kings and called police. Mike called my house because he thought Freeman was supposed to pick Derek up. I guess he thought I'd be in the car too. When I got home at about 6:00 a.m., I tried to call Mike at his house, but there was no answer. I called when I woke up, about 3:00 p.m. He told me there was a shooting at McDonald's—the police have Derek downtown. That was about it. I ate and cleaned up and left home and went to Pockets. I'm not sure if I called Mike from home or at Pockets. I talked to him twice. I called Freeman before 4:00 p.m., and I asked him, 'Did you hear that Derek was at the police station?' I think he said no."

As the questioning continued, the persistence of Trickett and Lambe finally broke Muise's resolve about the route he and Freeman MacNeil took that night, and he gave them one that he felt kept him and Freeman safely away from McDonald's and matched what his friend had already told them—at least, he hoped so. Dave Trickett had been in Cape Breton long enough to know the route Muise showed him made no sense—not if Freeman MacNeil had been in a hurry to get his girlfriend's medicine, as MacNeil had told police. According to Muise, he and MacNeil had driven along the Sydney bypass as far as McDonald's, where they took the turn-off—but that part of the drive was a blur, because he wasn't paying attention. It was after the bit about the turn-off that Dave Trickett started thinking that a lie detector would be a good idea; the quickest way to MacNeil's house was to drive past the restaurant and turn at the intersection—where, indeed, the killers had gone after the crime. Muise said he and MacNeil took Highway 4, away from Sydney and McDonald's, circled back at Blackett's Lake to take Coxheath Road in as far as Mountain Road, and then continued to MacNeil's. That certainly was the long way around; even if they hadn't gone past McDonald's, they could have stayed on the bypass for two more exits, then cut back across Beachmont Road.

The trip to the detachment to look at maps was becoming rather serious. After interviewing Muise for more than five hours, Dave Trickett asked if he would consider taking a lie-detector test, something being done with a number of witnesses as an aid to the investigation, he said. Muise wanted to know if he *had* to take one and was assured he did not, but Trickett explained that it would be helpful, and emphasized the severity of the crime. Glen Lambe noticed that Muise became nervous when any details were mentioned.

Although he would not commit himself to a lie-detector test, Muise agreed to go for a drive with John Trickett; he could show him the route he believed he took, and they could talk about the polygraph.

• • •

As DAVE TRICKETT and Darren Muise headed along Highway 4, away from the scene of the crime, they drove past the rear of Our Lady of Fatima church. The church was huddled below the Sydney bypass, at the same exit as McDonald's and opposite the restaurant on a one-way section of road below the secluded spot where the getaway car had been parked on the night of the murders. Because of the access ramps leading to and from the bypass, you had to drive in front of the church and under the bypass to get to McDonald's and Sydney, or drive behind the church if you were coming from Sydney and travelling away from the restaurant—as Trickett and Muise were. They could see a crowd of people entering the church as they drove silently past. The people were going to a multifaith ecumenical service for members of the community who wanted to pray for victims of the McDonald's murders, and for the police hunting their killers.

I walked in the front door of the church as a familiar-looking unmarked police car rolled past at the back. Cars like it were everywhere I had been in the past few days, and I figured one of the detectives was either swinging around to come to the services or just heading home. It was the second time since the killing that Darren Muise had passed me in a car; the first incident had occurred about a hundred metres away, when we were both on the bypass in the ninety minutes after the tragedy. Inside the church, I stood at the rear and said a silent prayer—my opportunity to do what many in the area had already done. I found myself standing beside Dave Roper, someone I was seeing more of than my own family at that point. Roper looked like I felt: he was certainly spending more time with reporters than with anyone else. We talked quietly about the excitement the RCMP were feeling after the discovery at the brook, where I had seen him a few hours earlier. We smiled at the realization that we were not really having a break; we were both still working. Roper was in full dress uniform—the postcard red-serge Mountie attending the service on behalf of the force. Still, we were relieved to have an hour of peace in the quiet of the church. Apparently, we weren't alone in that feeling:

At the multifaith service in the small church near McDonald's. Restaurant owner Garfield Lewis is at the centre, beside the minister. [Print from ATV video tape.]

hundreds of people were jammed into the church, and those who could not get in were gathered in the large foyer and on the walkway outside, where they could hear the words of Father Stan MacDonald coming from a small speaker. Father MacDonald told the group that a safe community gathering-place had been violently taken away from the people of Sydney River. Roper and I both knew that no-one, ourselves included, would ever feel the same about the Sydney River McDonald's.

I remained standing in the rear of the packed church, taking notes on Father MacDonald's comments; Roper went forward to participate in a candle-lighting ceremony. Once the candle was lit, Father Mac-Donald called on everyone to join hands and pray for the victims, their families, and the police officers working so hard to solve this horrible crime. I had just finished trying to get a head count so I could report on the size of the crowd, when everyone stood and began holding hands for the prayer. I was a little taken aback when another re-porter standing near me reached over and grabbed my hand; he was a young radio reporter, and I figured if he wanted to take part in the prayer, that was fine. Switching my notepad to my left hand, I looked around and noticed that the other people at the back of the church had joined hands; and I realized that the young reporter had linked the two of us to this chain of people. Before the prayer began, a short, dark-haired woman left the back row of the church, came over and stood on my left, and reached for my free hand. I quickly stuffed my notepad in my pocket and took her hand. I recognized her; she owned the house next door to the Sydney River McDonald's and had been deeply moved by the carnage that had taken place beside her home. I was a little puzzled by the silent look she gave me. She squeezed my hand hard and looked into my eyes as if to thank me. Because I had been so caught up in the story for the past week, I had not fully grasped how desperate the community was for any news of the murders and the resulting investigation.

Outside the church, several other people approached to thank me. They said that every evening, they waited to find out what the RCMP were doing and felt reassured when I showed them the search teams and reported on the latest briefing from Dave Roper. A few metres away, people were also shaking Roper's hand and wishing him well. Then, a couple of people I knew came forward to say that they too had made it a point to tune in every evening to see what news there was on the murders. Finally, Father MacDonald, who had been talking with people at the back of the church, came outside. What he had to tell me was what the others had been implying: "I know any day you'll tell us it's all over, and those responsible are in jail. I'll continue to pray for that. Good luck."

I had a new sense of why I was working late nights and early mornings tracking the movements of the RCMP. People in Cape Breton needed to know what the police were doing. They needed to feel secure after such a violent shock.

Nine

AFTER DRIVING ALONG Muise's route, Dave Trickett persuaded him to go to North Sydney to talk to the polygraph operator. He assured Muise once again that he did not have to take the test, but said he felt the polygrapher could better answer some of the questions the young man had about the machine and how it worked. At the North Sydney detachment, Trickett was told that the polygraph operator had not arrived, and Muise saw his chance to get away from this persistent policeman, who had, after all, told him that he could leave any time. The eighteen-year-old complained that he was tired, and offered to call Trickett in a day or so if he still wanted to talk to the polygraph guy or if he thought of anything that might help the investigation. The two headed back to Sydney.

Back in Sydney, Constable Pat Murphy was sitting in a small room at the detachment, staring at a tape recorder. He had finally waded through the mounds of paperwork and made his way to a judge willing to allow wiretaps to be placed on four telephones Derek Wood was believed to use. Two were pay phones; the others were at two of the places where Wood was known to spend the night. The tape machines in the room were activated automatically if someone picked up the phone at any one of those locations. Murphy stayed in the room just in case something was said that officers could act on immediately. If they knew Derek Wood was on his way to a coffee shop, a bar, or some other public place, one of the observers could be sent there ahead of him. He was not likely to be suspicious of someone who was already in a bar when he got there—at least, not as suspicious as he might be about a stranger who walked in after he had arrived. Kevin Cleary also wanted to know if anything said over one of those phones could lead him to the gun. Murphy had listened to every call; nothing worthwhile had transpired. Well, not much, anyway; he would be able to tell the observation unit to relax—Wood had told friends he was staying in for the night to watch a video of the movie *Boyz in the Hood*.

In another room, Kevin Cleary was staring at his flow charts again. He had talked with Dave Trickett and Glen Lambe before Trickett left with Darren Muise, and he was now looking at four names: Muise, Wood, MacNeil, and Campbell. Freeman MacNeil was still believed to be a helpful witness by some, but others looked at where he lived, and where the evidence had been found that day, and wondered. Mike Campbell was generating a lot of interest among the police because he was spending a great deal of time with Wood; in fact, they were pretty much living together. Clearly looked at the names and wondered: why had Campbell phoned Muise? Why had Wood phoned MacNeil and Campbell? What were MacNeil and Muise doing in the vicinity of the restaurant that night? Time to talk with MacNeil's girlfriend, Michelle Sharp, about that asthma condition of hers.

MacNeil and Sharp were spending a relaxing evening together. Earlier, they'd driven Derek Wood home, and they were worried about him—he was making comments about committing suicide if Arlene MacNeil died. Michelle didn't understand why he felt so bad. It wasn't his fault. Freeman had told her they didn't rob the restaurant that night. Someone else got there first—it had to be true. Freeman wouldn't lie to her; she loved him.

Darren Muise might have been expecting a routine evening, too, now that he was finally on his way home. But it was not to be. As the police car left North Sydney, Dave Trickett got a radio message: the polygraph operator had arrived. Trickett persuaded Muise to return with him, emphasizing how important it was for Muise to be helpful. Muise said he wanted to help but was getting tired. Trickett pointed out that it was only eight o'clock—early for a guy who normally stayed out all night. The two headed back to North Sydney.

At 8:16 p.m., Darren Muise met RCMP Sergeant Phil Scharf. The head of RCMP General Investigative Services in the Metro Halifax area, Scharf was one of many experts assigned to the McDonald's case. The sergeant's specialties were the polygraph machine and interrogations. Short for a Mountie, under five-ten, Scharf had thick, wiry hair, probing eyes, and an intense personality. He immediately tried to assess the character of anyone he encountered, and his findings were generally clouded by years of working with criminals. Phil Scharf didn't trust people until they gave him a reason to; he was not easily fooled, nor was he a particularly patient man. His size and temperament made the senior investigator the kind of cop a lying criminal likes to avoid. He was a cross between a fireplug and a pit bull: it was pointless to expect him to move; you could try to go around him, but if he caught a piece of you he wasn't going to let go.

Muise was discovering a whole new kind of policeman. While he might have felt Dave Trickett was persistent when it came to detailing the route, he soon realized that Trickett was a laid-back pussycat by Phil Scharf's standards. Trickett had befriended Muise, calling him "bud" or even "my son" in his downhome Newfoundland manner of speaking. Trickett's antennae had tweaked a couple of times at Muise's reactions to questions about the route he and MacNeil had taken, but he hid his feelings and bided his time. Phil Scharf had no time to bide. He was there to work on a serious case, and everybody around him had better understand that. Scharf was friendly enough when the two were introduced, but began to get impatient when Muise informed him that he wasn't sure he wanted to take a polygraph; he just wanted to ask a few questions about it. Phil Scharf wasn't here to play schoolteacher to some kid in a sweatshirt and walking shorts. The sergeant explained that part of taking a polygraph exam was an extensive information session during which the machine and its functions are completely outlined for the subject. The information session could last more than two hours, and Scharf was certain any questions Muise had would be adequately addressed.

Muise explained that he was really tired; he had been with the police since getting up that morning, and he wasn't up to taking the test. That was fine by Scharf, who knew that a tired subject was not an ideal subject, so he asked Muise to give him a time when they could do it—maybe the following morning. Muise refused to be pinned down on a time, and then the real Phil Scharf surfaced. Scharf began to lecture as Muise sat cross-legged in the oversized polygraph chair, his elbow on the wide arm of the chair, his hand over his mouth. Muise leaned forward, nodding agreement and trying to figure out how he could get the hell out of there. The sergeant told Muise he only knew of one reason why someone would refuse to take a polygraph. "It's one of the most horrible things that ever happened in Canada, Darren. They are senseless, cowardly killings. You're making me think you have some information; you're being evasive. I look at you and I see a man with a lot of turmoil. The only way I'll know is to get you on a polygraph. It's the best way for us to eliminate you from this." Scharf spoke quickly, leaning close to Muise and bringing his points home with such emphasis that it was hard for Muise to get a word in edgewise as the sergeant pressed on, wanting to know when he would return to take the test.

"May I contact you?" Muise hoped he could leave with a promise to call later.

"Yes, of course."

"Then may I leave now? I'll get some rest and see if I can remember anything."

Scharf did not understand why Muise wanted to leave without committing himself to a time. Here was a kid with no prior history of criminal activity, who claimed he wanted to help but did not want to take the test. To Scharf that meant only one thing. "Look, Darren," he said. "You should be saying, 'I want to help.' You've never been in trouble, but if you would protect someone like that... Those McDonald's workers would do anything to help in this case if they could, but they were killed in cold blood."

Muise wanted to make it clear he was not protecting anyone. The officer was making him nervous. "I wouldn't care if it was my brother that did this. I'd tell. That's why I stayed all day, but if you don't mind, can we stop this? Can we go?" He leaned forward in his chair, trying to get closer to the door. The room was set up pretty much like the one where he'd been in Sydney, but when this Scharf character came in, it sure got crowded. Muise wanted Dave Trickett to come back; he said he'd only be a few minutes. If Dave came back, he could get out of there. Dave Trickett was in a room near the polygraph suite, watching the proceedings on a TV monitor. All activity in the suite was recorded, and officers could watch from the monitoring room.

Trying to get Scharf off the topic, Muise pretended to be interested in the machine. Well, it was more than a feigned interest; he was becoming intimidated by the machine and the man who operated it. "Is it accurate?"

"It's very, very accurate. No one could fool it." That was all Muise needed to hear. As long as they said he did not have to take the test, he wasn't going to. Scharf persisted: "I see a young fellow scared to death."

"I just don't want to take it."

Scharf leaned back in his chair. "I think I see someone involved in this crime," he said. "Maybe not pulling the trigger, but involved after the fact. You have information. You got to have courage. Stand up and be counted; help us catch these vicious cowards. The investigators will track down those involved—if the people on the jury had ropes, there'd be no judge and jury. They'd take them out and hang them. This is something you would expect from someone like Clifford Olson or Ted Bundy."

This was not really something the RCMP thought a young man like Darren Muise would be involved in, but they were beginning to wonder. They felt fairly certain he knew something; they just weren't sure what. Scharf told Muise that criminal behaviourists at the FBI and Interpol were putting together profiles of the killers. He warned Muise that when those responsible were caught, and the courts learned of people who had the opportunity to help but refused, the system would not be lenient on those people. It would be too late to decide to help after the arrests. This argument might have worked if Muise had been protecting someone other than himself, but Muise had had enough. He didn't want to know what judges or juries were likely to do to him. "When would I be able to leave?" There was agitation and a hint of panic in his voice. "I had nothing to do with it. You said I can leave when I want to."

"You can."

"Can I leave?"

"Yes."

Both men stood. "I'll call you," Muise offered.

"Give me your word."

"Yes."

"Give this some thought," Scharf urged as Muise walked away.

Dave Trickett and Darren Muise returned to Sydney shortly before 9:00 p.m. On the way, Muise told Trickett he did not like Sergeant Scharf or his approach; he wanted to help in the investigation, and it wasn't fair for Scharf to treat him like he was involved. Trickett explained that sometimes people just don't hit it off, but insisted it wasn't a problem; the RCMP were working with two polygraph operators—would Muise meet the other operator the next day? Muise said he'd think about it, and told the officer to call him in the afternoon. Then he asked to be taken to Pockets; he didn't feel like going home. A few hours later, Muise did head home, with a lot on his mind.

At home, Muise took a razor blade and cut his left wrist; it was not a deep cut and did not threaten his life. He also took some pills and wrote a lengthy suicide note:

To all my love ones,

I was told I know too much and they said they are going to get me! To my mother, I love you with all my heart. As the years went by I've been a pain in the ass but you have got me through many things. I learned to love and feel kindness.

To my Father, I also love you. I love you! I hope you can forgive me.

Muise's note contained messages to his three brothers, his former girl-friend, and other friends and relatives. He offered some of his belong-ings to the people he loved and asked them to remember him fondly, but it was clear he expected the note to be read by the RCMP. He knew they were closing in, and he used his suicide attempt, genuine or faked, as a means to mislead them. Dave Trickett was included in the list of people he wanted to say goodbye to:

To Cst. Trickett—I told you everything I remember except about the guys trying to kill me. I thank you for being my friend. I hope I helped you. I don't know the names of the guys who did it but I know they are from the Hali-fax area. It did matter if I told you that before, they would still get me.

To all my friends—I love you and try not to hate me. I have to do this. I'd rather do it than them doing it.

My last requests are to be buried with a Tae Kwan Do uniform on. And let the public know I had nothing to do with the murders. I never pulled a trigger. I want my parents to be left alone. They are the nicest people in the world. By the way the polygrapher was good I did hold back so I could pro-tect myself.

To God! I know will never forgive me but please let my family live long and healthy. I'm doing this for them. It's a cruel way to kill myself but I guess I deserve it.

I also give my deep regards to the family of the victims. Don't worry the police will get the guys. They just have to look in Halifax.

Mom I leave my love. You're the hardest to say goodbye because I know you don't want to be alone. Please treasure this—this is the most important thing I have had to left you my courage. I want you to go out and get two bottles of Whiskey, gather the family and have a drink. Remember me in a happy way. The other bottle I want to save it as a reminder of your past. And keep it sealed to reminder of what the future holds. Please do not open it.

I guess this is it. I love you everybody.

Muise signed this letter, folded it, and placed it in a tennis-racket cover in his bedroom. While the kind and amount of pills he took isn't clear, he may have been high as he wrote his farewell, as the rambling nature of the letter indicates: he suggested he was in danger, yet hinted at his own guilt by saying God would not forgive him.

Muise's parents had asked him to stay close to home after his long day with police; instead, he slipped out his bedroom window and went to a nearby ball field, where he smoked, contemplated life, and considered his situation. He concluded that he would not kill himself after all; he would ride it out. He returned home but did not destroy the suicide note.

• • •

THE MORNING OF Thursday, May 14, brought an upbeat briefing at the RCMP detachment. It had been a week since the murders, and the investigative team was on the right track; they could sense it. Two officers assigned to brief the victims' families continued to assure them that the investigation was proceeding. The officers could not say anything about the suspects, or even that there were specific suspects, but for the relatives of the slain McDonald's workers, more contact from the RCMP was reassuring enough. Their questions were being answered, and they felt they were part of the process.

For me, Thursday marked the first opportunity to walk through the McDonald's restaurant at the centre of the story I had been working on night and day, for a week. The restaurant had been turned back over to the company by police, and its doors had been opened to the public that morning. Getting inside the restaurant with a camera was a tough sell—McDonald's did not want to expose the restaurant or its employees to that kind of attention—but fortunately I had developed a relationship with Garfield Lewis years before. He knew me and trusted me, and after the first rejection I spoke to him directly about the story I wanted to do. It would look at the corporate response to the crisis, how counsellors had been hired to work with the employees. One of those psychologists was Dr. John Gainer, who with Constable Dave Roper had accompanied employees on a walk-through at the restaurant before it reopened. He agreed to an interview, and he discussed the problems being experienced by the hundreds of teens who had taken part in the program in the past few days. Dr. Gainer concluded that it was not surprising for the employees to want to return to work. Rather than prompt a mass exodus, the crime had brought the employees closer together, he said; they had become a tight-knit group, who drew on each other's strength.

For me, walking through the kitchen and down to the basement office for the interview was strange. The polished ceramic tiles showed no sign of what had happened, but I felt as though I was violating something. Innocent lives had ended where I stood, and now the space had returned to its everyday, utilitarian purpose. The significance of the victims seemed somehow diminished. I had been at murder scenes before, but never had I felt anything quite like it.

Later that day, Dave Trickett was instructed to pursue his relationship with Darren Muise—get him over to see the second polygraph operator and get him hooked up to that machine. The police were now convinced that he was a young man with something to hide, that perhaps he was trying to protect his friend Derek Wood. They did not think he was involved in the crime itself; in fact, many officers still believed Wood was only an accessory, who left the door open for someone. But police believed they could get to the killers by focusing on Muise and Wood, and they decided someone should talk to Free-

McDonald's employees at work hours after the restaurant reopened—a week after the murders.
[Print from ATV video tape.]

man MacNeil again, to find out what he had to say about the strange route Muise claimed they took that night. Muise's story did not match MacNeil's; maybe they could both be persuaded to take polygraph exams.

Constable Trickett decided to phone Muise and take him up on his offer to consider talking with the new polygraph operator—would he come and meet with Sergeant Mitch Soucie? Muise said he had a cold and was not feeling well enough to take the test or meet the operator that day. Dave Trickett did not believe him; he left the detachment and drove to Muise's house. When he arrived and went in to see Darren, he noticed there were no signs of a cold—no sniffling or coughing or watery eyes. "Look, Darren, you're not sick. You're just trying to avoid this test. Come on, man, you've got to help us on this."

"No, no, I want to help. I helped ya yesterday. It's just I'm not feeling good, that's all."

"Don't make excuses, Darren. Let's get this thing done."

"Well, I can go over and meet this new guy, but I don't have to take the test if I don't want to, right?"

"I already told you, Darren, you don't have to take it—but we're asking all witnesses to do it. You know how serious this thing is."

Once again, Darren Muise and Dave Trickett went to North Sydney, but Sergeant Soucie was not ready for them, so they headed out for a coffee. The two were in a drive-through line at a nearby Tim Hortons when Muise rolled up his sleeve and pulled a bandage from a cut on his wrist, showing Trickett what he'd done the night before but not admitting that the injuries were self-inflicted. Trickett looked at the cuts and immediately thought that Muise was misleading him; those straight cuts were not likely to have been accidental, although he could see that they were only superficial. The two were driving along, drinking coffee and talking, when they got a message on the car radio. It was time to go meet the new polygrapher. While they were returning to the detachment, Muise had some questions. "I know the sentence for murder is twenty-five years, but is the sentence for three murders three times twenty-five years or just twenty-five?"

"Why are you asking that?"

"Oh, I'm just curious. I was wonderin', too—does a plea bargain mean a shorter sentence?"

"I'm not a lawyer, Darren, I'm a policeman."

The two drove to the detachment in silence. Darren Muise found himself back in the polygraph suite, but the officer he met was more low-key, more like Dave Trickett. They got along, and Muise agreed to take the test. Muise allowed himself to be hooked up to a machine that two experts had already told him would hang him out to dry if he lied. The eighteen-year-old believed he knew better than they did, though. Muise was a fairly accomplished storyteller, and he knew how to concentrate—something his extensive martial-arts training had taught him. He could fool the machine, and then he'd be home free. Maybe avoiding it had been a mistake in the first place. After all, if the machine was as good as these guys claimed, it would be allowed in court. No, he figured people could fool them, and he was going to try.

Before the test could begin, the operator and the subject would have to get to know one another. They discussed how the machine worked and then began to talk about Darren—things he did as a child, things he thought and felt as a young adult. Darren enjoyed this part of the test; he loved talking with people, especially when he was the subject of the conversation. He told Sergeant Soucie that the only time he had broken the law was when he took a bag of chips from a candy store as a child. He said he did it for his brother.

Finally, at a little after three in the afternoon, Sergeant Soucie connected Muise to the lie-detector machine. Soucie may have been more easy-going in his manner than Phil Scharf, but he was still all business. Like Scharf, Soucie was a little on the short side for a policeman, but his demeanour made him less-threatening. He had the solid build of a man whose work could entail physical exertion, but who wore a business suit. His slightly thinning, wavy hair made him look a little older than he was, and the whole image was more like a middle-aged banker, or even a schoolteacher, than a man set on catching a killer. Muise was at ease as the sergeant tightened black straps across his chest and lower abdomen, and as sensors were placed on the fingertips of his left hand. On his right arm, an inflatable strap—the kind used in blood-pressure tests—was tightened between his elbow and shoulder.

With the sensors in place, Soucie demonstrated the effectiveness of his machine. He conducted a sample test, asking Muise to select a numbered card from a small pack of test cards he kept with the polygraph kit. The sergeant then told Muise to memorize the number from the card and return it to the pack. Muise seemed happy to take part in the fake test; he chatted with the sergeant as the cards were shuffled and the machine was readied. The test might be intended to show how effective the polygraph could be, but it also would give Muise a dry run at attempting to fool it. Soucie told the young man to

answer no as he was asked if each card from the pack was the one selected; Muise closed his eyes and sat perfectly still in the oversized
polygraph chair. He did as instructed, and he concentrated on relaxing and keeping his breathing, pulse, and sweat glands under control.

"Was your card number 16?"

"No."

"Was your card number 5?"

"No."

Soucie continued through the deck of cards and then told Muise
to relax. The test was over. He looked at the results on the sheet of paper streaming from the polygraph, then sorted through his pile of
cards, selected one, and dropped it to the table. It was the card Muise
had chosen; the machine had worked. The sergeant showed Muise
where his body had reacted to the lie. "If you look here, you get an ar-
tificially high reading when I asked you about the number 16. That's
normal, because it was the first question. There is no number 16 in
my deck; it's just a way to ease into the test—the same way I will ask
you control questions during the real test. But if you look further
along here, the readings get high again when I ask you about this
number—it was your card, and you were lying, as I told you to."

Muise leaned over the chair, getting closer to the machine and examining the chart. "That was pretty cool. Can I try it again?" Muise
wanted another practice run.

"No, it's a waste of time to allow people to try to fool the machine.
You know now how it works. It's time to conduct the real test." The
sergeant removed the sensors from Muise's fingers and dried them.
Then, for a second time, he told the young man what he would ask
him during the exam, assuring him there would be no trick questions.
It's important for a subject to be relaxed during a polygraph test; if the
person being questioned expects a trick from the operator, the anxiety can skew the results. That's why the operator always asks, at some
point during the test: "Do you think I will ask you any questions other than the ones we reviewed?" This allows the polygraph technician
to determine whether or not the subject had such a concern, and prevent the subject who fails a text from arguing that it was because he
was afraid of what might be asked.

At 3:14 p.m., Darren Muise was ready to be questioned again by
Sergeant Soucie, but this time there would be no card trick. Muise
concentrated, trying again to will his body to ignore the anxiety he
was feeling. Soucie asked the control questions that he had worked

out during his lengthy preliminary discussion with Muise—questions such as: "Aside from the time you took a bag of chips from a store, have you ever committed a crime for which you were not caught?"

"No," Muise answered.

Mixed in with the control questions were the ones Muise was afraid of, but had tried to prepare his body to ignore. "Last week, did you rob McDonald's restaurant?"

"No."

"Last week, were you involved, in any way, with the robbery at McDonald's?"

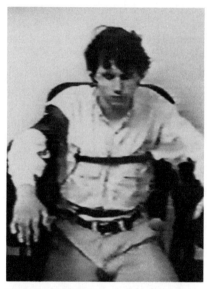

Darren Muise, hooked up to the lie-detector equipment, considers his answer to the police question: 'Were you involved with the robbery?'

"No."

"Are you now hiding anything from the police about this robbery?"

"No."

Soucie wanted to run through the test a number of times; between each session, he removed the finger sensors and dried them, talking casually with Muise, who leaned over in his chair looking at the paper and machine. Each time, the key questions were repeated, but the sequence and order were altered. Finally, the sergeant felt he had enough data. He told Muise it would take a few minutes to analyze the results and asked him to remain in the room. If Darren Muise was afraid he'd fail, or was nervous about what would happen if he did, it was not apparent from his actions. Muise slouched back in the chair, drinking water and enjoying a cigarette; he blew smoke rings into the air and played with the cigarette on the edge of a Styrofoam cup he was using as an ashtray. Sitting in his blue cotton button-down shirt and watching smoke rise to the ceiling, Muise looked as if he did not have a care in the world. But his posture and demeanour were about to change.

Sergeant Soucie returned to the polygraph suite and informed Muise that he had failed the test. The sergeant told him how disappointed he was; he thought they had a good test, and now he wanted to know why Muise had lied to him. Soucie neither raised his voice nor appeared angry as he began to debate with Muise; for his part, Muise reacted innocently, as though it had to be a mistake. Soucie wasn't buying that routine; he'd seen it too many times before. "From these charts today, there's no doubt in my mind you're connected with this situation—the murders at McDonald's," he said.

"I'm not," Muise answered, his tone surprisingly calm, considering he had just been told by a senior member of the RCMP that he was a suspect in one of Canada's most serious multiple murders. Although his voice remained even, his manner had changed. Earlier in their conversation, Muise had been like a typically energetic teenager, moving constantly in his seat, leaning one way and the other, interrupting the sergeant with questions, and making humourous remarks to keep the mood light. Now, Muise was leaning forward slightly in the chair, his left leg locked tightly across the right knee, his right elbow propped on the arm of the chair, and his hand covering his mouth— the way it had when Sergeant Scharf challenged him the night before.

While Sergeant Soucie computes the results of the polygraph, Darren Muise relaxes with a cigarette.

As he sat facing the young man, Soucie remained calm, not wanting to provoke an argument. The police had no legal ground to keep Muise; they wanted him to help voluntarily. "You know something about it," he said, "and if you can sit here and deny that, there's something going terribly wrong up there in your head."

"No, I have a conscience, and I'm telling you that I didn't have anything to do with it." Muise shifted in the chair, now leaning on his left arm and still covering his mouth with his hand, as though he was trying to keep the panic that must have been racing through his mind from bursting out in a confession or a plea for mercy.

"Well, there's something wrong with that conscience, Darren, because people don't do this—normal people don't do this—and you came in here today, and you didn't pass the polygraph test. What's that gotta tell me? It's gotta tell me that—" Soucie leaned forward, pointing a finger at Muise's chest—"that test result shows me something inside your body is reacting to those particular questions in relation to that murder."

The officer and Muise continued to go around in circles, with one imploring the other to tell the truth. Soucie felt Muise could have become involved sometime after the crime—although the test indicated he had been in the restaurant—but the officer still wanted the young man to tell what he knew. The discussion became heated as Muise insisted on his right to leave. In the other room, Dave Trickett could see it was time to step in, to settle Muise down and keep him from leaving. As Trickett came in, he was briefed by Soucie, as though they had not observed the testing procedure and the resulting conversation. The constable told Muise he was really shocked, and asked him why he had failed the test. As Soucie stood to leave, Trickett sat in the chair across from Muise—who wanted to leave. But Trickett wanted just a minute to try to understand what was going on. He asked Muise if there was something he was trying to hide. Darren Muise wanted no part of another debate with another officer; he just wanted to leave. About then, the friendly tone Dave Trickett had used since the two had met the previous day began to change. Trickett was losing patience with Muise, and he wanted some answers. He did not yell or display anger, but he made it clear he expected an explanation.

Muise objected to his persistent questioning, saying it upset him. "Well, when you start drilling at me and that..." Muise's voice trailed off as Trickett interrupted. He wasn't ready to hear about this kid's problems; he had a multiple murder to solve. "I'm not drilling you," the constable said. "I'm telling you straight to your face that you know something about it."

"I told you right back, I don't."

"Now come on, Darren, be honest with me, boy."

"I am, I told you."

"You're not. Who are you afraid of?"

"No-one." Muise's tone was one of exasperation as he leaned back in the chair, throwing his arms apart in a gesture that suggested he did not understand how the misunderstanding could have arisen. But Trickett wasn't buying the answer or the body language that accompanied it. "There's gotta be somebody, Darren. Holy jeez, boy, there's so many inconsistencies."

Then the officer decided he would change tactics. Instead of suggesting that Muise was merely hiding information to protect someone else or because he was afraid, Trickett began to treat him as though he was the one responsible. He knew that the description of the injuries to the victims had upset Muise the day before, so he headed down that road—only this time he took Muise along as he described what he believed had happened to Neil Burroughs: "He was over there working on his stuff, when he was shot in the back of the head, when his neck was cut, when he was shot *there*—" Trickett used his finger to point to his own head, as if his hand were a gun—"when he was shot through the ear because he wouldn't stay down. Were you there?" Muise's hand went over his mouth again, and once again he crossed one leg over the other, rocking back and forth in a steady rhythm that belied the anxiety he must have been feeling. "Or the poor bastard, when you were going out the door and he was coming in," Trickett continued. "Were you there when he got drilled right *there*?" And he pointed to his head again.

"I wasn't there." Muise lowered his head as he answered, reaching back with his hand and running it through his thick black hair.

"Tell me. Tell me."

"I wasn't there."

"You weren't there," Trickett repeated after him. Muise flung his arms apart as he looked at the angry officer and, raising his voice a little, he insisted: "I told you I had nothing to do with it. I wasn't there."

"Nothing to do with it. You weren't there. Did you have knowledge of it?"

"No!"

Trickett tried to change the mood again, this time attempting to appeal to Muise's conscience. "Come on, Darren, you've got three people killed. Does that bother you?"

The answer was not what Trickett expected: Muise yawned, leaned back in the chair, stretched, and ignored the remark.

"Look! A big yawn. So what. Big deal." Trickett looked incredulous.

"Sorry," Muise said. "I'm tired."

The conversation continued, but after twenty minutes or so, it became clear who was going to win this round. Muise began to take a firm stand. "I just want to say one thing. You told me when I came here, right?"

"Yeah." Trickett knew what was coming.

"If I wanna leave I can leave, and you said you'd leave then and there."

"Yeah, sure..." But Muise interrupted before the officer could say more. "I asked you five times," the young man said. "No, six times."

"Yeah, we can go. We can go—" and as Trickett uttered those words, Muise stood up. The officer did not like looking up at him, so he too got to his feet, but Muise had already turned towards the door. Trickett knew he was beaten, but wanted Muise to know it wasn't over yet. "We can go, but just remember that there are three people dead. We don't believe you, O.K.?" Muise responded with an affirmative "Mmm-hmm" and a nod, but no words. He wasn't going to be drawn back into the debate.

Trickett wasn't quite finished. "We don't believe you one little bit," he said. "You're not pulling the wool over our eyes. Someday, some policeman's gonna come to your door, and I'd suggest to you that day is not too far away."

The two walked out of the polygraph room and to the parking lot as Trickett continued to impress upon Muise that he had not won, that he had not fooled anyone. Muise sat quietly in the car as the officer continued his lecture and they drove towards Sydney. Trickett noticed that his passenger had started to cry quietly. Muise wanted sympathy. "It's a sad day when a machine is taken over the word of a man," he said.

"It's more than just the machine, Darren, and you know it."

As they drove on, Muise told Trickett that the wounds on his arm had in fact been self-inflicted, and that he had also taken pills. Then he said he was afraid, not because of what he'd done but because of what he knew. What if—he asked—what if he had overheard two men talking about "doin' a job at McDonald"? Not "McDonald's" but "Mc-Donald." This hypothetical conversation, he said, took place at the food court in the Sydney Shopping Centre, and when he got up to leave, the two men looked at him. Then there were the dark cars that had been following him since the night of the murders; he was afraid they were after him. Trickett told Muise he would have had to hear more than that, if they were really out to get him, but Muise insisted he knew only that they were from Halifax. The fiction he had created in his suicide note the night before was now helping him to explain why he had failed the polygraph—the problem was, Dave Trickett didn't believe the story.

When the two arrived at Muise's home, Trickett went in to talk with his parents. He told them that Darren had attempted suicide, that he had failed the polygraph, and that police believed their son was withholding information about the murders. Darren repeated his claim that he had overheard a conversation and was afraid; that was why he failed the test. The Muises were frightened by what the officer had to say. They wanted to believe Darren. This had to be a mix-up. He might have failed the test, but that didn't have to mean that he was involved in the crime. They urged their son to be honest, to tell police the whole truth; Trickett said he hoped Muise would listen to his parents, at least, if not to police. Muise went to his room to think about it. A short time later, at the insistence of his parents, the eighteen-year-old phoned Trickett to apologize for upsetting the officer.

Dave Trickett left and returned to the Sydney detachment to report to Kevin Cleary and Sylvan Arsenault. Late Thursday afternoon, it was decided that a wiretap should be put on Darren Muise's phone. And if Muise was involved, then Freeman MacNeil's alibi was no longer solid; at least, it required a much closer look. It would probably be a good idea to tap MacNeil's phone, too. Even if he wasn't involved, he was certainly connected to the two people police were now certain had key information. Constable Pat Murphy got to work on the court documents again, and this time he was able to get a judge to approve the wiretaps the following day—the depositions obtained for the tap on Derek Wood were already before the courts, and police simply had to show why further surveillance was needed.

• • •

FREEMAN MACNEIL had no idea he was still on the minds of the investigators probing the murders. He had not heard from them since the day of the killings, and that was fine by him. Muise and Wood were spending a lot of time together, trying to second-guess the RCMP, but MacNeil was staying away from his colleagues in crime. He spoke with them and saw them once or twice, but for the most part he was reacquainting himself with old friends. Still, he was glad he had spoken to

Wood shortly after the crime; otherwise, he might not have found out about the gun. It hadn't been missed, and now it was back where it belonged. MacNeil's relaxed attitude was obvious when he encountered a friend at a local convenience store. The friend, who had once worked as a security guard with MacNeil, asked him where he had been on the night of the murders; Freeman said he had been at McDonald's. The two laughed at the macabre humour, then went their separate ways.

On Thursday, MacNeil and a friend were visiting another stereo store in Sydney. This time he was getting a better set of speakers for the system he was installing in Michelle's mother's Impala. The car was sounding great, but he knew it could be even better. When he purchased the speakers, Freeman cashed his unemployment cheque at the store; the McDonald's money was running out. That was O.K., though. Freeman had a new plan for making money, and this one did not involve breaking the law. He was going to become a taxi driver.

Freeman MacNeil was driving through Sydney, heading to Whitney Pier, at about the same time Dave Trickett was briefing the chief investigators. When MacNeil got to Michelle's place, another car was just pulling in. Constables Rod Gillis and Wayne MacDonald had been sent to interview Michelle Sharp to see what she remembered about the night of May 6 and the early morning of May 7: had she in fact sent her boyfriend to his house to collect her asthma inhaler? Gillis was a thin, almost frail-looking man with red hair and an easygoing manner; the shorter, stockier MacDonald seemed deadly serious most of the time, and his thick black hair and dark moustache emphasized his stern military look.

Freeman MacNeil recognized the unmarked police car, but not the man inside it. Gillis introduced himself to Freeman and asked if they could talk while his partner was meeting with Michelle. She was the one they had come to see, he explained, but as long as Freeman was there, he could help clarify something. Freeman agreed; he wanted the police to know he was cooperative and open with them. Gillis asked MacNeil to review the route he and Darren Muise had taken on the night of the murders, but MacNeil's answers did not establish which one of them was telling the truth. Gillis believed MacNeil, but he knew that a lie-detector test was the only way to clear the matter up. Muise was supposed to be taking one that day, but Gillis did not know that the young man had failed it. "Look, Freeman, we're giving a number of the witnesses lie-detector tests, and I was wondering if you could take one for us this evening. It's not that you're a suspect or anything; it's just a way for us to be sure everyone is telling the truth."

MacNeil did not want to take the test, but he was equally unwilling to convey to the RCMP that he had anything to hide. "Well, I'm going to look into a taxi permit tonight. Can we do it some other time?"

"How about tomorrow morning?"

"Well, I guess so. Where do I have to go?"

"I can pick you up. We'll be going to North Sydney for the test. It should only take two or three hours, and then you can leave. Will you be here tomorrow at around eight o'clock?"

"No, I'll be at my place on Beaton Road. Do you know where it is?"

"Yeah, no problem. I'll meet you there at about eight, then."

"O.K." Freeman left the officer and went into the trailer. Rod Gillis waited in the car until Wayne MacDonald finished taking a statement from MacNeil's girlfriend. Then the officers headed back to the detachment.

"MacNeil's a nice kid. Can't see him involved in this." Gillis was as impressed by Freeman MacNeil as Lambe and Eagan had been a week earlier.

"Yeah, his girlfriend backs his story about the asthma inhaler. What did he have to say about the way he drove home that night?"

"Same story he told last week."

TRUE TO HIS WORD, Rod Gillis arrived at Freeman Mac-Neil's house shortly after eight o'clock Friday morning, May 15. It was the beginning of the most successful day the RCMP investigators would have since the murders occurred, a little over a week before. The road to that success would be marked with a string of conflicting and misleading statements from Freeman MacNeil, who would be working with a handicap as he tried to fool the police.

What MacNeil did not know was that as he was getting ready to go to the North Sydney detachment to take the lie-detector test, his friend Greg Lawrence was making arrangements to meet Sergeant Gary Grant. Lawrence did not want to go to the police station to make his statement; instead, he insisted on going to the Sydney Holiday Inn. As an added precaution, he drove his car to the Sydney Shopping Centre and parked there, taking a taxi to the hotel. Grant and Lawrence met, and the heavy-set young man with the dark eyes and dark hair told his story. In his version of what led to the Mc-Donald's robbery, Greg Lawrence implicated Freeman MacNeil as the primary player, the man who controlled the conversations and took the lead in asking Lawrence to participate. Lawrence also told Grant that he had seen a small silver handgun in the trunk of the car Freeman was driving. Grant was surprised to learn that the robbery was to have happened a week earlier, but that it was cancelled when a fourth robber failed to show up and Lawrence refused to take that person's place. Lawrence didn't phone the police at the time because he said he simply did not believe they were going to go through with the plan.

At the MacNeil home, Rod Gillis told Freeman's mother not to worry; her son would be home in a few hours. They travelled in the police car, stopping at Tim Hortons for a coffee, and then went to the detachment, where Freeman MacNeil was introduced to Sergeant Phil Scharf and agreed to take the test; Darren Muise's failure had apparently made no impression on him—if in fact he had heard about it at all. MacNeil too failed the polygraph, and Phil Scharf expressed his surprise and disappointment. Then he read MacNeil his rights, telling him he did not have to answer any questions. But Scharf wanted an explanation, and he made that clear. When he suggested that MacNeil failed the test because he was afraid rather than involved, MacNeil took what he saw as a lifeline out of the pit into which the polygraph had plunged him. In reality, MacNeil was about to begin a descent into an even deeper pit. He began by agreeing to give the officer a statement; he had been afraid for the safety of his mother and his girlfriend, but now he was prepared to tell the truth.

MacNeil's story implicated Darren Muise and Derek Wood in the robbery and killings. He stuck to his original claim that he drove home to pick up his girlfriend's asthma inhaler, that he didn't leave her place until after 1:00 a.m., and that on the way, he saw Muise at the side of the road and picked him up. The new part was that Muise allegedly said and did certain things after Freeman picked him up—things that made it clear that Muise and Wood had just robbed the restaurant.

By early afternoon, MacNeil and Scharf had discussed his new statement and his reasons for not talking to police earlier. Sergeant Scharf asked MacNeil if he would meet with Constable Gillis and his partner, Constable Wayne MacDonald, and go over the details in a formal written statement. MacNeil said he would be happy to do so; he believed that once he gave the statement, he would be able to leave. Then he could help prosecute the other two, or maybe get in touch with them and make a run for it as soon as he got out. But whatever he was planning as he prepared to make a formal statement implicating his partners, the RCMP had something else in mind.

MacNeil left the polygraph suite and entered a nearby interview room. At 1:42 p.m., MacDonald read Freeman MacNeil his Charter rights and asked if he understood them. MacNeil said he did, and MacDonald and Gillis began the questioning. MacNeil claimed that it was the Monday after the murders when he began to suspect Derek Wood of being involved; he and Wood were in a car, and Wood said he'd kill himself if the girl didn't pull through. Wood, he said, was all shaky and nervous at the time. That same day, MacNeil also picked up Darren Muise, who gave him ten dollars for gas—and that was unusual, because the guy never had money. Oh, and Muise also told him to say the two of them had spent Wednesday night together if he was asked. MacNeil said he felt threatened when Muise mentioned twins from Halifax who were checking on him daily to make sure he was O.K. Those twin bikers, he said, were only fourteen when one of them killed their father. That was why he lied; he felt forced to protect Darren Muise. Then there was the matter of Darren Muise getting enough money together to move to British Columbia, where he had a job lined up with the Hell's Angels. It sounded like bullshit when Muise said it, but now he wasn't so sure.

MacNeil added more incriminating evidence to his tale: on the drive to get the asthma puffer, Muise asked him not to drive out Kings Road, the route he usually took. *Then* Muise borrowed a pair of his sneakers at the house, because his were muddy, and *then* he asked Freeman to stop by the Grantmire Brook, where he got out to urinate. MacNeil told police Muise left the car with muddy shoes in his hand but returned without them, and that before he got in the car he threw something on the other side of the road. Maybe it was a gun, but MacNeil said he never would have picked Muise up if he thought the guy was carrying a weapon. When the officers hinted that they had information implicating him in the planning of the robbery, MacNeil claimed he had been there when the other two discussed it, but told them he wanted no part of it—their plan included putting people in the freezer if they were found in the restaurant. He didn't think anyone was supposed to be killed, but he knew that Derek had a gun, because he had left it in Freeman's car a few weeks earlier. MacNeil also suggested a possible suspect if police felt three robbers had been involved. He gave them Mike Campbell as an accomplice, saying Muise told him that Campbell had driven him back into Sydney after the robbery.

The officers wrote out this statement but let MacNeil know they felt he knew more. Then he began connecting Muise and Wood to other crimes; they'd been involved in break-and-enters before, he said. As the questioning continued, MacNeil began to wonder just what it would take to get him released. He painted a grimmer and grimmer picture of his colleagues. One time they borrowed his car to go buy a submarine sandwich—Darren even borrowed money to buy the food—and when they returned, two hours later, they had filled his car with gas. He wondered how they suddenly came into money that night. At the conclusion of this statement, the officers left the interview room and MacNeil relaxed, certain that he would be able to leave soon.

This information certainly gave police reason to pick up and question Darren Muise, Derek Wood, and Mike Campbell. But MacNeil hadn't offered an account of the discussions with Greg Lawrence, and something just didn't feel right. Phil Scharf decided he would have another chat with the young man, and while the new statement was being faxed to Kevin Cleary and Sylvan Arsenault, Scharf took over the questioning of MacNeil.

The new statement, coupled with the one from Greg Lawrence, gave police enough reason to prepare for arrests, and extra officers were brought in from other RCMP detachments. It would not be a repeat of the high-profile ERT raids in Glace Bay a week earlier, but the Mounties would take no chances; the gun was still out there somewhere. Pat Murphy had been listening to the wiretaps and learned Wood was planning a night of club-hopping to celebrate his nineteenth birthday. Afternoon briefings were held, take-downs were planned, and officers were assigned to conduct interrogations once the suspects were in custody. Dave Trickett would get another chance with Darren Muise, and his partner would be Corporal Brian Stoyek, the man who had questioned Wood on the morning of the murders. Jim Wilson and Karl Mahoney were assigned to interview Wood. They were fresh faces: Cleary didn't want Wood to think he was dealing with officers he felt he had already bested. And unfortunately, officers were also assigned to arrest and question an innocent man—Mike Campbell. Rod Gillis and Wayne MacDonald were instructed to push for more from Freeman MacNeil; questioning him further was critically important. So far police had enough time to hold the suspects on conspiracy to commit robbery, but not enough to tie them to the crime itself. They needed more.

It had become a habit for me to touch base with Dave Roper every morning at eight and every afternoon about three, just to see if anything new had developed. When I called that afternoon, Roper's voice sounded excited, but he was guarded about the reason for his exuberance. Roper almost always said the investigation was going well, but this time he said things were going *very* well. I said I wanted to head out to the detachment to get an on-camera interview with him saying just that, and told him I had heard there was an unusual amount of activity at the detachment. Roper confirmed that there were several new officers in the building, but asked me not to take a camera up there right away and said he would call back in a few minutes to explain. I asked George Reeves to get the gear ready; we might have something more compelling than the community-concern item we had prepared for that evening's broadcast.

Roper did call back, saying he had switched to a telephone that was not being recorded, as most of the lines at the detachment were. This was an arrangement we had made a few times in the past week, when the officer wanted to ask a favour and knew he might have to trade information for it. I pushed for confirmation that arrests were pending, but he could not give it, and asked that I make no reference to the reinforcements arriving at the detachment—something that our camera would reveal simply by panning across the packed parking lot. His tone of concern told me that police were about to make a move, and I knew reporting it could sound an alarm for the suspects. There was no way I'd do that, but I wanted something in return for assuring Roper that I would stay away from his back door. The best he could do was to say that if I didn't have anything important to do that evening, it might be worthwhile to hang around the station for a few hours; he would call me there with something new to report. I hung up the phone and asked George if he could cancel his plans for the night. He grumbled a little, reminding me—as he had several times in the past week—that he did have a life outside the workplace; maybe I should consider getting one myself, he remarked, heading into the equipment room to sort through the gear. I knew he was joking, and that like everyone else, he was looking forward to seeing this case resolved, but it reminded me to call home. I was going to be late again.

By the time plans for the arrests were readied, it was too late in the evening to make the move before Muise, Wood, and Campbell left their homes. Officers debated whether to make the arrests in public places and risk a violent confrontation, or wait until the suspects had returned home. While those issues were being worked out, Phil Scharf persuaded Freeman MacNeil to give yet another statement. Once again, he insisted that he had held back information earlier in the day because he was afraid that his mother and girlfriend were in danger. Scharf told him that if he was not completely truthful, Wood and Muise would remain at large, and his loved ones might indeed be put at risk. Then, Gillis and MacDonald took over again.

This time, MacNeil's statement was much more specific, and MacNeil hoped the details would convince police he was finally telling all, and should be allowed to go home. The new statement would run eleven pages in length; Gillis and MacDonald wanted every bit of information MacNeil was willing to give. "Freeman, you spoke to the other police officer, Phil Scharf. Do you wish to say anything further at this time?"

MacNeil was relaxed and his tone was casual as he began his newest tale. The officers had no inkling of the bombshell he was about to unleash. "Yep. Darren Muise didn't have anything with him…when I picked him up, but he got me to stop along the bypass and he picked up a steel can. I don't know what the contents were. I assume it was the contents from McDonald's. I asked Darren where Derek was; he said he went to call the police. He said that they robbed McDonald's, and when Derek got inside, that he went nuts and started shooting everybody."

That was it. Just before 5:00 p.m. on May 15, police heard for the first time who had pulled the trigger. It was a shock to the officers who had dealt with Derek Wood. They suspected him of being involved, all right, but was he really capable of that kind of cold-blooded murder? Was Derek Wood the gunman, and did he still have the gun? MacDonald and Gillis continued to question MacNeil, while Phil Scharf contacted Sydney to report that they had a statement implicating Muise and Wood in more than the planning of the robbery.

MacNeil gave police some truth and some fantasy as he continued to deliver the goods on his former partners in crime. "He got me to stop at the brook, and that's where he dumped it all. I don't know what was in the can; he just took it down to the water with him. He asked me if I wanted some money—he had about a hundred dollars on him. He said they got a lot of money but everything went wrong. He said the other guy got all the money, and I said, 'Who, Derek?' and he said no. I told him, 'Never mind, I don't want to know.' I don't know who the other guy is, but he said Mike dropped him off in town and I think that's who the other guy is. That's it."

MacNeil was not only willing to hand over his partners, but also more than willing to implicate an innocent man. He would say anything to get out of that interrogation room. But the longer MacNeil stayed, the more police learned about his real involvement. Part of the investigation involved finding and talking to the friends of those believed to be connected to the crime, and an interview with a friend of MacNeil's had yielded the interesting information that MacNeil had been shooting a handgun at a beach about a week before the murders. MacNeil had an explanation for this: Wood had left a small pistol in his car, and when MacNeil was at the beach with two friends, he discovered that it was loaded, so he decided to shoot at some ice floes. He said Wood took the gun back shortly afterward.

Police also wanted an explanation that would ease their concerns about the Greg Lawrence statement. "Did you yourself talk about doing this robbery with Darren or Derek?"

"I think I might have."

"Explain."

"They asked me a couple of times if I'd drive them out there, and I told them no."

"When?"

"About a week before and then the night of the shootings." This fit Greg Lawrence's time frame, but hardly implicated MacNeil in the way Lawrence had. Gillis and MacDonald continued the interview, and with each question, MacNeil handed them more and more; he was burying his friends.

"Do you know who did the shooting?"

"Darren said Derek did it, but I think Darren did it—or it could have been the third guy, because I don't know him at all."

"Why do you think Darren?"

"I don't think Derek would hurt anybody, and Darren was so calm and strange, and Darren keeps calling me, and I saw Derek, and Derek is a mess."

The officers asked MacNeil if he knew how it all happened, and he outlined what he claimed Darren told him, including the locations of some of the shootings. His description was accurate enough to convince police he had inside information, but contained enough errors to be seen as second-hand. He was telling what he knew but, after all, he hadn't been there at the time. The police also wanted to know if he had any theory on why they tried to kill everyone. "I don't know, Derek told them that nobody was there and Darren probably had the gun and freaked out because he was probably stoned," MacNeil said. Muise smoked hash a lot and must have been high that night, because he acted so calm after the murders.

Then, he dropped another bombshell: "Darren also said he finally got to slit somebody's throat. I don't know whose, but that's what he said." The RCMP had not revealed that a knife had been found at the brook, but now MacNeil had Muise claiming to use a knife during the robbery, and he had already placed Muise in the area where the knife had been recovered.

MacNeil again offered to tell the officers about the criminal histories of Muise and Wood. "I know they used to break into houses, but I don't think recently. Derek said when he was fifteen or sixteen, he used to break into houses and stuff, but he got away from it. I think that Darren got him back into it. I say this because it's Darren I would see broke one day and then have money the next, and he always had money to play pool."

"Did they ask you to go on any other robberies or thefts besides the McDonald's restaurant?"

"They used to get me to pick them up downtown and drive them home, but not to any breaks that I am aware of. I feel that probably there were times when they used me as a taxi service after they had done something without me knowing it." MacNeil was getting right into the role of innocent friend of the guilty—any part he played in past robberies was that of an unwilling patsy.

MacNeil signed his new statement, and agreed to take the officers along the route he'd driven that night and show them where he said he had picked up Muise and where Muise had disposed of evidence. Gillis and MacDonald decided to video-tape the trip. The three men stood in front of the North Sydney detachment as another officer recorded the start of their journey. Before they headed to Sydney, Constable MacDonald read Freeman his rights once more and asked if he wished to speak with a lawyer. MacNeil said no, and the three officers took their willing witness on a drive to Sydney. The camera began to record the re-enactment just outside Tim Hortons on Charlotte Street, where MacNeil claimed to have found Darren Muise that night. As the police car rounded the corner by the coffee shop, MacNeil began to recite the information he had already given police, but now he was pointing to locations and indicating where each comment was made.

As the car drove past Tim Hortons, I was just on my way out with a large coffee; it would probably be a long night, and I wanted to start the caffeine flow early. That brown Ford Taurus rounding the corner was probably an unmarked police car, but I didn't see the video camera being used by the officer in the back seat, and I had no idea that the car also carried one of the three men responsible for the crime. The car turned up towards the RCMP detachment, and it occurred to me that the four men inside were going to take part in whatever Dave Roper had hinted would be happening that night. It was a few minutes after 8 p.m. Time to go back to the station and try Roper again. At some point, I could also strike up another conversation with the

observation officer posted in the ATV parking lot. If an arrest was going to happen tonight, the observation team would have to be near
the suspect so police would know where to pick him up.

As Freeman MacNeil guided police along the route he had taken
with Darren Muise after the killings, Muise was back at the pool hall,
worrying about the lie-detector test and the disturbing promise made
by Dave Trickett. He wondered when that officer Trickett spoke of
would come to his door. Derek Wood and some friends of his were
also at Pockets, and a local youth counsellor, Barry Moore, was watching the group. He had been keeping an eye on Muise all week and felt
something wasn't right. Moore had played the poker machines with
Muise at Sanitary Dairy on the night of the murders, and since then
he had begun to wonder where his young friend had been before he
arrived at the store. And Muise was also spending more money than
he normally did.

Moore watched Muise laugh and joke with the group on the other side of the room. As the group broke up, Muise huddled and whis-
pered with Derek Wood. Moore knew Wood was the McDonald's
employee who had survived the attack, but he had no idea how much
the two had to talk about. Muise was worrying about the polygraph—
Freeman was taking one, and Wood figured police would soon want
him to do the same. When Wood got up and left, Moore confronted
his friend, who looked pale and nervous: "Darren, are you involved in
that McDonald's robbery?" Moore didn't think his friend was a killer,
but he could tell something was wrong. As a counsellor and a friend,
he felt Muise might want to confide in him, but Muise had no time
for caring friends.

"No." Muise left the pool hall and headed home.

Derek Wood had not gone home, but to the nearby Irish Club, a
small bar where he was going to celebrate his birthday with his cousin
Mike Campbell and a couple of friends. As he walked towards the
club, Wood had a feeling this would be the night. He knew Darren
was finally feeling the pressure he himself had felt ever since that day
with the police. But he wasn't going to let his premonition stand in
the way of his birthday party. At the Irish Club, Wood and his buddies
had a great time, drinking and joking; a friend even gave the karaoke
machine a try. The club wasn't considered the best spot in town to
find young women, but the guys figured they'd have a few beers there
and then go down to Daniel's Beverage Room or Smooth Herman's
and make a late night of it.

As they sat inside the club drinking, Freeman MacNeil was only a block away. He had finished showing Gillis and MacDonald the route, and now the three of them were parked in front of the Sanitary Dairy, where MacNeil had left Muise on the night of the murders. The officers figured they would be able to take MacNeil home, but first they wanted to stop at the Sydney detachment to see what role they would play in the arrests about to take place. At the detachment, they were told not to allow Freeman MacNeil to go home; Kevin Cleary was not satisfied with MacNeil's statement. MacNeil must have played a more active role: Greg Lawrence was certain that he had acted as the ring-

leader, and that didn't fit with his contention that he was aware of the crime but did not even want it discussed in his presence. No, Gillis and Mac-Donald had to push a little harder. MacNeil had changed his story twice already that day; he might do it again.

The two officers returned to the car and apologized to Mac-Neil; no point in letting him they think they were responsible for keeping him in custody. The officers wanted to maintain a friendly rapport with MacNeil. But MacNeil was furious. He had given the police enough to hang Muise and Wood, but they still would not let him go. He sat silently in the car as they drove back to North Sydney.

Freeman MacNeil points towards Grantmire Brook as he shows Constables Wayne MacDonald, centre, and Rod Gillis where evidence had been disposed of.

This time he was not going to cooperate; he wanted to go home. When he was taken back to the interrogation room and told about his Charter rights, MacNeil said he would exercise one. He wanted a lawyer. The police helped MacNeil contact Legal Aid lawyer Art Mollon, the man who had advised Derek Wood a week earlier. On the phone, Mollon told his new client that he was not to talk with police, no matter what they asked. "Just be quiet and wait until I get there," he said.

On the night of May 15, Freeman MacNeil became the first of the three killers to be placed in custody, at the North Sydney RCMP detachment.

"I already talked to them. I just want to go home."

"Well, don't say anything else until I arrive; it will take me about a half-hour. Just sit tight." MacNeil returned to the interview room, where he told the officers he would not make any comment until his lawyer arrived. Wayne MacDonald then placed Freeman MacNeil under arrest and told him he was being charged with being involved after the murders. MacNeil was taken to a holding cell and locked up. He could wait for his lawyer there.

While MacNeil waited for his legal counsel, I was out in the ATV parking lot, chatting with the lone Mountie. It was about 10 p.m., and police were getting ready to bring in the others, but if this officer knew that arrests were coming, he wouldn't admit it. We talked about how the crime had changed people in Sydney, and the officer told a story that had him convinced not enough people were getting the message. Earlier in the day, he was at a local store to purchase cigarettes when he was asked to wait while the clerk cleared out the cash register. He couldn't believe it: the money was right in front of him, yet the clerk seemed completely unconcerned about the prospect of being robbed. She had no idea the man at the counter was carrying a gun. The radio in his car interrupted our conversation; the observer team was using a frequency that our newsroom scanner could not detect. Much of what was said was in code, but I did recognize the places named at the end of the transmission. The officer said he had to leave, and I rushed back into the station newsroom.

"Let's get ready, George. It looks like the arrests are going down. I'm not sure where, but the guy out front was just told it would be at the Irish Club, Daniel's, or Smooth Herman's." The wiretap information had given the officers the itinerary for Wood's birthday bash, and now officers were preparing to interrupt it. Another car from the observer's unit was in place at a church parking lot about a kilometre from the ATV lot. The car trailing Darren Muise had "put him to bed," and with Muise at home, that car was left to watch his street while the others prepared to "take down" Derek Wood and Mike Campbell.

We decided not to take a station vehicle—not much point in drawing the attention of the police while we tried to find out where the arrests would be made. We drove through Sydney, passing all three clubs. No sign of unusual activity at Smooth Herman's or Daniel's, but as soon as we rounded the corner and headed for the Irish Club, I saw what we were looking for. I had contacted a former member of an RCMP emergency response unit, who told me team members would try to blend into the area where they would be attempting to make the arrests. And there they were, six plainclothes police officers, mingling on the sidewalk outside the club, trying to look like other late-night revellers deciding where to head next. They would not have stood out in any way, but I knew half of them and recognized the unmarked police four-wheel-drive parked at the curb. The car we were driving was too cramped for George to work from, so we borrowed a half-ton truck from the duty engineer at the station. As George prepared the gear in the back, I started out of the lot. He had his camera pointed out the side window of the cab; suddenly, he pounded on the window separating the two of us. "Hold on, hold on. I don't believe it," he shouted. "This recorder is not working." George jumped out and ran for a new recorder; he was back in less than a minute, and we raced down the road, reaching the corner near the Irish Club just as the unmarked cars pulled away. We had missed the arrest by seconds. I swung the truck around and raced towards the RCMP detachment; maybe we'd be lucky enough to get a suspect being taken into the building.

There was no sign of activity there, so we headed back downtown to look for witnesses to the arrests. The coffee shop where Freeman MacNeil, Derek Wood, and Darren Muise had planned much of the robbery was on the same block as the Irish Club, and there we found the two men who had been with Wood and Campbell at the club. They were shocked, and they were telling everybody about what they'd witnessed. It didn't take too much persuasion to get them to repeat the story on camera. They said they were walking out of the club when suddenly a couple of big guys grabbed Wood and Campbell, leaned them up against the car, and told them they were under arrest for murder. The two were quickly placed in the back of separate cars and taken away.

The name Derek Wood was not much of a surprise; I had heard he was the employee who ran away to call police after the killings, and I had confirmed that he had been kept at the RCMP detachment for twenty-six hours after the shootings. But Mike Campbell? I had met Campbell years earlier, and in the past year he had received media attention when he acted as a key player in resolving a conflict among teens in the community. Some kids in Campbell's neighbourhood of Hardwood Hill had been tossing around white supremacist slogans, and Campbell and a few others responded by meeting with Black community leaders and teens from the Pier, making it clear that the troublemakers were not representative of young people in the area. It made no sense that a bright young man, compassionate enough to help out in such a situation, would turn around and start murdering people. (Incidentally, this was exactly what Campbell would try to convince the RCMP, when he gladly agreed to take a lie-detector test and clear his name.)

Although the interviews were great, we were furious about the bad luck that kept us from getting video of the arrests. We returned to the station and called Dave Roper, who told us he would call as soon as he had a statement prepared. In fact, he was delaying us so that officers could inform the victims' families about the arrests. It was almost three in the morning before the Mountie was finally ready to stand in front of the camera and release the good news: three men had been arrested, two in Sydney and one in North Sydney. The Mounties were not ready to include Mike Campbell as an arrested suspect; they were questioning him, but by that time it was becoming clear that he was not a suspect. Roper didn't release any names, nor did he say what charges these suspects might face or when they would appear in court. We returned to the station to edit a report that highlighted the arrests at the bar and the 3 a.m. press briefing with Roper. At five-thirty in the morning, I went home for a few hours' sleep before returning to find out everything I could about the suspects now in custody.

● ● ●

DEREK WOOD WAS not surprised when he was handcuffed and placed in the squad car, but he demanded to know why Mike was being taken away in another police cruiser. Wood insisted that Mike had nothing to do with the crime, adding that it was lame to try to use his friend to get at him. The officers said they would talk with Wood when they arrived in North Sydney, where he was being taken for questioning; Mike was going to the Sydney detachment. As the police cars left the club, the backup teams prepared for another arrest. Just after 1:00 a.m., Dave Trickett knocked firmly on the door of Darren Muise's house. He informed Darren's startled parents that he was there to see their son again. But this time he was not asking Darren to come along to help the investigation; he was placing the eighteen-year-old under arrest. Muise was cuffed and lead to the waiting police car, just as Trickett had promised he would be. Muise was taken to the Reserve Mines detachment of the RCMP to face questioning.

Kevin Cleary felt more relaxed after the final arrest was made, but the real work was yet to come. There was no strong physical evidence linking the suspects to the crime; the police needed confessions, and they would have to be properly obtained. Those selected to conduct the interrogations knew the case depended on it.

When Derek Wood arrived in North Sydney, he was taken to the polygraph suite where both Muise and MacNeil had tried to lie their way out of the mess they were now in. Wood was not going to be asked to take a lie-detector test, though; he was simply going to be asked to confess. Wood did not realize that he just about passed Freeman MacNeil in the hallway, coming back from a meeting with his lawyer, Art Mollon, in another area of the North Sydney detachment. Mollon had told MacNeil that he should continue to remain silent when questioned; he had already told police enough. MacNeil took the advice, and when Rod Gillis and Wayne MacDonald realized further questioning was pointless, MacNeil was placed back in the cell to spend the night.

The first of the three to see the inside of a jail cell, Freeman Mac-Neil found himself in a large, sterile room with marbled floors that curved up to form rock-hard benches on three of the four sides of the room; the cell could sleep three or four drunks on a busy night. A lidless stainless-steel toilet, with a moulded seat that could not be lifted, was located at the end of one of the benches. On top of the rear wall were small, thick, opaque glass windows that offered no view but allowed a bit of natural light into the gloomy cell. The huge brown steel door had a slot cut in it to allow officers to hand food to prisoners; it also had a window, to allow guards to check on the inmates, but a sliding steel plate could be placed over the opening to prevent prisoners from seeing out. Constable Wayne MacDonald checked behind the brown door every fifteen minutes, all through the night, to make sure his prisoner was all right. At one point, MacNeil asked MacDonald for a blanket, then made himself as comfortable as he could on the marble bench. A little after two in the morning, MacDonald opened the cell and allowed Freeman MacNeil's mother and sister to visit with him. It was an ordeal for the two women: Freeman was the baby of the family, much-loved by his mother and sister, who were helpless to get him out of the trouble he was in.

Meanwhile, Derek Wood was in the polygraph suite, where he was being advised on his legal rights. Dressed in a black T-shirt and loose-fitting pants, Wood did not look like the killer the RCMP now believed he was. The outfit, along with his sandy hair, pouting lips, and sullen eyes, made him look a little like the late Rolling Stones guitarist Brian Jones.

After he was informed of his rights, Wood told the two constables with him that he wanted to speak with his lawyer. One of them, Jim Wilson, left the interrogation room to look for the phone numbers for Legal Aid counsel and was surprised to learn that Art Mollon was already in the building; he came back and told Wood, who said he wanted time with the lawyer. The two met in a separate interview room, and Mollon again told his client to remain silent. But Wood said he wanted to talk; he was ready to get it over with. Mollon told him to wait until he had a chance to speak with his partner, Allan Nicholson; the two of them would decide what was in Wood's best interest. Wood gave his word, even signing a piece of paper stating that he would not discuss the matter with police. But the tall, stocky Jim Wilson and the slight, fair-haired Karl Mahoney had other ideas.

The police interrogation is probably the most complex task an officer ever faces. The sole aim of the interview is to persuade suspects to abandon their instinct for self-preservation in favour of a soul-cleansing confession. The most-effective interrogators are able to bring suspects around to their line of thinking, actually making them feel good about telling all. While the moment of confession can be a wonderful unburdening, however, suspects usually come in contact with attorneys, whose job it is to explain that such a moment of catharsis will almost certainly rob them of their freedom. Such was the challenge facing Jim Wilson and Karl Mahoney. They had talked over their options and approaches before entering the polygraph suite. Wood was involved, they knew; Freeman MacNeil had given that much to police. But they also knew he would not be convicted of murder based on the testimony of MacNeil, who still maintained he had not had direct involvement in the crime. The dedicated police-men felt the burden as they approached the interrogation: this vital case could depend on what happened in that little room. The kid waiting for them would be no easy sell—Brian Stoyek had tried for more than twenty hours to convince Wood to tell his story, and Stoyek had failed. Wilson and Mahoney vowed they would not.

In the room, Wood informed the officers that he had been ad-vised by his lawyer not to comment, and that he planned to follow that advice. Wilson and Mahoney tried to shake the pressure and fo-cus on their work as they considered Wood. Although all the officers involved in the arrests were feeling this pressure, Karl Mahoney felt something the others did not. His colleagues knew what he was go-ing through and felt for him, but they could not share the strain. When it became clear that Darren Muise was not a witness but a sus-pect, word quickly spread through the investigating team. Muise had dated Mahoney's daughter for about nine months. Both Mahoney and his wife disapproved of Darren Muise and were relieved when their daughter ended the relationship. Neither parent had any inkling that Muise was capable of a crime like this; it was just that he had failed high school and was drifting into an aimless life that the cop in Mahoney knew would lead to no good. He was not looking forward to telling his little girl what he hoped to learn from Derek Wood. He was angry; this crime had hurt a lot of people, and now it was going to hurt his daughter. Mahoney tried to put those thoughts out of his head, but as the questioning began, it would quickly be-come apparent that his anger was going to make him the aggressor in this interrogation. Jim Wilson was much bigger than his partner, but he would be the one to befriend the suspect. Putting a killer at ease and making a personal connection with him was something most interrogators tried to do, despite what it made them feel like af-terward. If the job was better done because you showed compassion and understanding to someone whose actions made you sick inside, then it was what you did; you could always deal with your own emo-tional baggage later.

Mahoney began the process of questioning Derek Wood. "There's a few things I want to talk to you about—just to tell you what has to be done here." Wood did not want to hear anything; he just wanted to clear something up: "The only thing I gotta say is that Mike, I know for a fact, 'cause when I called him he was asleep." Mahoney ignored the interruption and showed Wood a list of the charges he faced, among them three counts of first-degree murder and one of attempted murder. The list was placed on the table in front of him.

As the officers began to question Wood about the murders, he insisted he would not be making any comments, at least not tonight. Seeing Jim Wilson place a notepad on the table and begin to take notes, Wood told him not to bother wasting his time. "You might as well save your hand," he said. "If there's anything I know, it's gonna be said to my lawyer. There's nothing I'd say tonight."

"Why's that?"

"If I know anything, it will come out in time. But as of right now, I have nothin' to say."

"Why don't ya just get it off your chest now?" More than six feet tall and over two hundred pounds, Jim Wilson was careful to take a soft, friendly approach with Wood; he did not want his size to intimidate the teenager. Wood did not want to be questioned, either in a gentle or a harsh tone, so he hinted that if the officers would wait, they'd get their statement: "I have nothing to say. If—if there's anything that I know that you want to find out from me, probably find out tomorrow morning. I have nothing to say until my lawyer's here. We're just going to sit here all night saying the same thing, and I'm not saying anything. You guys are going to be asking me, 'Why not?' I know this already. I have nothing to say."

Mahoney realized they would have to convince Wood that he had not fooled police a week earlier, that this was different. The officer told Wood that the only reason he had been released the first time was that police were sent on a wild-goose chase by someone who decided to call and give them false information. But Wood stuck to his position. The only topic Mahoney was able to get him to open up on was Mike Campbell. Wood was clearly upset that his cousin was being detained. "All you're gonna do, you gonna arrest him, maybe charge him. I mean, he won't even be held here—probably until tomorrow."

"Do you think anybody that's charged for murder is gonna go anywheres?" Mahoney wanted Wood to know his friend was facing the same serious charges. The police, operating on the information from Freeman MacNeil, considered Mike Campbell at the least an accessory, and possibly a participant in the killings.

"Okay, say you hold him," Wood said. "He's gonna get off. All you're doing is ruining his public name."

"Yeah, but how's he gonna get off? You're the one that can prove that. If that's the case and he's not involved, tell us, and that's the end of it." If Wood was worried about his friend, the police wanted him to believe that the only way to help Mike was to tell them exactly what happened. Not only would a confession be good for Wood's soul, but it was also needed to clear his friend.

Changing course slightly, Wilson and Mahoney told Wood they'd been talking with Darren and Freeman, casually dropping the names and hoping for some effect. "We know much more about this case, now," Mahoney said. "That's the reason Mike is here." Wood remained defiant: "Then I know you're bullshitting me," he said, laughing at the officers, confident that if they knew the truth, they would not have arrested his cousin.

Once again, the officers changed their approach, asking Wood about his family, trying to get him to open up. He told Wilson he loved his baby sister most of all, but he also said he loved Mike, so the officers worked on his feelings, even asking how he would react if his little sister grew up and took a job at McDonald's, only to be shot and killed for no reason. They told him to be a true friend to Mike, to tell them what happened so that Mike could go free if he was not involved. For hours Wood remained defiant. The tension in the cramped room continued to build. There was nowhere for the officers to pace or otherwise ease the physical strain, so they remained seated, occasionally shifting in their seats as they talked to Wood. The officers wanted to scream, and reach across the table to shake some sense into Wood, but knew they had to stay in control.

At one point, Mahoney decided to use the victims—Wood's former co-workers—as a way to reach him: "Donna layin' there after workin' with ya and treatin' ya well. She was a friend. Neil was there, he just came back to work. Arlene—you were standing alongside of he not ten minutes before. And Jimmy, comin' through the door, not expecting anything at all...for whatever little bit of money that you got out of it."

"I don't know what you're talking about. I got no, no money for anything." Wood was adamant; he had not taken the money and wanted to make that clear. Money might have been the motivating factor for the others, but for Wood the robbery was more about being accepted, being in control.

"Mike is involved because he's stickin' up for a friend." As Mahoney searched for the right buttons, the ones that would convince Wood to open up, he was greeted by a long sigh. Wood was tired of listening to him. Then Wilson tried to show how serious the crime was.

"I cried. I cried when I went home that night, an' I still cry…I just, you know, get choked up." It was true; in the days after the murders, Jim Wilson had gone to see Olive Warren to obtain a photograph of her daughter for the police file. At the time, Olive had asked for assurance that Donna had not been sexually assaulted; it was something that had been nagging at her, and the officer reassured her that nothing like that had happened. It was little consolation, Wilson knew, and it was a painful moment for him.

Jim Wilson might have been choked up, but Derek Wood was not. The longer the officers pressed, the more defiant he became, seemingly enjoying the conflict. It was more than Karl Mahoney could tolerate, and the exchanges between the two became more and more heated. There was no shouting, but the verbal sparring made it clear that there was no love lost here.

"You know, like, if you wanna sit here and, like, do your stupid games with me, then you have to," Wood said.

"I'm not doin' no stupid games with ya."

"No?" Wood's answer was more of a challenge.

"I'm doin this 'cause it has to be done."

"Do you honestly think Mike Campbell had something to do with this?"

"With what we have, yes."

"Hmph. Well then you're a bigger fool, then…"

The two continued to debate the issues, and Wood continued to refuse comment until the conversation returned to Campbell. Mahoney kept pressing; if Mike was innocent, Wood could prove it by saying what had really happened. Wood could see through the approach: "I give up. I don't even know how you made it through college, then, 'cause you're not too bright."

"You figure you're the brightest one in the room here, or what?"

"Well, I'm smart enough to know that Mike doesn't have anything to do with this."

Mahoney continued to try any approach he felt he could break down Wood's defences, but the harder he pushed, the more resistance he met. "You don't care about Mike. You don't care about your little sister. You sure as hell don't care about those four people that you tried to snuff out. How do you live with it, anyway?"

"No offence, man, but you gotta take better psychology classes." Wood was unmoved; his posture and tone suggested he was impressed with his ability to berate the officer. Mahoney pressed on regardless: "How d'ya live with it?"

"No, seriously. You should take better classes."

"How d'ya live with it?"

"I don't know what you're talkin' about."

Finally, after a seemingly endless cycle of debate, Mahoney left the interview room to cool down and give Constable Wilson a chance to try the quiet, friendly approach by himself. Outside, Mahoney moved around the detachment, pacing and fighting to regain his composure. His body was rebelling against the stress he was feeling, and he tried to walk it off, bring himself back to the focus he knew he needed. Meanwhile, Wilson tried to relax Wood by making small talk about school, his experience with the militia, and other unrelated topics. Very gradually, he returned to the McDonald's murders. Wilson also tried to give Derek Wood an avenue towards a confession by telling him he was really two Dereks—one sitting there, talking, and one responsible for what happened at McDonald's. Wood laughed at the suggestion that he had a split personality, but Wilson continued with the approach and adopted an almost evangelical tone as he told the young man that Donna was watching him from heaven—that she forgave him, and the officer also forgave him, because they both knew there were two Dereks. Wilson moved his chair closer to Wood's and lifted his hand heavenward in an effort to depict Donna's perspective. Wood lowered his head and leaned forward in his chair, weary from the hours of constant questioning. Wilson brought his hand down from on high and placed it on Wood's head, trying both to keep the suspect awake and make contact with something he hoped was inside.

As Wood started looking as if he was literally falling asleep in his chair, Wilson became more dramatic, more animated. "You can't forget things like that. Donna, with the gun shoved up to her nose. Boom! Boom!" He was shouting now, and the sound reverberated through the room, startling Wood and bringing his attention back. But no matter what techniques or approaches Jim Wilson tried, he couldn't bring Derek Wood to the place he wanted him to be. Wood was not going to talk about the murders. In the next room, Karl Mahoney and Sergeant Phil Scharf were monitoring Wilson's progress. By then, Mahoney's focus and energy were back, and he decided to return to the room to give Wilson his chance for a break. Wood changed his posture at the changing of the guard; the movement in the room awoke him.

Mahoney decided to try to convince Wood that Mike Campbell was indeed in trouble. The officer had never left the North Sydney detachment, but Wood didn't know that. Mahoney's voice was loud and confident: "I just got back from talkin' to him," he said. "I told you I was gonna see him. He's tryin' ta take the fall for ya."

"Who?"

"Mike."

"Why? What's he sayin'?" Wood was interested now.

"He said, 'Gimme twenty minutes with Derek, and I'll get the gun for ya.' He knows you were there, and he's trying to take the blame." The remarks did bring a reaction from Wood, but not the one Mahoney had hoped for. "Can I call my lawyer?"

"Whaddya wanna call your lawyer for?"

"I wanna talk to him for a second."

"Do you wanna call him right now?"

"Yes."

"You figure you're gonna get a hold of him now?"

"What time is it?"

"Twenty after five." Mahoney reminded Wood that Mike was trying to take the blame.

"Can I talk to him?"

"Who do you want to talk to?" If Wood answered that he wanted to talk to his lawyer, it was over. The officers knew they would be starting all over again, once the suspect was reassured by Art Mollon that remaining silent was in his interest, that he should stop worrying about Mike Campbell. If Mike was not involved, they'd deal with that later.

"Mike," Wood answered. He had stopped asking for his lawyer; the questioning could proceed. Mahoney told Wood that no, he could not talk with his friend, and continued asking questions. Later, Wood's lawyer would argue that nothing he said after he asked for his lawyer could be used against him in trial. But in the early morning of May 16, 1992, legal issues didn't seem to be the point. Anyway, Wood was sticking to his guns, resorting to the same verbal one-upmanship he had used with the officer earlier: "Excuse me, did ya say somethin' ta me?" was his answer to one question.

"How's that make you feel?"

"What?"

"What you've done, how does it make you feel?"

"Are you talkin' ta me?" In the monitoring room, Phil Scharf had had enough. He could see they were going nowhere, and as long as Wood tried to be clever and play word games, they would continue to go nowhere. He decided it was time for him to get involved. Shortly before six, Sergeant Scharf walked into the room, introduced himself, and began to lecture Wood—not question him, just preach at him. If Jim Wilson was good cop and Karl Mahoney was bad cop, then Phil Scharf was righteous cop—a new spin on the old police interrogation technique.

Scharf pulled no punches as he tried to make it clear to Wood that it was not the time for games: "This is one of the worst tragedies I've ever investigated. It's probably the worst tragedy that many of us will ever see in our service. You are the author of that tragedy—part of that tragedy. There is no doubt in our minds from what Darren has told Freeman—what Freeman told us. Darren said, not to me, but he told Freeman that you went crazy. Ya made Donna open the safe, then you shot her. Then you went looking around the building for anybody left....If you got any pleasure outta this at all...Derek, my God, it's gonna happen again." Scharf leaned closer to Wood, accusing him of being sick, of enjoying what he did, relishing the power of playing God and watching the life drain from his innocent victims. Karl Mahoney remained silent, all but disappearing into the wall as Scharf drilled his points home again and again; he did not want to interfere with the flow. Scharf had Wood's full attention, and he wasn't letting up. Scharf's lecture continued with no sign of abatement; his words came fast, and his disgust remained apparent.

After a little more than twelve minutes, Derek Wood had had enough of righteous cop. At one minute past six in the morning, he interrupted the monologue: "Can ya shut up for a second? Whaddya want?"

"I want the truth."

"Well, if you'd shut up an' let me talk."

"All right, then. Talk. An' be truthful. What happened?"

Derek Wood leaned over to the table and picked up the list of charges Mahoney had placed there hours earlier. "Guilty. Guilty. I'm not sure about that one. Guilty. Not guilty an' guilty."

"Why, Derek?"

"I got scared." A visible relief came over Derek Wood as he told the officers where they could find the weapon. He told them it would be at Michelle's stepfather's trailer, where Freeman had gotten it. Scharf was surprised. He had believed Freeman's claim of having only been involved after the crime, when he took Darren to the brook. When he asked Wood about Freeman's involvement, Wood again lifted the paper from the table, pointed to the charge of first-degree murder in relation to Jimmy Fagan, and said, "Guilty." He then told the officer that Darren had used the knife, but he was not sure if he pulled the trigger or not.

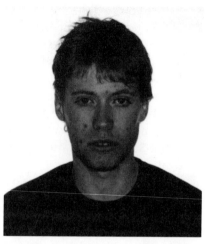

Derek Wood at the North Sydney RCMP detachment, shortly after his confession.

Jim Wilson returned to the interview room and began a lengthy written statement from Derek Wood, and police got their first glimpse of the nightmare that led to the deaths of three innocent people and the permanent, disabling injury to a fourth. Throughout the night, they had told Wood that the others had already confessed—although they had not—but now police would use the Wood statement as leverage against MacNeil and Muise.

Surprisingly, with the drama and tension behind them, Derek Wood and Karl Mahoney talked as though they were friends. After the written confession was completed, they chatted as they waited for an Ident officer to come to North Sydney. Wood had agreed to take both officers to the place where Freeman MacNeil had thrown his shovel handle after the murders, and to the pond where he himself had submerged Darren Muise's bag of money. At the pond, Jim Wilson tried to get the money but could not find it as he teetered on the edge of the log. Wood offered to find it, and after the handcuffs were removed, he crawled out to the end of the log and fished out the money. All this was much more than the officers had ever hoped for—and certainly more than Wood's lawyer had expected.

Eleven

O N SATURDAY, MAY 16, Cape Bretoners awoke to news of arrests in the McDonald's case. It was the news many longed to hear. Dave Roper's voice came at the beginning of CJCB radio reports each hour, as the tape of his early-morning briefing was replayed. It would be evening before television audiences got their first glimpse of what had happened overnight.

After a few hours of sleep, Roper had returned to the detachment to discover that one of the men had confessed and that Mike Campbell was no longer a suspect. He had, as Wood had insisted, been home in bed at the time of the crime, and he was released early Saturday morning, as soon as police were able to verify that alibi. As word of the Wood confession spread through the detachment, excitement filled the investigating team: one down, two to go. Roper knew he would be releasing the names of the suspects to the media at some point, but when reporters called him—every hour, on the hour—he told them to try later. The names could not be released until all three were remanded into custody by a justice of the peace, and by Saturday afternoon the RCMP had only one confession.

We at ATV already had two names, Derek Wood and Mike Campbell—the witnesses from the Irish club had told me about them in the pre-dawn hours following the arrests—and when I returned to work, shortly after noon, I was expecting to be tracking down the others. That was not the case: Greg Boone had already done the research, while preparing a report on community reaction to the arrests. Greg, the senior reporter in the ATV newsroom in Sydney, is one of the most-respected journalists in Cape Breton. When I arrived that afternoon, my head was still buzzing from the late night and lack of sleep over the past week; a session with the meticulously organized Greg Boone was exactly what I needed. Always exceptionally cautious with information, Greg closed both doors to the newsroom and returned to his desk. He was going to brief me, and he didn't want anyone to hear what he was saying—not even the two cameramen we were working with. He would not openly discuss information that had yet to be confirmed, and he was not going to have anyone say they heard Greg Boone identifying the suspects.

Greg and I had worked side by side in the Sydney newsroom for ten years, and our relationship was one of mutual respect and trust; it had also grown into a strong friendship. I had learned a great deal from Greg's conservative approach to information-gathering; our styles differed considerably, but we had the same measure of a reporter's worth. Truth was the bottom line, and we'd both seen too many reporters who never let truth get in the way of a good story. I sipped my first coffee of the day and watched as Greg read through his notes. A few of us at work had often joked that if a movie were ever made about Greg's life, Al Pacino would have to play the part. There was a strong resemblance, which was particularly apparent at times like these, when he was intensely focused.

As usual, Greg had done his homework. When he arrived in the newsroom early that morning, he found out that there had been RCMP activity on East Broadway, in the Pier, so he headed over there. The cameraman who went with him recorded images of officers taking evidence out of a mobile home; neighbours gathered to watch, and he found out from them that a young man named Freeman Mac-Neil often stayed in the trailer, and that he had apparently been arrested in connection with the McDonald's murders. Later, he picked up a second name; word of the arrests was spreading quickly through the community as the families and friends of the accused men found out what had happened.

"I read from your notes that you have identified Derek Wood and Mike Campbell as the suspects arrested at the Irish Club," Greg told me. "Well, we have a problem; I've also been given two names—Darren Muise from Patnic Avenue, and a Freeman MacNeil. He lives somewhere on the North Side, but stays with his girlfriend in the Pier as well. We have video of police searching her place." It was clear why Greg had closed the door; we had one too many names, and that meant one of them was innocent. "There is good news, though," Greg continued. "None of them are young offenders." That was a relief. Reporters and police alike had been talking about the possibility of suspects under eighteen being involved, and if that had happened, they would have been protected as young offenders—their identities would never have been released, and they would not have been behind bars for more than five years.

"O.K., I'll try Dave Roper to see if there are four men in custody now." I called Roper, and he assured me there were only three men in custody, but added that a fourth had been picked up for questioning; this man had been released, and was not a suspect. But he wouldn't say who the fourth man was; he needed clearance before he could comment on any of the identities. I turned back to Greg: "I guess we're going to have to build bio's on all four and drop one when we get the names. I'll do Campbell—I know him, and I hope I'm wrong—but I think I can get some background on Muise, too."

"Do you know him, too?"

"No, but I'm pretty sure my mother does."

"I'll see what I can get on MacNeil and Wood, then," Greg said.

"Actually, leave Wood for me as well. I have an idea on that. If you can find out who MacNeil is and try to track some pictures." Greg turned to face his desk, and lifted his phone; I did the same. I hoped I was wrong about Darren Muise too; while I needed background information on all of the suspects, I did not want to confirm that one of them was the son of a woman I had known since I was a child.

My mother and Gail Muise had worked together in the same clothing store before my mother retired, and Gail is someone I really like. She has four sons, and I thought I'd heard the name Darren mentioned. I phoned my mother and asked for the names of Gail's sons. She bristled, wanting to know why I was curious about her friend—my mother knew what story I was working on. I told her that one of the boys might know someone involved. That was probably Darren, she said; she had heard that he knew one of the McDonald's workers. I asked what school Darren went to, and she told me he had quit but that he had attended Riverview High.

My throat was dry when we ended the conversation. I sat back and realized that the killers I'd been reporting about all week were not evil phantoms that had slipped into Cape Breton under cover of darkness and then disappeared after completing their grisly work. I had met Mike Campbell, and knew he was a nice kid from a nice family, and now I was finding out the same thing about Darren Muise. The report I was working on was going to hurt a lot of people, I thought, realizing—for the first time since the tragedy—how deeply scarred the community would be by this crime. I reflected on Dave Roper's confidence during the 3:00 a.m. press briefing; there was little chance these were false arrests. I knew Muise could have been the suspect who was questioned and later released, and that would mean Gail would be spared such tragic news. On the other hand, I didn't want to hear of Mike Campbell being involved, either. I later learned there were friends and relatives of Derek Wood and Freeman MacNeil who were praying that afternoon—praying that those young men had been picked up by mistake. But no matter who was released, it meant three families were not going to have their prayers answered.

I forced myself to put Gail Muise out of my mind and get back to work. "Greg, we need a yearbook from Riverview." I called to my colleague. "We'll get Muise's picture there." Then I phoned Garfield Lewis at home. The owner of the restaurant would certainly be able to tell me something about his employee, Derek Wood, and he might even have a photo. Lewis didn't want to reveal anything, but he had more questions than I did. He was consumed by the tragedy, and police had not told him who was in custody; he did not even know that Wood was among the suspects. I told him I could answer some of his questions, if he would answer some of mine. Wood was among those arrested, I said, but didn't identify the others. He gave me some background on Wood, who had just passed his employee evaluation. The young man was a relatively new member of the staff, and didn't have many friends at the restaurant, Lewis said, but his work was up to standard and he had just been made a permanent employee. I thanked him and hung up.

"Wood should be a Riverview student too," said Greg, who had also just hung up. "He may have graduated last year, so we'll need a couple of yearbooks. I don't know about high school, but I know he went to Malcolm Munroe junior high—and Freeman MacNeil is not from North Sydney, he's from the Coxheath area. He also went to Riverview." Greg had called a cousin who attended Riverview; he was trying to get the yearbook I had mentioned. She told him she didn't know Darren Muise, but Freeman MacNeil and Derek Wood were familiar names. And she had a junior high school yearbook with a picture of Wood, and her Riverview yearbook from a couple of years of ago had MacNeil's picture in it. Greg rushed out to get the books and talk to his cousin about the suspects.

We now had three pictures to go with three names. I had recovered a photo of Mike Campbell from the newspaper report on his intervention in the neighbourhood clash the summer before; all that remained was to find a current yearbook with a photo of Darren

Muise. I called a student I knew who was about to graduate, and she not only had the book, but also knew Darren and had heard that he was in custody. I was surprised how quickly the word had spread—and even more surprised when she told me that people at school had been talking about Muise and Wood all week; the local teens were certain the two were involved. I asked her why no-one had called police with information, and she said they figured the police knew—they had talked with Wood. Besides, the kids were not 100-per-cent sure, and didn't want to report the wrong people. The young woman also gave me names of a few other people who knew Darren Muise, and she said would drop off the yearbook on her way into town. I called a few teachers from Malcolm Munroe and Riverview. They were shocked that I was asking about Muise, Wood, MacNeil, and Campbell. It turned out all four had attended the same junior high and secondary schools, and all four were well-liked by the teachers, who could not believe their names were connected to this case. By late afternoon Greg and I had assembled photos and brief biographies on all four young men.

Having the names and pictures was one thing; releasing them to the public was another. Without police confirmation, the names could not be used. A check with Dave Roper showed that the Mounties were not yet ready to release names, but Roper did say again that police were now dealing with three suspects, not four. Mike Campbell had been released, but Roper could not reveal his identity, either. We were still working with four pictures, one of which would have to be dropped. That ruled out prepackaging a report on the suspects; I couldn't commit anything to tape until I knew who the innocent party was and pulled him from the group.

Reaction from the victims' families would have added strength to Greg's report on community response to the arrest, but it was not to be. The Burroughs, Warrens, MacNeils, and Fagans had been advised by the RCMP not to speak with reporters, and they made it clear they would follow that advice. It was frustrating for us, but trying to convince most people that they don't have to do what they are told by police in a case like this is fruitless.

• • •

AT THE RCMP detachment in Reserve Mines, Darren Muise was playing hardball with Dave Trickett and Brian Stoyek. During the interrogation, Muise maintained a degree of control, asking for a glass of water and a pack of cigarettes. Later, he asked for another glass of water but instructed the officers to run the tap a little longer this time to make the water colder. While Derek Wood had occasionally argued and become defiant, Muise, at times, was almost abusive—not so much what he said, but what he did. His every comment was polite, but he kept blowing smoke rings at Trickett and Stoyek, making it clear to both officers that they were not reaching him.

Darren Muise at the Reserve Mines RCMP detachment shortly after being arrested. He was the last of the three to tell his story.

After being taken to the detachment, Muise spoke to a lawyer on the phone for about an hour, then sat down to face Trickett's and Stoyek's questions. Muise refused to comment on the McDonald's case, and held his ground for hours as the police tried to persuade him to get his side of the story on record. Trickett lectured in the style of Phil Scharf; that is, he conducted lengthy monologues as he tried to explain the importance of the truth to Muise. The monologues had little effect. Muise responded when Trickett insisted on an answer, but stayed away from the particulars of the case. Telling the truth might be a good idea, but he wasn't about to volunteer any.

While Wood had made it clear he did not want to be talking with police, Muise seemed to have no problem with this; in fact, he encouraged Brian Stoyek to talk with him about his past. He might be under arrest for murder, but Darren Muise still liked to be the centre of the conversation. The officers were amazed as he talked of his future and how he planned to correct the mistakes he'd made since leaving high school. "I'd like to go back to school. I wanna get my high school diploma."

"How ya gonna get that? Goin' back full time, or classes?" Brian Stoyek was curious about how Muise thought his future would unfold.

"I might even write my G.E.D., or, um, go to night school, or go back to school full time, 'n then, hopefully, get somethin' to do with fitness, or anything really to do with computers, 'cause computers is kind of the way of the future." Muise did not appear to be grasping the significance of the situation, or else he simply liked to hear himself talk about things that were not going to occur. He knew he was guilty, and he knew the police knew it, but he was still willing to talk freely about his ambitions.

In North Sydney, Wayne MacDonald and Rod Gillis had examined Derek Wood's confessions and decided it was time to question Freeman MacNeil again. They took MacNeil from the holding cell, but no matter how they pleaded or what approach they took, he simply informed them he would follow his lawyer's advice and remain silent.

Anger seethed in Rod Gillis as he leaned over the interview table. He knew now that MacNeil had fired the gun that killed Jimmy Fagan. "You're so low, you could walk under a snake with a top hat on. You're so tough, attacking women with sticks and guns, but you don't even have the guts to come over the table after me." Gillis looked at his partner and then back to MacNeil. "Don't worry about him, he won't stop you."

Both Gillis and MacDonald were outraged that MacNeil had so successfully lied to them the night before. They were also beginning to show the signs of a sleepless night and the stress of the investigation. MacDonald realized it was over—things had simply deteriorated too far—he too let MacNeil know what he thought of him. MacDonald stood and told his partner it was time to leave, and he told MacNeil why. "I'm sick of looking at the likes of you. I couldn't sleep last night, but you had no trouble—I watched you in that cell. We're through with you, but there will be other officers in here and they'll get to the truth."

The officers put MacNeil back in his cell, but not before photographing and fingerprinting him. MacNeil hung his head as he was booked, but he still felt he had won the session with Gillis and MacDonald. He was convinced his lawyer's advice was working; he was remaining silent, and the police were being frustrated. This was better than giving them more and more information and still ending up being kept here. MacNeil figured he'd stay with the new technique. He was worried, though. Constable Gillis had read a list of information to him that made it clear the police were not lying when they said his partners in crime had confessed. In fact, only one of them had confessed by this point, but the police wanted MacNeil to know they had the inside information, and they needed him to believe

Wood and Muise had given him up. He was certain of one thing as he sat in his cell: someone had given them the goods on what had happened at McDonald's.

At the Sydney detachment, Kevin Cleary reviewed the information he had. Derek Wood had given a full account of his activities inside the restaurant, but claimed he shot Arlene MacNeil, Neil Burroughs, and Donna Warren each once. If he was willing to admit shooting them in the head, it made no sense to deny the number of times he'd pulled the trigger, and Cleary knew the autopsy reports well; both Donna and Neil had been shot more than once. If Wood had indeed cleared his conscience, then either Darren Muise or Freeman MacNeil must have delivered the second and third shots that hit Burroughs and the second shot that struck Warren. Wood did say Muise took the gun from him while he cleared out the safe, but added that the next time he saw the gun, MacNeil was using it to kill Jimmy Fagan. In fact, Wood said MacNeil wanted to take the weapon downstairs and finish off Arlene. If MacNeil was that intent on using the gun again, maybe he was the one responsible for the other shots—but if Muise took the gun from Wood, and MacNeil ended up with it, there was a good chance all three had used it. The Wood confession was a great break in the case, but Cleary knew it raised as many questions as it answered. He needed more. The officer wanted to know who was responsible for every injury suffered by the four innocent restaurant workers.

Cleary considered his next move. Brian Stoyek and Dave Trickett wanted to continue their work in Reserve Mines with Darren Muise, but it was clear that Rod Gillis and Wayne MacDonald were finished, so Cleary decided he would try his luck with Freeman MacNeil. He chose Pat Murphy as his partner for the interrogation. It was time MacNeil met with officers who were his size; until this point he had towered over every Mountie who had questioned him. The investigators didn't want to intimidate the young man, but they didn't want him looking down on them, either. Murphy and Cleary headed to North Sydney, agreed on a friendly, low-key approach. They would try to befriend MacNeil and convince him it would be in his best interest to get his story out.

At 3:30 p.m. Saturday, Cleary and Murphy led MacNeil back to the interrogation room, showed him their badges, and asked if they could be on a first-name basis. MacNeil agreed. He liked these officers. Pat Murphy reached out and shook MacNeil's hand, and at that very moment he felt the interview would succeed; he could feel in MacNeil's grip that the young man was reaching out to him. He could also see it in MacNeil's eyes. Murphy sat at the end of the table in the small room, Cleary beside him, and MacNeil in front of Cleary, facing the officers. The three stayed very close, in an almost-intimate grouping, with MacNeil's and Cleary's knees within centimetres of touching. MacNeil told the officer he was following his lawyer's advice to remain silent. Cleary said he knew what MacNeil's lawyer would have told him, but his lawyer was at home and MacNeil had to deal with the predicament he was in. "We've had three funerals already," he said. "We may have a fourth. Are you proud of that?"

MacNeil, who had become emotional at times with Gillis and MacDonald, now began to fold himself into a fetal position in the chair; he did not want to listen. Cleary remained firm but calm as he reached for the young man's folded arms, taking one of them and pulling it down to his leg. "Don't fold up on me now, Freeman, you've got to be open." Moments later, MacNeil again folded his arms and lifted his legs, and this time Cleary kept his hand on the young man's arm as he gently eased it back to his lap.

Then, the officers tried to emphasize how serious the matter was. Murphy read the charges MacNeil was facing, and while he spoke, he was overcome by emotion, his voice cracking as he was flooded with memories. Kevin Cleary sat back in surprise when he realized where his partner was going. On the verge of tears, but just managing to remain controlled, Pat Murphy told Freeman MacNeil that he knew very well what the victims' families were going through. Seven years before, he had been summoned to identify the body of his own teenaged daughter, who had been killed in a car accident.

"I can never erase that terrible memory, and I know the families of these kids will carry this with them forever. You can help ease their pain by telling the truth, by making sure they know what happened." Murphy looked down at the pen in his hand as he spoke. It was a powerful moment, and there was no question he was looking deep inside himself. There was no pretence here; there was real pain and genuine human compassion. Murphy had never told a suspect about his personal tragedy before—and has never taken that approach since—but at the time he wanted to remove all barriers, to somehow let MacNeil know he too was human, to make it clear that he considered this a horrible tragedy. This could not be about gamesmanship or talking in circles; this was just too serious. People were dead, and it was time to deal with that.

"You'll never find a more compassionate officer than this," Cleary told MacNeil as he looked at Murphy. The mood in the room was not what it had been moments before. Murphy had breached something; there were no longer two men trying to persuade a third to do something he did not want to do. Now three men were grieving together. The officers explained that they were not there to judge MacNeil, but rather to help him forgive himself for what he'd done. They quietly asked him to be truthful for his mother's sake—she was now a victim in this, and at least she would know that her son told the truth when it mattered.

Cleary continued to remind MacNeil that police had all the information about the crime but felt it was important for him to get his version of the events on the record; it would be better for him in the long run if he told his story now. Cleary painted the picture of Mac-Neil and Muise and Wood heading to the rear door of the restaurant, with Muise wearing a mask and Wood holding the gun. Just before 4:30 p.m., Cleary was describing the scene inside the basement door: "...And you had a stick in your hand," he said. At that remark, Freeman MacNeil began to cry. He cried hard, engulfed in emotion. Cleary tried to reassure him. Pat Murphy reached out and took his hand, holding it on the table between them. The three were very close now; the circle was complete, with Cleary holding Freeman's arm—their knees almost touching—and Murphy holding MacNeil's other hand. He had had enough. Freeman MacNeil wanted to tell these men everything; he wanted to get it all out.

Cleary asked MacNeil to take himself out of the picture, if it was too disturbing to remember what happened while thinking of his own involvement. "Just be like a movie camera," the officer said. "Move along one frame at a time and tell us what you see." With Mac-Neil in such an emotional state, the officers could not stop him and ask him to repeat things, as Wilson had when taking the written confession from Derek Wood hours before. Pat Murphy worked furiously, his free hand writing everything he could, and his other hand tightly squeezing MacNeil's. As his confession proceeded, MacNeil became less emotional, but occasionally he would start crying again, and Murphy would squeeze his hand again, looking up from his notes to comfort him. At one point, encouraging him to continue, Murphy told MacNeil he forgave him.

The picture that emerged—the movie Freeman MacNeil describ-ed—was painful for all three. MacNeil had trouble describing it, Cleary found it tough to hear, and Pat Murphy tried not to think about what he was writing. MacNeil's camera conjured up images from hell—a sobbing Donna Warren, on the floor beside her friend Arlene; blood pouring from Arlene's face and spreading on the tile floor; a blood-soaked Darren Muise, standing over the body of Neil Burroughs. He described himself, hitting Burroughs with his shovel handle and knocking him back to the floor; and Muise again, running for the gun and returning to fire a shot into the head of the fallen man.

When MacNeil finished, all three men relaxed in a brief, awkward silence, which Kevin Cleary broke by asking MacNeil to go over it all again in a detailed written statement. MacNeil agreed, saying he wanted to get it all done at once. The tension and emotion in the room had left Pat Murphy parched, and he felt it probably had had the same effect on the others. "Can I get you a glass of water or anything?" He was talking to MacNeil, but both Cleary and MacNeil said they were thirsty.

Murphy walked out of the interview room and was called over by another officer; MacNeil's lawyer had arrived and wanted to see him. David Ryan had been contacted earlier by Art Mollon, who could no longer handle the MacNeil case because of possible conflict with his client Derek Wood. Ryan had met briefly with MacNeil in the morning and was back to see his client again. Pat Murphy's heart sank, and he silently cursed his thirst. They had the information, but a sworn, signed statement, including a written police caution and Charter of Rights proclamation, would be better—and that was what MacNeil had just agreed to give them. In the interview room, Cleary was reading MacNeil his rights; they had gone through the process earlier in the afternoon, but the officer was now writing them out and asking MacNeil to sign, confirming that he had been informed of and understood his rights. Pat Murphy opened the door and summoned Cleary. The senior officer immediately shot an impatient look at his partner; whatever it was, it was not important enough to interrupt this confession. Murphy insisted, and the two left the room. As David Ryan entered the interview room, it seemed the two officers had reached the end of the line.

At 5:45 p.m., David Ryan emerged after spending about twenty minutes with his client. Cleary and Murphy went back into the room to try to convince MacNeil that it was too late to remain silent, because he had already told them everything. To their surprise, MacNeil told them he would go ahead with the written statement; he just wanted to get it over with. MacNeil's written statement confirmed some of the information in the Wood confession, but also answered some of Cleary's questions about the number of shots. Wood had said that after shooting Arlene MacNeil, he ran upstairs and shot Neil Burroughs once. MacNeil claimed he heard two shots from upstairs when Wood went up there, and another two as he was walking upstairs later, after Wood had taken Donna Warren up to open the safe. That was in line with the autopsy report that both Donna and Neil had been shot at least twice.

MacNeil also identified Darren Muise as the one who used the knife. "When I got to the top of the steps, there was a guy holding himself up by his hands and knees, and he was saying, 'Help me.' His throat was cut and there was blood everywhere and Darren was standing there with the knife in front of him and there was blood all over the knife and all over his gloves and arms. Darren said, 'The guy won't die...Derek shot him, I cut his throat, and he still won't die.' Darren hit him six to eight times with the knife, and he bent the knife, stabbing him with it in back of the neck." This claim puzzled the officers. The autopsy on Neil Burroughs showed no sign of multiple stab wounds; there was only one cut to the side of the victim's throat. Was MacNeil trying to lessen his role by painting a crueller picture of Darren Muise?

MacNeil went on to say that he tried to help the man, telling him he would call an ambulance: "The guy was trying to get up, saying, 'Help me, please help me.' I told him to lay down...and he laid down, but he started to get back up again. I hit him with my stick because I tried to knock him out, so he wouldn't be in so much pain." The officers allowed MacNeil to justify his actions in any way he wanted; they needed the information now, not an explanation of why he did what he did.

He did, however, provide an explanation of a third shot on Burroughs: Darren, he said, had run to the safe and come back with the gun. This matched Derek Wood's version, but MacNeil picked up Muise's movements where Wood could not see them. "He said, 'The bastard won't die, he'll fuckin' die now'—and he shot him from about one-and-a-half to two feet. He stood right over him and shot him."

But MacNeil was not quite so vivid when it came to the moment he shot Jimmy Fagan. "Darren said, 'Shoot him,' and I think he put the gun in my hand, and I think it was my hand that pulled the trigger. Derek took the gun and said, 'We got to get the hell out of here.'"

The shocked and confused participant MacNeil described as he implicated himself did not quite fit with Wood's portrayal of a man who wanted to return to the basement to ensure that Arlene MacNeil was dead, but it was a confession that tied him to the murders of Burroughs and Fagan.

After the statement was completed, Cleary wanted to know why MacNeil had become involved. Wood had told Scharf he shot his co-workers because he was afraid, and now Cleary wanted to know what led Freeman MacNeil to take part in such a grisly crime. "They asked me to drive, and I needed money," he said. "I am unemployed."

"What do you feel?" asked Cleary.

"Terrible," MacNeil replied.

This wasn't an explanation that satisfied Cleary, but there was no time to consider it; there was still work to do. With confessions from two of the suspects in hand, investigators began to concentrate on Darren Muise, whose interrogation had been proceeding without success for a very long time—more than twelve hours. After talking freely with Corporal Stoyek about his past and his plans for the future, Muise had returned to his tough-but-polite stance, which he maintained hour after hour, each time the officer tried to move the conversation in the direction of the McDonald's murders.

At one point, when Stoyek tried to explain the need for getting his side of the story out, he interrupted with: "Ah, 'scuse me, could you tell me what time the food will be here—do you have an approximate time?" Muise was interested in breakfast, not in answering questions about the case. As Stoyek continued to press the issue, Muise began ignoring him blatantly, playing with his pop bottle and other items on the table, and even picking at the cut on his wrist. He was not being budged one inch by the big officer. He went so far as to joke about the inconvenience the police had caused him in the past couple of days. When Stoyek tried to suggest that Muise was losing sleep over the murders, the young man insisted he slept just fine—then quickly corrected himself: "Well, actually, I haven't, 'cause people keep waking me up in the morning...I'm a night person."

Knowing that Muise wanted his approval—that was clear from the suspect's casual conversations—Stoyek tried to appeal to his sense of responsibility. "None of this bothers you at all?" he asked. "There's only two ways you can have it, Darren. There's only two possible ways you can have it, O.K.? Does what happened at McDonald's bother you?" There was no answer. The eighteen-year-old looked at the officer, deeply inhaled his cigarette, and blew smoke rings.

Brian Stoyek and Dave Trickett had been in and out of the interview room for hours. By 7:30 a.m., Stoyek was alone with the suspect, but he decided he too needed a break, and left Muise to have his breakfast. Outside, the two officers regrouped, and shortly before eight, Trickett returned to the interview room. He tried to explain the situation to Muise, telling him he was the only one left who had not told his side of the story. That wasn't true; Freeman MacNeil's confession had not yet been obtained by Cleary and Murphy, but the police wanted Muise to feel he had nothing left to protect—and they did have MacNeil's statement from the previous day, implicating him. Again and again, Trickett tried to make the point that police already knew what Muise had done, but just wanted to be fair and hear his version. But it was no use. Muise was apparently under the delusion that the police were lying to him, trying to trick him into confessing.

Trickett could not believe this young man with no criminal record could possibly be this tough. "Darren, do you believe what I told ya? Answer me. Answer me, Darren. Do you believe what I told ya? Don't play your games with me, trying to stare me down; that's garbage. I'm not even gonna play your silly games, bud. You've lost. You've played the game, you've given it a good shot, but you've lost. You can blow your smoke."

"I don't mean to blow smoke in your face."

"I don't care whether you blow. That doesn't bother me in the least. I'm tellin' ya I know your games. You can blow your smoke, you can play with your matches, you can play with this, you can play with that."

"Believe what you wanna believe."

Trickett soon realized that he, like Stoyek, was not getting through to Muise, and he left the interview room just before 9:00 a.m. As Muise dozed off in the room, police planned a new approach. How could they make Muise see that it was in his best interest to tell his side of the story? Although Derek Wood's confession placed Muise inside the restaurant, Wood had said he was not sure if Darren ever used the gun, or if he even used his knife. Even if Wood had placed all the blame on Muise, it was unlikely Wood would testify against him—and there was very little physical evidence. The police decided they would use what little they had to shake Muise's confidence. Henry Jantzen got a call to bring over some of the exhibits he had collected—the bag of money retrieved by Wood after his confession, and the deck shoe that had been found at the Grantmire Brook. Muise's parents, who had been at the Reserve Mines detachment all night, identified the shoe as their son's.

Sandy and Gail Muise had been sitting for hours in an open area in the detachment office, watching officers come and go, and wondering what was happening to their lives. At one point, Darren walked past with an officer and smiled at his parents. His voice confident, he told his mom not to worry. But how could they not worry? The police wouldn't even let them talk with Darren. It took a long time for them to accept that their youngest son would not be coming home with them, but the Muises were finally convinced by police that Darren had in some way taken part in the McDonald's murders. Back home, incredulous and shocked, Sandy Muise took some of his son's belongings to the back yard and burned them. As the heartbroken father stood there and watched the smoke rise, he was fully aware that burning the items would not remove Darren from his life; in fact, he knew he didn't want to do that. He just needed to act out in some way, to direct his anger at something. For the past week, he had heard a continuous stream of comments from passengers in his cab, a common theme being that whoever was responsible for those brutal McDonald's murders should be taken out and killed. No punishment was too severe, he agreed, although that was an easy answer—like everyone else, Sandy Muise had an image of the killers as hardened criminals who had managed to find their way to Cape Breton. But now everything was different.

Across the street, Kris Granchelli's mother woke him to tell him that his friend had been arrested for the murders; word of the late-night visit by police to the Muise home had spread quickly through the tight-knit community. Kris looked over towards the house and saw smoke billowing from the back yard. He had to reach out to the Muises somehow, so he went over to their house. Darren's parents welcomed him to their home, as always, but the visit was filled with an awkward silence. Kris could say nothing to comfort them; he could see the shock they were experiencing, and he felt some of it himself. He left them to their grief. Gail Muise later said she thought it would have been easier if Darren had been one of the victims; she could not understand how her son could be involved in such a horrid crime. But whatever role Darren played, the Muises decided—even if he held the door open or drove the car—he should be punished.

Meanwhile, Muise remained defiant. Even when Brian Stoyek returned, at about 11:30, to tell Muise it was all over—they had evidence, they had the deck shoe, they had the money, and they had confessions from his partners—Muise just wasn't buying it. He knew they had his shoe, because he had heard about the evidence recovered from the brook and seen TV reports showing divers searching the area. It didn't seem to matter to him. About twenty minutes later, Constable Henry Jantzen entered the room. He said nothing, just looked at Muise, went over to the table, and plunked down the shoe, the plastic bag filled with money, and the shovel handle used by Freeman MacNeil. Muise looked at the items but said nothing; Jantzen picked them up and walked out. Now Dave Trickett pressed ahead, hoping the evidence had shaken Muise's confidence, weakened his resolve to remain silent. They didn't even need Muise's statement, Trickett told him; everything was falling into place: "Freeman has been in, Woody has been in; Greg Lawrence, Michelle, Kristine—everybody has said their piece, and it's time for you to do the same thing, Darren. It's time for you to tell the truth, my son." Trickett was trying to persuade the young man that it would be better for him to tell his story now, because if he waited for his trial, a judge would be more inclined to believe his partners' versions. They were giving their side now; why would a judge give any credence to someone who was only telling his story at the last minute?

Muise's confidence was broken by the sight of the bag of money. He knew there was only one way the police could have found that. Still, he couldn't believe Derek had sold him out. Muise decided he'd better talk to his lawyer again, and told the officers he might make a statement, but that they had to turn off the video camera beforehand. He also made sure there were no reporters outside the interview room before he left the room. Muise met with his attorney for about an hour and a half. He was obviously trying to determine if in fact his partners had sold him out, because his lawyer left the meeting and asked police if he could see what Wood and MacNeil had said. He was shown copies of the Wood confession and the statement taken from Freeman MacNeil the day before; although that statement didn't include MacNeil's own involvement, it clearly implicated Muise. While the lawyer read through the papers, Muise returned to the interrogation room with Stoyek and Trickett. Shortly afterward, he came and told his client that police were telling the truth; he had been implicated in the statements by Derek Wood and Freeman MacNeil. But even then, Darren Muise was not ready to give in. Maybe he would say something, but first he wanted to be left alone to eat supper and think. He was given a meal and left alone for an hour.

Muise was sitting in silence with his food at the very moment Freeman MacNeil was finally giving his full written confession to Pat Murphy and Kevin Cleary. When word from the North Sydney detachment reached the officers in Reserve Mines, they felt renewed pressure to somehow persuade the young man to stop going around in circles. It wasn't going to be easy. At Muise's request, the video camera had been kept covered while he ate his meal, but the audio tape was left running. Muise knew the microphone was live, and spoke into it at 4:50 p.m., saying he wanted to go to the washroom. Brian Stoyek took him there, and Muise told Stoyek he wanted to talk with Dave Trickett alone. Clearly, Darren Muise was in complete control of the situation: he was not free to leave, but he was making sure the police did exactly what he wanted. And they were willing to give in to his whims because, no matter what they were telling him, they needed that statement.

Dave Trickett tried again, but it quickly became apparent that Muise was not in the mood to give a statement. He just wanted company; he tried to get Trickett to talk about other things but avoided discussions of the murders. "Nothing about police," he said. "I wanna talk about your average Joe stuff. I wanna relax for a minute."

"O.K., I can appreciate you wanna relax, Darren, but the reason we're still here is to take this statement. We don't have time to relax." Still Muise avoided the issue, questioning Trickett about where he would be kept in custody. Earlier in the day, police had told him it would probably be in the detachment building, and now he wanted to make certain that had not changed. Trickett said he thought that was still the case, but that it was not his decision.

Finally, the officer got Muise on track and had him sign the written police warnings. Then he asked, "Darren, what can you tell me about the robbery and shootings at McDonald's Restaurant in Sydney River?"

"O.K., you understand I'm nervous."

"Yes. I understand you're nervous."

"Um, it all started, um, two or three weeks ago, when Derek mentioned about McDonald's. I guess we all agreed, but I was wary. One thing I'd like to say is that I never pulled a trigger...I kinda remember when we first went in. I knew Derek had a gun, but I never thought he'd use it. I remember hearing shots and my mind went blank...I feel sorry for the families. F' some reason it seems like my fault, but I know it wasn't."

Dave Trickett was not satisfied with the statement. It was a start, but Muise was claiming he had blacked out in the restaurant and could not recall anything that happened. Trickett pushed for more detail, but Muise insisted his statement was over; he wanted to talk one-on-one with Trickett, but not about the robberies. Trickett refused, and Muise declined to answer any more questions, so the officer left the room. He and Brian Stoyek, like many veteran police officers, had heard similar confessions involving supposed amnesia, and they felt Muise was still trying to protect himself and his partners in crime. Stoyek decided he would make one last attempt to reach Muise before a new team of interrogators was sent in; he walked back into the interview room at 6:20 p.m. Angry and frustrated, he aggressively challenged Muise about his blackout—but the suspect remained adamant in his indifference, informing the officer that he had said all he was going to say.

The pressure of the week-long investigation, and the long night and day with Muise, had reached a peak. For a moment, Brian Stoyek the man took the place of Brian Stoyek the police officer. Stoyek knew from personal experience to what extent violent crime leaves permanent scars on those left behind. Years earlier, when he was stationed in Newfoundland, his wife had been staying with a friend in Halifax when a masked man broke into the apartment and beat her viciously. She had been left permanently disabled, and he had been left feeling helpless. Now, Stoyek felt helpless again, and that it shouldn't be that way. He had enough of this emotionless kid and he wanted Muise to know it. As emotion and adrenaline surged through him, Stoyek suddenly blew: "You're a cold-blooded fuckin' killer." Muise was unmoved by the outburst; he slouched in his chair and ignored the officer. Stoyek was finished with Muise, and he knew it. He left the room for the last time.

At seven-thirty that evening, a new team began questioning Darren Muise: Sergeant Tony Penny and Constable David Hadubiak. Muise told Hadubiak he remembered him from the brief meeting in the parking lot in North Sydney a few days earlier. At first, it was the same old story; Muise would not comment. Then, Hadubiak tried to make casual conversation while at the same time exploring one of the theories police were considering. He asked Muise about the game "Dungeons and Dragons." The officer said he had played it, and was wondering if Muise had. The teenager was willing to discuss the game, but rejected the notion that any kind of fantasy had been involved in the McDonald's murders, that it was a case of people losing touch with reality. Muise liked Hadubiak, and when Sergeant Penny was called from the room, the young man asked if the constable would like to go over his suicide note with him. Police had found the note during a search of Muise's home and presented it to him during questioning. Hadubiak moved closer, and Darren read him the note, saying that most of it was true, except the references to guys from Halifax—that part, he said, was made up. At times Muise cried as he read the note, then asked if he and Hadubiak could talk privately. Well, they could talk, Hadubiak said, but as a police officer, he would have to testify about what was said.

When finally Muise agreed to tell Hadubiak his side of the story, it seemed so easy—no pressure from the young constable; Muise just decided to give him what he wanted. And then, the last of the three partners to implicate himself in the murders, Muise began his confession. This time he gave a very detailed statement, filling in some of the blanks left by Wood and MacNeil. Like MacNeil, Muise also said he heard two gunshots from upstairs when Wood ran up there, but he had an altogether different version of what happened to Neil Burroughs. According to Muise, he and MacNeil went upstairs together and found Burroughs struggling to get up. The look in Neil Burroughs's eyes was very disturbing, Muise told the officer. "I felt for him," the young man said. "I guess I didn't know what to do. There was lots of blood. I knew he was dying. Freeman hit him in the head with a bat. That wasn't stopping him. I knew where the jugular vein was, so I went over and cut him. He stopped moving, so I thought he was dead and felt no more pain."

Muise was then called to the safe by Wood and told to help pack up the kitbag, he said. MacNeil yelled for the gun, so he took it from Wood and brought it to MacNeil before returning to the safe, where he heard another shot. Then they left and MacNeil shot another guy at the door. Now, police were unsure who had shot Neil Burroughs the third and final time: in fact, it was not even clear whether Derek Wood had shot him twice or only once. The only thing they now knew for certain was that Burroughs had been shot three times, and only one person had admitted to shooting him. The other two killers had fingered each other as the source of the final shot.

In concluding his statement, Muise reiterated this point: "I am glad that people will know I wasn't a shooter. In my mind I feel that I am not responsible for the shootings of these people. I couldn't stop Derek or Freeman, I was in such shock at the time." It was a bizarre comment. Muise was trying to lessen his own guilt by putting it off on the others. He did not understand how appalling it was that he had deliberately tried to cut the jugular vein of an innocent man—ostensibly to put him out of pain. That he saw such a horrible action as somehow better than what MacNeil and Wood had done just made it all the more shocking.

Muise cried several times while telling his story. He signed his confession at 10:24 p.m.

• • •

AT THE PRECISE moment that Darren Muise was signing his confession, his name and picture were being broadcast around Atlantic Canada. Saturday May 16, had been a frustrating day for those of us covering the story. We knew the suspects were in custody, and we at ATV even knew who they were—by 8 p.m., I had verified through a police source that Mike Campbell was the fourth man, who had been questioned and released. But we still could not identify those in custody. Dave Roper was holding the media at bay, awaiting confirmation from Sylvan Arsenault, the investigation's coordinator, that the identities of the accused men could be made public. Charges had to be laid, and Roper also needed to keep the victims' relatives up to date.

Officers were sent out in the early evening, after Darren Muise made the statement admitting his involvement but claiming he had blacked out. The families were told that charges were being laid, and court appearances would follow shortly. As the evening continued, I pressed Roper to release their identities in time for our 10:00 p.m. newscast. The decision to lay charges had been made, but the officers sent out to talk with the victims' families had not completed their task. Only a couple of officers had been assigned to explain matters to a great many relatives, who had a great many questions. The biggest question—and the one police laboured to explain—was why the men were only being charged with conspiracy to commit robbery. The decision was a legal one: the Mounties had to lay charges of some kind so that Muise, MacNeil, and Wood could be remanded in custody; but investigators wanted time to confer with the Crown after reviewing the statements, and then decide exactly what additional charges each suspect would face.

As newscast after newscast informed the public that the suspects had been arrested and that their identities would soon be revealed, media pressure on Roper grew more and more intense. Finally, he arranged a 10:00 p.m. news conference at the Cambridge Suites—he would release all the information then. It was close, but I knew that if we kept an open phone line to Halifax and sent the video tape of the suspects' pictures ahead, we could still get the names and pictures on the show. Although it had been a relief to find out that Mike Campbell was not involved in the crime, I still felt the awful apprehension that came from knowing I would have to broadcast the identity of the son of a woman I'd known most of my life. Facing Gail Muise would be difficult, not because what I was doing was wrong, but because I knew it would hurt her.

Roper had not arrived at the hotel by 9:55 p.m., so I phoned the detachment from one of the basement pay phones. Roper said he would make the announcement in a matter of seconds, so I asked if he would stay on the line while I waited. He wanted to tell all the reporters at one time, but reluctantly agreed to release the information that way. I grabbed a second pay phone, dialled the newsroom in Halifax, and asked to be patched through to the anchor—but she was already on the air. The identities would be confirmed in a matter of moments, I told the director, and we could break into the newscast live. It seemed an eternity that I waited with a phone pressed to each ear, but finally, just after 10:20 p.m., Roper was told that the last of the victims' families had been notified. He read a brief prepared statement into the first pay phone, and I placed the other receiver down to take notes.

"This information is a supplement to the news release given earlier this morning," Roper said. "The three persons presently in custody are: Derek Anthony Wood of Sydney, date of birth 73-05-14; Darren Frederick Muise of Sydney, date of birth 73-09-18; Freeman Daniel MacNeil of Cape Breton County, date of birth 68-08-24. All three persons have been charged with conspiracy to commit robbery contrary to section 465.(1)(C) of the Criminal Code of Canada. All three have appeared before a justice of the peace and have been remanded in custody. This is the initial charge only; other charges will be laid to coincide with the suspects' court appearance on May 21, 1992. That's it. I'll see you down there in a few minutes."

"Thanks, Dave." The identities I had were confirmed. I hung up the first pay phone and shouted into the second, as Dave Roper left the RCMP detachment and headed to the hotel to reread the release to the other reporters and camera operators. While he was getting into his car, the school yearbook photos of all three suspects were being displayed, one after the other, on regional television; and I was being heard from a hotel pay phone, as I gave a brief audio sketch of each young man and explained that friends, neighbours, and teachers were shocked to hear their names associated with this crime. With the broadcast complete, I headed upstairs in time to see Roper being interviewed by the other reporters. I went over and asked my own questions; the ATV cameraman, Gary Mansfield, was already recording the "scrum," as we call that tangle of reporters and microphones around a person being interviewed after a major news break.

After the briefing, Roper and I walked outside. I was surprised to see him excited; his standard briefings were always given in a direct, unemotional tone, but now he was beaming with the pride of a job well done. But he became more sombre when he made reference to the reality of what had happened at McDonald's in the early hours of May 7. Roper had read Derek Wood's confession; he would not give any details, but told me the people of Sydney would be shocked when this case came to trial.

Gary and I loaded our vehicle and returned to the station to feed the taped RCMP briefing to the Halifax newsroom; it would be used on the late-night and Sunday newscasts. While Gary cued the tape, I sat back and enjoyed a coffee at my desk. The May 21 court date meant there would be a few days to relax after the late nights and early mornings of chasing the RCMP. I'd be able to do a community reaction item for Monday and then get away from the story for a couple of days. Sipping the coffee, I looked through the pictures of the accused men and stopped at the yearbook photo bearing the name Darren R. Muise. There were some humorous remarks from classmates, and one of those "Goals for the Future" type of entries—Muise wanted to be a social worker. How had this young man's plans gone so far off track? He had been interested in a career helping others; how could he have turned into a killer? This was not someone whose childhood differed so dramatically from mine. We had grown up in the same general area, and our mothers had worked together. I looked at the picture and wondered how Gail Muise was feeling, now that word of her son's involvement had been made public.

Suddenly, my stomach turned as the name Darren R. Muise seemed to jump off the page. I grabbed the RCMP release from the desk: Darren Frederick Muise. *Oh, no. It's the wrong Darren Muise, and we've just shown his picture on TV as a suspect in this case.* I screamed, grabbing for the phone to call the teenagers who had identified the person in photo. They did not understand why I was upset; they had just watched my report, and they were absolutely positive that was the Darren Muise who had been arrested. Yes, they knew him and had talked with his friends. He was in jail, and they were sure he was the right Muise. It was some relief, but not enough; how could I have believed teenagers on such an important matter? I phoned Greg Boone, who had also confirmed the Muise I.D. through separate sources. He wasn't sure about the middle name. Finally I contacted Roper, who said it was possible the "Frederick" was a mistake. He checked it out for me—yep, the name is Darren Richard Muise. I hung up the phone exhausted. In less than an hour I had gone from the agonized clock-watching of impending deadline, to the triumphant feeling of getting the identities and pictures in time for the newscast, to believing I'd made a career-ending mistake, to realizing that everything was all right. I sat back and stared at the oversized clock that dominated the rear wall of the newsroom. That large white face could be most intimidating as its hands marched along towards the next newscast—whether you were ready or not.

Gary walked back into the newsroom after feeding the tape from the control room. Reports assembled in the Sydney bureau of ATV are transmitted via a designated phone line to the ATV edit suites in Halifax, where they are recorded and rushed to the playback room before a newscast begins. Feeding tape this way is considerably cheaper than the satellite technology we used earlier in the week for our live reports from the RCMP news conference and the disturbance at the courthouse.

"Someday, that thing's going to kill me," I said, without looking away from the wall clock.

"*That's* what's going to kill you," Gary said, pointing to the coffee.

"Everything in-house?"

"Yep."

"Let's get out of here."

By midnight, Darren Muise, Derek Wood, and Freeman MacNeil were in custody at the Cape Breton County Correctional Centre, where they were locked in the special isolation wing to await their first court appearances on Thursday. Shortly after the suspects were safely behind bars, the members of the investigating team began heading home for some much-needed rest. For the first time in ten days, the pressure was off. They had the killers behind bars, and a search of the East Broadway trailer where MacNeil had stayed with his girlfriend had produced the gun. The weapon looked surprisingly harmless—a tiny chromed .22 with brown plastic handles. It didn't even look like a real gun. A starter pistol, maybe, but not a weapon capable of delivering the fatal shots that had been fired in Sydney River.

Twelve

BACK AT THE SYDNEY RCMP detachment, a few members of the investigative team were discussing the case and feeling pretty good about their success. But as they started looking through the confessions, the officers became quiet. They couldn't believe the horror the victims had gone through, how detailed the descriptions were, how Muise and MacNeil had excused their brutal acts as being humane gestures designed to relieve Neil Burroughs from his suffering. Like many of the investigating officers, Pat Murphy was exhausted as he arrived home, but he could not sleep. Constable Murphy sat on the edge of his bed and kept thinking about taking Freeman MacNeil's hand and holding it tightly as MacNeil confessed. He could see himself reaching out, consoling and forgiving a man who had clubbed an innocent man and shot another. Murphy felt very bad about befriending the killer; he knew it was part of the job, but in the loneliness of the moment he could not rationalize what he had done. Pat Murphy sat in bed in the dark and cried.

Murphy was not the only officer to react that way. Later in the week, two members of the team were discussing the confessions and wondering which version was closest to the truth, when one of the men began to cry, right there in the office. No one felt that was unusual; everyone understood that the team had worked under unyielding pressure, and now, with the pressure off, the strain was beginning to show. An RCMP psychologist was sent to Sydney to offer group sessions and private counselling to officers who wanted to express their feelings to a professional. During one group session, both junior and senior officers filled the room, listening to the counsellor and discussing what they felt inside. At the end of the session, there was not a dry eye in the room. For many, that cathartic release was enough—they had dealt with the anxiety, and the pain—but others took longer to get over the experience. More than a year later, Pat Murphy was returning from a vacation with his family and some friends when they stopped in the town of Antigonish to take the kids to McDonald's. As the group approached the restaurant, Murphy stopped. He looked at his wife and said he had changed his mind and was going to an adjacent Tim Hortons. He'd meet her back in the car. A travelling companion was about to question him, but Murphy's wife insisted they all go in and allow Pat to go have a coffee. She understood that her husband just didn't want to be reminded of the case by going to McDonald's, in Sydney River or elsewhere. Some members of the team took their families back to the Sydney River restaurant as soon as it reopened; others still avoid it. John Trickett remains haunted by the image of the bent knife-blade and the bloodied Neil Burroughs. A year after the case, he joined a snowmobile club, only to learn that meetings were in the basement of the restaurant—in the training room behind the black steel door used by the killers to get inside. When a friend who had joined the club with him phoned to ask if he was coming to the meeting, he declined, making excuses. He just couldn't bring himself to go back in there.

For other officers, the effect of the experience has been entirely different. Kevin Cleary, for example, has developed a renewed respect for the little things in life. Always a deeply religious family man, Cleary now constantly finds himself reminded of the value of time with those he loves. Crawling around a deserted restaurant, finding one innocent victim after another, has made him truly appreciate what he had in life.

The community of Sydney was also shaken by the murders and the intense investigation that followed. The Monday after the arrests, I began to interview people, asking them how they felt now that the suspects were in custody and life was returning to normal. Many said that things would never return to normal, that what happened in Sydney River had entirely changed the community. It wasn't so much the violence of the crime itself, although that certainly was being discussed. But what seemed to disturb people most was that three apparently average young men from the area had been involved in such a crime.

The increasing numbers of people filling the ranks of the unemployed in Cape Breton, and the grim economic forecasts for the future, had hardened some people; yet those same conditions had drawn others close together. It was difficult to understand the hows and whys of it. Reverend Mel Findlay, a local community activist who worked providing food and other essentials to those who could no longer support themselves, shed some light on the issue when he said the McDonald's murders were a symptom of something gone very wrong in the community. In an interview, he pointed to the harsh economic realities facing Cape Breton, and said they naturally led to an increase in crime; people in need were sometimes forced to take what they could not get any other way. Findlay felt programs like the "Loaves and Fishes" soup kitchens and a newly opened shelter for the homeless could address part of the problem by providing help to the most desperate, but those programs could not deal with whatever drove people to such extreme violence. The McDonald's murders did not mark the start or the end of a rash of violent crime in Cape Breton, he said; they just focused attention on what had been a steadily growing problem. Indeed, within weeks of the murders, there were two more killings in the area. In Sydney Mines, two brothers got into a fight after a card game and ended up outside, rolling around in the driveway and stabbing each other. One brother died, the other was hospitalized. Later, a young mother was brutally murdered in her apartment in Sydney. And in the months before the McDonald's murders, there was the savage stabbing death of convenience-store clerk Lorraine Dupe in Sydney—a crime that many felt was connected to the McDonald's case. That the two tragedies were unrelated only served as a nagging reminder that the end of the Sydney River investigation did not mean the problem would go away.

The escalation of violence had been gradual, but journalists could see its course just by the way we handled violent crimes over the years. When I first started working as a reporter at a Sydney radio station, more than ten years before the McDonald's murders, a routine phone check with police that revealed a stabbing had occurred the night before would become a lead item in our newscast. We would want all the particulars from the police—whether anybody had been charged; where the stabbing had occurred; how police had been notified; what the victim's condition was. By 1992, a question usually had to do with whether the victim was going to survive. If the injury was not life-threatening, the story might not even get reported—unless, of course, it was an otherwise slow news day. Emergency-room workers at local hospitals had also observed a rise in violence, and were becoming more accustomed to seeing ambulances arrive late at night, carrying someone injured in a violent confrontation. The situation was still far from what hospital workers in large cities faced, but it was also far from the image of "downhome" Cape Breton.

Police noted that most of the violence was linked to alcohol abuse; however, social workers from the local addiction-treatment centre found that alcohol abuse was often linked to the desperate state of the economy. People were hiding from the circumstances in which they found themselves, and while alcoholism is certainly not limited to those who have fallen on hard times, neither is violence. The pressures of an uncertain economy were felt by the employed as well as the unemployed. There were very few people in Cape Breton who felt secure in their jobs. All in all, the explanations—the economy, its hardships, problems like alcoholism or drug abuse—had relevance, but were not answers to the overwhelming question: Why?

What is certain is that the arrests of Derek Wood, Darren Muise, and Freeman MacNeil shook the foundation that had always helped Cape Bretoners work through the tough times. People's inner strength had always been a source of fierce pride; islanders had been through extreme hardship in the past and had always pulled closer together. The mining communities had proved they were stronger than the powerful mining companies during the bitter disputes over workers' rights in the 1920s. They could "stand the gaf," as the expression went—a rallying cry in times of apparently insurmountable difficulty. The term had its origin in a remark made by a mine owner when company stores were refusing to provide food to the miners and their families; the owner had commented that the people did not have the strength to "stand the gaf"—to endure in the face of hardship. But Cape Bretoners proved they had what it took; as long as they stuck together, they could conquer anything. And they won their rights. Working conditions in the mines would improve, as would the meagre salaries paid to men who worked from before dawn until after dark. The companies running the mines began to show more respect to the men who worked underground. The songs and stories of Cape Breton artists have always celebrated the dignity of people such as coal miners, who risked their lives underground to support their families; fishermen, who headed into unpredictable waters to do the same thing; and steelworkers, who stood proud in the extreme heat and dirt of an ageing plant to produce one the highest-quality steel rails in the world.

That people shared an experience of struggle against forces beyond their control became a unifying force for the communities of

Cape Breton, and in the early days after the McDonald's murders, people once again began to unite to help the family of Arlene Mac-Neil. A foundation and trust fund were set up by caring members of her community, on the north side of Industrial Cape Breton, who staged door-to-door canvassing campaigns, dances, and other community events to raise money to help the MacNeil family cope with the financial strain brought on by the hospitalization of their daughter. The North Sydney–based committee and the hundreds of volunteers who helped in the fund-raising efforts managed to collect more than $100,000 in an area hard hit by job losses and economic uncertainty. It was the kind of thing Cape Bretoners did without question. They were experiencing hard times, but someone in the community needed their help, so they gave.

The economic hardships of the 1980s and '90s were not the most severe the island had ever seen, and people who had lived through tougher times were outraged at what had happened in Sydney River. Cape Bretoners were supposed to pull together, to help their neighbours. It had always been that way. How could islanders stand tall if three of the young men who should have represented the future could have decided that a lack of pocket change was reason enough to kill? The fear and sadness that had prevailed in the community since the murders began to give way to a powerful anger.

• • •

FOR SOME OF THE investigators, the McDonald's case ended with the confession of Darren Muise, while others, including Kevin Cleary, conducted follow-up interviews as the Crown prepared its case. One of their first priorities was to visit the correctional centre to clear up some loose ends with Freeman MacNeil and Derek Wood. During that visit, Wood told police he had been given the gun by Freeman Mac-Neil before he went to work that night, that he was not sure how many times he had shot Donna Warren, and that the three men had indeed discussed the possibility of using the gun during the robbery, although he didn't think they knew what they were talking about when they discussed it. Freeman MacNeil revealed where he had left the ropes that were to have been used to tie up employees in the original plan, and where and how he had burned the evidence.

On Monday, May 18, prosecutor Frank Edwards reviewed the statements made by the accused men and decided what charges would be laid during the first court appearances, which had been put ahead to May 20. Wood faced first-degree murder charges in the deaths of Donna Warren and Neil Burroughs and attempted murder in the shooting of Arlene MacNeil. Muise would be charged with first-degree murder in the deaths of Neil Burroughs and Jimmy Fagan, the second charge arising from Freeman MacNeil's contention that Muise had put the gun in his hand and instructed him to shoot Fagan as they were leaving the restaurant. By enabling MacNeil to commit the murder—handing him the weapon—Muise had committed an act the courts consider to be as culpable as murder itself. MacNeil would also be charged with the first-degree murders of Burroughs and Fagan. All three would also face robbery and conspiracy charges, and a count for the unlawful confinement of Donna Warren.

On May 20, the Cape Breton County Courthouse once again drew hundreds of curious and angry residents wanting a look at the three men charged with the island's most grisly crime. Police barricades were placed in a large arc twenty metres from the door where the suspects would be taken in and out of the building. Sydney police officers walked through the parking lot, making a highly visible show of force; they did not want any trouble. Security inside the courthouse was coordinated by Sydney police and sheriff's deputies, who would use metal detectors to check anyone entering the small provincial

Derek Wood, left, is escorted from the courtroom by Karl Mahoney after the trio's first court appearance. Freeman MacNeil is just behind them. [Print from ATV video tape.]

courtroom where Wood, Muise, and MacNeil would be arraigned. Courtroom Four was usually filled with petty criminals who had fallen on bad luck or broken some law out of frustration or drunkenness; it was a room where, every Monday, an array of minor charges were handed out to a new line-up of residents in conflict with the police. But on this day, Courtroom Four was to be used to lay the most serious charges in the Criminal Code of Canada. Because the room is small, court officers decided to restrict access to relatives of the four victims, relatives of the accused men, and reporters.

About twenty minutes before the suspects were to arrive, police parted the barricades to allow an elderly couple, a young woman, and two young men to walk through—the Fagan family. For Al and Theresa Fagan, this was their first exposure to the criminal courts, and they were nervous. The Mounties had explained the process to all the victims' families, but there was still that uneasy sense that accompanies an unknown quantity. The family was escorted to the front door of the courthouse and quickly taken to an empty courtroom that had been set aside to keep them and the other families out of the media glare. All the relatives of the victims had followed the advice of the RCMP up to that point, refusing to do more than politely acknowledge reporters and then decline to make any comment related to the murders.

Excitement rippled through the crowd outside as a motorcade approached the building. The RCMP was providing an armed escort for the sheriff's-department vans transporting the three young men to court. Marked and unmarked RCMP squad cars and police-dog trucks swept into the courthouse parking lot as onlookers, forced to stand behind those who had arrived early and lined the barricades, craned for a better view. Dozens of officers jumped from their cars, looking over the crowd as the vehicles carrying Wood, MacNeil, and Muise backed close to the prisoners entrance.

The young men were hustled into the courthouse, past a phalanx of television crews and newspaper photographers. Cape Breton County Sheriff Wayne Magee had set aside an area for photographers in order to prevent a last-minute dash by some overzealous camera operator trying to get a better shot. He wanted everyone to have the same access, and he wanted no-one getting in the way. Derek Wood came first, clad in a dark, conservative suit, white shirt, and tie. Wood ignored the cameras as he walked, his hands cuffed in front of him, an officer on either side. I noticed no emotion, no sense of fear or shock at being where he was. Freeman MacNeil was next, also wearing a stylish, conservative suit and ignoring the cameras. Had it not been for the handcuffs, MacNeil would have fit in quite comfortably with the police officers guiding him. He looked casual and relaxed, with a slight edge of seriousness that matched the expression of the police escorts. The final suspect led inside was a different story: Darren Muise pulled a blue blazer over his head to hide from the throng of photographers and the hundreds gathered outside. He was whisked to the holding cells behind his two co-accused, and the three men awaited their appointment with the judge.

For the relatives of the victims, the court appearance would be the first opportunity to see what kind of people had brought so much pain into their lives. Julia Burroughs, clearly still in shock over the loss of her husband, slowly made her way towards the courtroom. The Fagan family paused in the courtroom doorway to allow deputies to quickly search them with metal detectors, a process that was repeated for everyone entering the room. Because of the large numbers of relatives—in particular the angry young men, brothers of James Fagan and Neil Burroughs—extra precautions were also taken inside the courtroom. Courtroom Four is a small, carpeted room with churchlike benches lining both sides of the centre aisle. The victims' relatives were instructed to sit on the right side of the aisle, and only five members of each family were permitted to enter; there were not enough seats to accommodate more. The few relatives of Derek Wood, including his brother, were placed on the left side, behind the front rows, where the suspects would sit. They sat huddled in the centre of the row, not looking towards the twenty people crammed into the seats on the other side of the aisle. Reporters jammed the back row on the left side and stood at the rear. Before the court went into session, a line of RCMP officers walked into the room and stood one behind the other, creating a human wall down the centre aisle. Other officers took up positions in front of the seats the accused would use, and in the row behind. Then the doors swung open, and the three men were brought in. They conferred briefly with their lawyers. I was standing near the door where the three had entered, and I watched as Al Fagan and his sons craned forward to see beyond the wall of Mounties separating them from the killers. After a few minutes, some of the other family members in the section similarly attempted to get a better look at the three suspects.

Everyone stood as the judge entered and opened the court. The process took only seconds: the charges were read, and dates were set for the next appearance, when the suspects would enter their pleas. A first appearance in a murder case usually includes a Crown request for the court to order psychiatric assessment of the suspects with the agreement of defence counsel. But in this case, the question of sanity or fitness to stand trial would not be an issue. The judge read the charges and adjourned the matter until June 11; the span between arraignment and plea would allow defence lawyers to confer with their young clients.

The atmosphere in the tiny courtroom was intense as the RCMP prepared to take the suspects back to the correctional centre. From the perspective of the victims' relatives, it was all too much; these three well-dressed young punks showed no sign of remorse, no sign of anything. Pandemonium broke out as the victims' relatives began to shout, then jostled the Mounties in an effort to get closer to the killers. "You took my baby's father away!" came a woman's voice. The agonized cry of Julia Burroughs could be heard in the hallway outside, as could another cry: "Five minutes! Just give me five minutes with them!" Sheriff's deputies stationed outside the courtroom moved towards the closed doors, but the hallway was full of people, and they

The procession of police vehicles leaves the Cape Breton County Courthouse after the first court appearance by the three men charged in the McDonald's murders. [Print from ATV video tape.]

soon had trouble there as a young man lunged towards the doors. One of Neil Burroughs's brothers, who had been unable to enter the room because of the limited number of seats, heard Julia's cries. It was more than he could bear. Johnnie Burroughs is a small man, but it took three sheriff's deputies to drag him away from the door as he screamed: "I'm your worst fuckin' nightmare! Do you hear me, you pricks? I'm your worst fuckin' nightmare! I'm gonna get you, do you hear me?"

The Mounties assigned to transport the prisoners literally lifted them from their seats as soon as the trouble started, and raced them out past the TV cameras and towards the waiting vans. The three suspects no longer looked calm and in control. They looked shocked, and Darren Muise forgot to hide from the cameras. As the glass doors swung open, the crowd outside began yelling, as though they had somehow picked up on what was going on inside. "Killers!" "No-good bastards!" "May you rot in hell!" "Fuckin' killers, hope you hang!" These people had kept silent when the three suspects were taken into the court, but their anger built as they talked about how terrible the crime was, and how much shame they felt that it had happened in Cape Breton. One of the subjects of discussion along the barricades was the rumour, still circulating around Sydney, that torture and ritualistic abuse had been part of the murders. Despite the insistence of the RCMP that robbery was the motive, many in the area felt there had to be more, and were ready to believe anything said about the killers—for example, that Muise, MacNeil, and Wood were the founding members of a Satanic cult lurking beneath the surface of the teen subculture. By the time the crowd outside had discussed this and all the other prevailing theories on what had precipitated the murders, many no longer thought of the suspects as three young men. They were monsters, and they should be dealt with as such. That opinion was not shared by everyone outside the courthouse. A small group of young men stood quietly aside, watching the procession and the outburst. They were friends of Derek Wood and Darren Muise. I talked to them briefly and interviewed one of them for my report. He was shocked, and said he could not understand how his friends had become involved in this crime. He insisted that they were normal kids, not unlike the group he was with. They had never done anything to suggest they were capable of shooting innocent people and then proceeding to cover up their acts with no signs of remorse.

In the history of Cape Breton, there had never been so much security surrounding a court appearance, but the outburst inside and outside the building convinced police they had made the right decision, one they would make again as court proceedings continued. For the Mounties who had found themselves trying to restrain the relatives of the victims, it was a painful and draining experience; they understood the anger but had to protect the suspects. Back inside the courtroom, defence attorneys and prosecutors felt similarly numb, but prosecutor Frank Edwards soon recovered, and had the room cleared of everyone but the victims' relatives. Edwards explained to them that he understood what had happened, but told them it could not be repeated. The court process that had begun would be a long one, he said, and the families would have to be patient if they wanted to see justice done. There would be no deals in this case, he told them; it would be first-degree murder all the way, and he would make sure these three men got what they deserved. But the families would have to help him by controlling themselves. Many of them had seen Frank Edwards before; he was regularly interviewed on TV at the conclusion of major trials in the Sydney area. He was the senior prosecutor on Cape Breton Island, and if he was going to get first-degree murder convictions in this case, then they would have to do their part to make sure he succeeded. Ken Haley remained quiet as his boss talked about getting first-degree convictions, but he worried about the remark. The police file was not yet complete, and he knew that it was a problematic claim to make. Well, he had not made the promise, and he would not be the lead prosecutor, so Haley figured he wouldn't have to explain anything to the families if Edwards found that the evidence didn't support the promise.

The suspects' June 11 court appearance was much quieter, although security remained tight. The families of the victims kept their word and remained silent, while outside the courthouse, only a few shouts were heard; the community was beginning to set aside some of its anger. But the curiosity remained. People wanted to know exactly what had happened at McDonald's, and they wanted another glimpse of the young men who had been charged. Inside the courthouse, very little was accomplished. In the weeks since the arraignment, Darren Muise and Freeman MacNeil had hired new lawyers. The conflict within the Legal Aid office, which arose because Art Mollon had been retained by Derek Wood, prevented them from choosing a local Legal Aid lawyer, but under Nova Scotia Legal Aid provisions, suspects can obtain certificates to finance a defence with an outside attorney. Mac-Neil's new lawyer was Kevin Coady, a Cape Bretoner who now prac-tised in Halifax, while Muise retained Joel Pink, a high-profile defence attorney from Halifax, who had handled many murder cases. Pink at-tended the June 11 court appearance and spoke to reporters after-ward. I asked him how Darren Muise felt about the anger he'd seen on the first court date; Pink replied that his client was afraid, not only be-cause of the public outrage, but also because of what was happening at the Cape Breton County Correctional Centre—inmates were open-ly joking and making bets about which of the three suspects would be killed in jail first. The three were still being held in isolation, and that kind of jailhouse banter ensured that they would remain in protective custody. In the interview, Pink also stated categorically that there was no evidence to suggest any of the three were involved in a cult.

Because new lawyers were involved, the case was adjourned until August 12 to allow attorneys time to review the Crown evidence and decide how to proceed on behalf of their clients. Meanwhile, Corpo-ral Kevin Cleary was adjusting to the new focus of his involvement. As the legal informant in case, it was his job to prepare the police file to the satisfaction of Frank Edwards. The Crown had based its charges on the confessions of the three suspects and the statement of Greg Lawrence, but much more would be needed before the file was com-plete. Edwards had a reputation as a tough courtroom attorney who won most of the major cases he handled; he was also a stickler, and insisted on knowing everything there was to know before he got to court. Cleary worked on the file every day until the end of July, when he was finally ready to present it to the prosecutor. By then, the file had more than six hundred subfiles—interviews with prospective wit-nesses, from taxi drivers and police officers who had entered the restaurant, to friends of the accused men who could reveal what they said and did before and after the murders. The file was a good one, but a detailed examination made it clear that the success of the trials would depend on the confessions being admitted in court; there was no physical evidence linking Muise, Wood, and MacNeil to the crime itself. One set of footprints in the basement matched the tread pattern on Derek Wood's sneakers, but that was not enough; he *had* been working at McDonald's, after all.

Experienced police officers know it is often easier to persuade a man to confess than it is to persuade a court to hear what he has to say when he finally does. The intense pressure of the police interrogation process is not considered by defence attorneys, who carefully look at how their clients have been treated by police and search for any behaviour a judge might construe as a violation of a suspect's rights. While getting a confession is vital to a solid police investigation, getting it thrown out on a technicality is critical to a solid defence. And defence attorneys have a distinct advantage: officers must obtain a statement in a matter of hours, but lawyers take months to examine the circumstances in which the statement was obtained. If an officer makes one slip-up during an interrogation, a good defence lawyer will find the mistake and attempt to portray it as the most critical moment in the interview—to convince the court that the suspect would not have given a statement, but for the one moment when the officer did or said something out of line. It's a system that keeps police under constant scrutiny and guarantees the rights of an accused above all else.

As the legal issues around the case were being worked out, prosecutor Brian Williston offered to lighten his boss's workload by taking over the lead in the prosecution of Darren Muise. He knew Edwards planned on handling all three cases as lead prosecutor, but Williston wanted that file. He had put in long hours at the RCMP detachment with Pat Murphy, and he didn't want to walk away from this one. Williston asked if he could act as lead counsel in the Darren Muise prosecution; Edwards agreed, and Williston began preparing his case. He was the first to discover a potential problem with the confession obtained from Muise. As he reviewed the police notes, he realized almost all contact with the accused had been either video- or audiotaped, which was great; the court would be able to see how Muise had behaved with police, and Muise would not be able to claim that he confessed out of fear. But Williston wanted to know what happened between the time the tape machine was turned off, and Sergeant Penny and Constable Hadubiak began their questioning of Muise. Brian Stoyek and Dave Trickett would have to be interviewed.

Frank Edwards was also having a problem—with Derek Wood's videotaped confession. It concerned the moment when Wood said he wanted to talk to his lawyer: how might a judge feel about that? Constable Mahoney had not exactly prevented Wood from calling his lawyer, but he had not stopped and gone for a phone, either. In parts of the United States, this would not be an issue, because a suspect is required to categorically state his wish for an attorney to be present before further questions are asked; but this was far from the case in

Canada. It would be important to show the court that, a week earlier, Wood was given access to a phone whenever he asked for it—that he knew he could use a phone if he wanted to. It was a sticky point, and careful legal arguments would have to be built to support the admission of Wood's confession as evidence. Freeman MacNeil's confession looked better. There were no problems in how it was obtained; in fact, MacNeil met with his lawyer between the oral and written statements. Still, the circumstances surrounding his hours of custody before his confession were examined in detail. Frank Edwards knew that MacNeil's new lawyer, Kevin Coady, would be doing the same thing, and the prosecutor had to be sure that Freeman MacNeil was never treated improperly by Rod Gillis, Wayne MacDonald, or Phil Scharf. His case could depend on it.

These issues were being examined by lawyers on both sides of the case as the summer dragged on. The August 12 court appearance for the suspects came, and again high security was in evidence throughout the courthouse and in the parking lot outside. But there were fewer people gathered at the courthouse this time: people in the Sydney area were beginning to move on, and they were trying to put the murders behind them. In the courtroom, dates for preliminary hearings were set for MacNeil and Wood. Muise had waived his right to a preliminary, a sort of pre-trial trial during which the Crown presents its evidence and a judge decides if the evidence supports the charges—if so, the trial proceeds, usually on a much later date. The process is like that of a trial, with Crown lawyers introducing the evidence through their witnesses, and defence lawyers cross-examining. Some defence attorneys present witnesses, but others use the preliminary to get a sense of the Crown evidence without offering prosecutors a preview of how they will approach the case.

Joel Pink said later that his client didn't want a preliminary hearing because he accepted that there was evidence to support the charges against him. Pink also explained a decision that had generated much speculation—Darren Muise had been moved from Cape Breton County Correctional Centre to a facility in Halifax County, so that the two could confer as they prepared their case. Some people thought that the move was intended to separate Muise from his co-accused because he had turned them in; that the last of the three men to give his statement was really the first, the one who led police to the others. But Pink explained that the move would allow him to confer with his client more easily—even though access didn't seem to be a problem for MacNeil's lawyer, who was also based in Halifax. And there was also another reason for the move: Muise, who was suffering from depression, was under the care of a forensic psychiatrist from the nearby Nova Scotia Hospital. All three suspects had adjusted to the jail routine and begun communicating with friends and family, although MacNeil and Wood, who were closer to home, could have regular visitors. For his part, Darren Muise began making calls and writing letters to some of his friends back in Cape Breton. He told one friend he expected to be out in seven years, and hoped to work on some form of computer training while he was inside. He also said he had become a more-religious person.

For the relatives of the four victims, the summer of 1992 was a time of adjusting to the loss but also of wondering what lay ahead. The families had agreed that they would attend all the court proceedings; they all wanted to be there to represent their loved ones from beginning to end.

Germaine and Howard MacNeil remember that summer as the beginning of a long uphill battle. Doctors had told the MacNeils there was a good chance Arlene would never regain consciousness. Back in her home town of North Sydney, the trust fund set up by the community group, called Friends of Arlene MacNeil, was growing. The money would be needed to allow the MacNeils to travel back and forth to visit Arlene in Halifax, and to help with her recovery, if and when she returned home. For Germaine MacNeil, every day started with a visit to hospital, where her still-unconscious daughter lay in bed, her beautiful black hair shaved off, her face a contorted grimace. Germaine would loudly announce her arrival each day: "Hi, Arlene— it's Mom. How are you, dear?" The days stretched to weeks, and it seemed Germaine was the only one who felt Arlene was ever going to come back. She claimed she could see improvements in her daughter's condition, despite the fact that the young woman still would not awaken. Back in Cape Breton, the word was that Arlene MacNeil was never going to regain consciousness, and that the story of her mother seeing improvement where doctors saw none was just another part of the tragedy.

One morning, Germaine entered the room and moved to the window to open the curtains and let the sun in. "Hi, Arlene—it's Mom," she said, as usual.

"Hi, Mom."

Germaine's heart stopped, her eyes filled with tears, and she turned to see that Arlene was awake. Her speech was laboured and difficult to understand, but she was awake and she knew her mother. In the days and weeks that followed, Arlene began to improve, slowly but steadily. Everything the doctors felt she would never be able to do again, she did. She sat up, she learned to feed herself, and she began to work towards a goal—to return to Cape Breton. Other patients in the rehabilitation centre saw her progress as an inspiration: if this young woman could recover from such a tragic and serious injury, then others, too, would work harder to get better.

Germaine MacNeil explained to her daughter why she was in hospital, what had happened, and who had done it to her. But Arlene remembered nothing about the incidents of May 7. She would never be a witness.

For the family of Jimmy Fagan, summer was a painful reminder of how deep the loss was. A summer cottage at the lake, usually the centre of family activity for the Fagans, was used very little in the warm months of 1992. Jimmy loved the times at the cottage, and going there without him left his parents, brothers, and sisters with an empty feeling. The fun in the sun just didn't have the same appeal any more. The landscaping company owned by one of the Fagan boys was kept busy through the summer months, but whenever a job took his brother to the Sydney Forks area, he would take the time to wander up to Jimmy's grave. Jimmy should be working with him, bringing his inimitable humour to even the most tedious jobs. Why was he dead?

The summer was no easier on the relatives of Derek Wood, Freeman MacNeil, and Darren Muise. They too were asking why. How could their boys be involved in something like this? The murders had thrown their lives into turmoil, as they offered love and support to their children and examined what they had done in raising them. Could they be responsible for what had happened? People always blamed the parents, didn't they? Friends and neighbours could see a difference in the parents of the three accused men. Smiles and casual, friendly greetings had been replaced by a stern, distant look. Unlike the families of the victims, who had found strength in each other, the parents of the accused suffered alone. I talked with Gail Muise periodically that summer; the first contact was awkward, especially because I had been covering the case, but when we met in a coffee shop she simply told me she understood that I had a job to do. After that, whenever we met she would talk about the case and about Darren. She visited him occasionally in the Halifax jail and accepted that he would have to pay a debt for what he did. She still did not know what his involvement in the case was, but was anxious to see the trial over and the challenge of rehabilitation begin. "Whatever he did—" and she reached over and touched my hand—"even if he just drove the car, or held open the door, we know he has to take responsibility for it." Gail Muise had always been an energetic, cheerful woman, but that was no longer the case. It was as though someone had pulled the energy—the very life—from her body. She was going through the motions, but the pain in her eyes was unmistakable.

As summer turned to fall, attention turned to the tiny provincial courthouse in Glace Bay, near Sydney. The preliminary hearings for Derek Wood and Freeman MacNeil were being held there because of ventilation problems at the old courthouse in Sydney. Because evidence brought out at preliminary hearings must eventually be heard by a jury, there is a ban on publication or broadcast of evidence. The October hearings gave the relatives of the victims their first chance to hear the evidence in the case, but did not thrust them into the centre of a media feeding-frenzy. Without the freedom to report on evidence being presented, many news organizations decided to monitor the hearings but not staff them full time. The hearings were short, and by the end of October both Wood and MacNeil had been ordered to stand trial.

Meanwhile, Muise's lawyer was busy working on another aspect of the case. Joel Pink wanted his client's trial moved out of Cape Breton. In a change-of-venue hearing, he presented the court with volumes of newspaper clippings, along with hours of television and radio reports on the McDonald's murders. Pink argued that the media attention made it highly unlikely that an impartial jury could be found in Cape Breton. Lawyers for the other two accused soon joined in the argument—all three men wanted their trials moved away from the anger they had witnessed outside the courthouse in Sydney. The change-of-venue applications outraged the Burroughs, Warren, Fagan, and MacNeil families, who felt it would be unfair for them to have to leave home to attend the trials. They were relieved when Nova Scotia Supreme Court Justice William Kelly decided to put his faith in the integrity of the jury system. The trials would be held in Cape Breton.

As 1992 drew to a close, there was a major change in the Crown Attorney's Office in Sydney. In the period between the preliminary hearings for Wood and MacNeil, and the arguments over where the trials would be held, Frank Edwards was appointed to the county court bench. Justice Edwards was not going to prosecute what would have been the biggest case of his career. However, he did move up rather quickly in the judiciary; soon after his appointment, the county court system was eliminated in a justice department reorganization, and Frank Edwards became a provincial Supreme Court justice. The appointment meant a scramble at the Crown office; someone else would have to handle the file—and face the promise made to the victim's relatives: first-degree murder convictions on all counts. While the job of regional Crown prosecutor would have to wait to be filled, the McDonald's file could not.

Ken Haley and Brian Williston added their names to the list of lawyers vying for the job. Within weeks, Brian Williston had a change of heart and withdrew his name from the job competition. He wanted to continue as a trial attorney, and he didn't want the extra paperwork that came with the regional Crown title. Ken Haley became interim manager at the office and took the lead in preparing the file. Both Haley and Williston agreed that a third prosecutor was needed, but it would be too big a drain on the Sydney office to designate someone from the limited pool there. Haley contacted the Attorney General's Office and said he wanted to borrow a prosecutor from elsewhere in Nova Scotia. Halifax-based lawyer Marc Chisholm, one of Nova Scotia's highest-ranking crown attorneys, volunteered to work on the case, and Haley and Williston welcomed him to the team.

The three men threw themselves into their work. They decided early on that each attorney would take the lead role in one of the prosecutions, but they would work together on each of the cases. Brian Williston, who had asked Edwards for the Darren Muise file, changed his mind. Muise's grandmother was a courthouse employee, and Williston felt it would be a little awkward for him to work on that case. Chisholm took the Muise file, Williston took Freeman MacNeil, and Haley began to prepare the case against Derek Wood.

As he sorted through the work Williston had already done on the file, Chisholm decided it was time to talk with Brian Stoyek. After the meeting, the prosecutor knew he had a problem: Stoyek had told him about letting Darren Muise know how he felt about him. A judge might see it as intimidation for a man the size of Stoyek to call an average-sized eighteen-year-old a "cold-blooded killer"—unless the judge saw and heard how Muise had reacted to the officer. And there was another problem. Dave Trickett, in his effort to persuade Muise to confess, had told the young man it would be better for him to tell his story before he went to court, if he expected a judge to believe him. Chisholm wondered whether a judge would consider that an inducement. The arguments over the circumstances of Muise's confession would be crucial to the case against him; the confession might not be ruled admissible as evidence if a judge ruled that either officer's comments were improper.

Ken Haley, who had worked briefly as a Legal Aid lawyer before joining the Crown office, decided to approach the Wood file from a defence lawyer's perspective. Williston tackled the MacNeil file with his usual penchant for detail, and the change of focus gave him a renewed energy. And the new guy in the office shared his colleagues' enviable work ethic. For a while, the prosecutors' family lives were put on hold; they had agreed from the start that they would give the file the same dedication the members of the investigating team had. But that didn't mean there was no room for the lighter moments, which often developed around Brian Williston's keen critical faculties. It seemed that every time his colleagues developed a theory or an approach, Williston would uncover an obscure item in the file, or some fine point of law, that put the new theory in question—a tendency that earned him the nickname "Black Hole."

Williston's intense concentration on the file also produced a running joke among the lawyers. It all started late one Wednesday night. The three prosecutors had been working on the file all day and into the evening, debating the strengths and weaknesses of the legal arguments ahead. They reviewed typed transcripts of the Derek Wood interrogation; watched hours of video tape, recorded the night he confessed; and searched the legal library for precedents for and against the admissibility of a confession. When they realized they were too tired to continue, Haley suggested they resume that particular review the following evening, but Williston rejected the idea. "I can't do it tomorrow—I've got a commitment," he explained. "Can we do it Thursday instead?" Haley and Chisholm looked at each other and laughed. Expressing their hope that the commitment wasn't too important, they informed Brian Williston that tomorrow *was* Thursday, and whatever he had planned for Wednesday night had already gone by the boards. As the weeks of late-night work continued, Haley and Chisholm got into the habit of ending the sessions with: "Well, we can't get back at this tomorrow. Let's do it Thursday." The remark worked best when one or all three of the hard-working lawyers had reached the point of being too tired to concentrate any longer. They could laugh a little, and relieve stress at the expense of Brian Williston's need for a social secretary.

The prosecutors were not alone in their work. Police were giving them all the assistance they could, and the Crown attorneys were especially impressed by the diligence of Henry Jantzen, who was responsible for all the exhibits to be used during the trials. If the attorneys needed a particular item or had a question about one of the interviews with the accused men, Jantzen came through quickly. He also helped prepare a detailed document that showed the similarities and differences in the confessions made by the three men; the big, burly officer had a bit of the paper-shuffler in him, and this surprised the prosecutors.

Once the prosecutors had clawed their way through the mounds of paper Kevin Cleary had provided, they began interviewing prospective witnesses as they prepared to work out the least-confusing way to present the cases to jurors. The prosecutors knew it was going to be a tough fight, but they would try to keep Frank Edwards's promise to the victims' families and go after first-degree convictions against all three accused men. Because of this decision, they rejected a feeler sent out from the office of Joel Pink, who wrote asking if lesser charges might be considered by the Crown. The prosecutors were not sure what Pink was implying by that request; they believed they might be able to work out a deal that would see Darren Muise take the stand in the trials of Derek Wood and Freeman MacNeil, but that offer was not made in the letter. However, the prosecutors felt it was a safe bet that Pink would at least discuss the matter with Muise if the Crown agreed to move down from the first-degree murder charge against his client. Muise, after all, had broached the subject of a plea bargain with Dave Trickett before he took his lie-detector test. Whatever the letter meant, though, they had no intention of making any deals.

• • •

IN THE EARLY winter months of 1993, while the three prosecutors were immersed in the McDonald's file, many residents of the community had put the tragedy behind them. A normal routine had settled in at the Sydney River McDonald's, where some of the workers organized a walkathon to raise money for the victim's families, and others had written a song in tribute to their fallen friends. "Whispers in the Wind" was a touching acknowledgment of the loss, but it was also a promise. The four employees who had so violently been removed from the workplace would not be forgotten by their colleagues at McDonald's.

I met the workers who had written the song, and interviewed them for an ATV feature. They rehearsed the song and played it through a few times for the camera; what was lacking in polished professionalism was more than adequately compensated by the genuine emotion expressed by the two young women and three young men from McDonald's. They had worked the same shifts and carried out the same duties as their fallen co-workers; they were well aware that it could have been them. For the TV interview, the group wore part of their McDonald's uniforms—not the formal pinstriped shirts, but bright pastel T-shirts emblazoned with the corporate logo. The name McDonald's was not neatly printed across the front of the shirts; instead, it was stylishly scrawled in an arc that had a flavour of fun and vibrancy. The contrast was striking—five young adults, who would ordinarily be enjoying the carefree energy of youth, were singing of death, loss, and eternity. Although the lyrics did not say it explicitly, the song spoke of what the murders had done to them. They had lost some of their innocence—they no longer could take life for granted—but they refused to accept that life could simply end for no good reason, that all the dreams and plans of youth could be wiped out by a single senseless act. "Whispers In The Wind" dealt with the anxiety the young people felt in their sudden awareness of mortality. In the song, the young people vowed always to remember the names and smiles of the fallen victims; the McDonald's workers wanted to be sure the lives of their friends meant something, that they would live on in the hearts of the people whose lives they touched.

After hearing their song, I called a friend who owned a recording studio in Glace Bay. Tom O'Keefe of Overtom Productions had told me that he, like many people in the community, wanted to do something to help the families of the McDonald's victims. When he heard that some workers from the restaurant had written a song, he immediately agreed to donate some studio time and production guidance to the group. He would help them make a cassette tape of their song, and they could sell it to raise money for the trust funds now in place for Arlene MacNeil and the families of Neil Burroughs, Donna Warren, and Jimmy Fagan. The hopes of the young McDonald's workers were realized: "Whispers in The Wind" was now a permanent tribute to the victims. The tape gave more meaning to their message. They could hold it in their hands—it was not as fleeting as they now knew life could be.

While I was interviewing them for the ATV feature, I was surprised at how many questions these young people had for me. The psychologist who had arranged to have workers taken through the crime scene before the restaurant reopened had hoped that the visit, and the explanations offered by Dave Roper, would eliminate some of the speculation and fear among the workers. That was not the case with this group. They asked me how much I knew about what had happened inside; they wanted to know if a knife had been used. Mostly, they wanted to know if their questions would ever really be answered. When I covered the murder trials, would I be allowed to reveal what had happened at Mc-Donald's? I explained that it all would become public knowledge, maybe not during the first trial but certainly after the last one. Then I asked them if they could tell me anything about the suspects. There wasn't much to say about Derek Wood; they had only worked with him briefly, and while he was friendly enough, he hadn't really made much of an impression. But it was different now, they admitted. Derek Wood had made a powerful impression on a great many people. The young men had a clearer picture of Darren Muise, whom they also knew. They said he was a nice guy, but had a very annoying habit. No matter what you told him, he had a story to top it—if you broke your arm, Muise would say he broke both. No-one really took him too seriously when he told his stories, but he was generally liked, despite this tendency to exaggerate.

The question I had been asked by the McDonald's workers was one I faced almost on a daily basis. Because of the severity of the crime, television coverage had been closely scrutinized, and many people in the community had come to identify me with the McDonald's case. I would be at a coffee shop, or out interviewing someone on a completely unrelated story, and someone would stop and ask: "Will you be able to tell us everything that happened?" I was asked this question by politicians who I thought would have an understanding of the court system, and by union leaders, housewives, and scores of other people I had never seen before. When the crowds at the courthouse later dwindled, during the preliminary hearings for Derek Wood and Freeman MacNeil, there was a feeling that interest in the case was dying off. That wasn't really true. The anger and shock had subsided, but people still had a strong desire to know what had happened at McDonald's. They were willing to wait, but they wanted to be reassured that the truth would finally come out.

thirteen

A S THE WINTER OF 1993 melted into spring, the first of the three McDonald's murder trials was set to begin. Derek Wood was taken first to the Bicentennial Gymnasium in Sydney, where he would enter his plea on the charges against him, and where jury selection for his trial would be made. The courthouse was not big enough to to accommodate the crowd of prospective jurors. Jury notices had been sent to 500 registered voters in the Sydney area, of whom 350 were asked to come to the gymnasium on April 21; the others would be summoned only if 12 impartial citizens could not be chosen from the first group. Of the 350 people expected, however, only 179 Cape Breton County residents gathered on the first day of jury selection. Because of the outdated voters list used for jury selection, notices had been sent to people who no longer lived in the area—and even to a few who had died.

The gravel parking lot outside the gym was enclosed by wooden barricades, watched over by security guards and Sydney police officers. Death threats against the accused men had been a part of this case for some time, and they were being taken seriously. The police and sheriff's departments had received anonymous calls saying that Wood, MacNeil, and Muise would pay for what they did, and while such calls often figured in high-profile murder cases, they were still a matter of concern. Along with the phone threats, there were persistent rumours in the community that the suspects were going to be killed for what they did—rumours fuelled by gossip and speculation, as people remembered the anger the three men had generated, and pointedly hypothesized about whether the trials would in fact be needed. As officers of the court, the deputy sheriffs were responsible for Derek Wood's safety, and they wanted to be sure that he would not be hurt on their turf. Sydney police were assisting the deputies by securing the perimeter of the gym, while private security officers, hired to supplement the sheriff's department workforce, stopped cars at the parking-lot entrance to ensure that the occupants were arriving for jury duty and to direct them towards the cordoned-off parking areas. A Sydney police barricade, preventing motorists from driving behind the building, was quickly opened as the blue van carrying the suspect rolled into the parking lot, flanked by RCMP and city police vehicles. As the van continued around the rear of the gym—and away from TV cameras and curious spectators—a huge loading-bay door swung open, and the vehicle ducked inside. Only when the door had closed was Derek Wood taken out of the van.

For prospective jurors, the process of getting inside the gym was a tedious one. Each person entering the building was searched with the aid of small portable metal-detectors, a procedure so slow that jury selection was delayed by an hour before everyone got in their place. Finally, a steel door at the front of the room opened, and a phalanx of burly law-enforcement officers entered. In their midst, unnoticed by many of the potential jurors, walked Derek Wood, clad in a light-grey blazer and pants, dark shoes, and a white shirt and black tie. As Wood took his seat, I watched from my vantage point off to the side and looked for signs that the strain of the year in jail and the prospect of a murder trial were wearing on him. On the contrary, Wood's bearing was relaxed and his expression nonchalant as he watched the goings-on around him. An image suddenly came to me, as Wood took his seat at the front of the gym—Derek Wood as a kid about to start a game of pick-up basketball. His chair was located in the "key," the area where free throws are taken, and above the young murder suspect's seat hung one of the basketball nets that had been pulled up to the ceiling as the gym was transformed into a makeshift courtoom.

Supreme Court Justice Gordon Tiddman began the jury-selection process by asking if anyone was unable to sit on a jury for reasons unrelated to the specifics of the Wood case. Exemptions were granted to people collecting unemployment insurance benefits, because jurors are not available for work and thus do not qualify for UI. Also exempted were people with medical problems, and those whose employers—though allowing them to take time off work—would not pay their salaries while they performed their civic duty. Because of the number of people requesting exemptions, the process was slow, so those of us covering the start of the trial went outside to question some of the jurors who had been excused. Surprisingly, many said they believed they could have judged the case fairly, and that their reasons for leaving were financial or medical. Others said they were very happy to get away from the case.

With the general exemptions out of the way, Justice Tiddman asked Derek Wood to stand and hear the charges against him. At 12:02 p.m., the remaining members of the jury pool listened as the judge read each count and the small blond man at the front answered. To the attempted murder of Joan Arlene MacNeil, to the unlawful confinement of Donna Alecia Warren, to the first-degree murder of Donna Alecia Warren, to the first-degree murder of Neil Francis Burroughs, and to the armed robbery, Derek Wood responded, "Not guilty."

Ken Haley then read a list of those who could be called to testify during the trial—151 possible witnesses, among them Darren Richard Muise and Freeman Daniel MacNeil. The prosecutors did not expect Muise and MacNeil to testify, but were keeping them on the witness list nonetheless; in fact, the Crown anticipated calling only 65 people to the stand—less than half of those on the list. Once again, the pool of potential jurors was drained—some had a relationship with one of the witnesses; others knew the accused, or one of the lawyers; still others worked for McDonald's or were relatives of McDonald's employees. By the end of the day, Justice Tiddman had excused 116 people, leaving a group of 63 for the final jury selection.

On May 4, back at the county courthouse, the defence team representing Derek Wood began the process of challenging for cause, a series of questions designed to determine if jurors could be prejudiced against a defendant. Art Mollon, who led the questioning for the defence, wanted to know whether the prospective jurors had closely followed media coverage of the McDonald's murders, whether they had a preconceived notion of the guilt or innocence of those charged, and whether they felt they could decide the case on the evidence and not on what they had heard in the community. Two other members of the jury pool then gave their opinion on the impartiality of the candidate, who was then considered one last time by Mollon and Crown prosecutor Ken Haley. Haley and Mollon were surprised that it was only 3:13 p.m. when they came to an agreement on twelve people acceptable to both sides in the case. The ten men and two women were sworn in by Justice Tiddman; the Wood trial was ready to begin.

Perhaps the most important part of the trial took place in the six days between the jury selection and the calling of the first witness. This was the time devoted to the *voir dire* hearing into Derek Wood's confession, which was key to the Crown's case. *Voir dire* refers to a trial within a trial, in which witnesses are called and evidence presented. But unlike a regular trial, there is no jury, and the central issue—rather than innocence or guilt—is the legality of the evidence in question. Can it be presented to a jury? Justice Tiddman heard testimony from the police officers who had contact with Derek Wood on May 7 and May 16, 1992; watched the video-taped interview with Wood, conducted by Constables Wilson and Mahoney; and listened to the lawyers' arguments. Mollon stated his case clearly: anything and everything that happened after Derek Wood asked for his lawyer could not be allowed as evidence. To allow the confession to be admitted, said Mollon, would be a violation of his client's rights. Ken Haley countered that Wood, who had been in custody little more than a week earlier, was well aware that he need only tell police he wanted his lawyer, and they would assist him. Besides, Haley said, Wood had asked for and been given legal counsel earlier in the interview in question. Neither lawyer got an immediate answer. Justice Tiddman reserved decision on the matter until the morning of May 10.

In the middle of all the uncertainty came the first anniversary of the McDonald's murders. The Sydney River restaurant was closed for the day and barricades, festooned with roses in honour of the victims,

From left, Karl Mahoney, Phil Scharf, and Jim Wilson chat after testifying during the admissibility hearing at the start of Derek Wood's trial. [Print from ATV video tape.]

were placed at the entrance of the driveway. Another ecumenical service was held near the restaurant, at Our Lady of Fatima church, and once again a large crowd listened as Father Stanley MacDonald repeated his earlier message—that the community was in desperate need of healing. For the families of the four shooting victims, May 7, 1993, was spent in painful reflection on the tragedy that had shattered their lives a year before. Prayers were said over the graves of Neil Burroughs, James Fagan, and Donna Warren, and an unspoken question lingered in the cool spring air: Why did this happen? Perhaps the trials would provide an answer.

Just after eight in the morning on Monday, May 10, Derek Wood arrived at the courthouse for the first day of his trial. He was left to cool his heels in the basement holding cell for some time—nothing would be happening in the courtroom until nine-thirty—but Cape Breton County Sheriff Wayne Magee had decided to bring the accused to court early, before the anticipated crowds began to gather outside. He needn't have worried. There were enough people to fill the courtroom, but not many had to be turned away. Still, security was intense: access to the second floor of the courthouse was restricted, and no-one could enter the courtroom without being searched. For the relatives of the four victims, it was an unnerving experience to stand with their arms extended as guards ran wandlike metal detectors along their sides and between their legs. Al Fagan did not like being treated like a suspect when he had spent a long, productive life as a law-abiding citizen, and he especially disliked being subjected to such treatment in front of the TV cameras, which were recording the searches. A throng of journalists huddled near the courtroom entrance, and every few moments one of them would glance towards the doorway at the end of the hall, where Derek Wood and the security entourage would emerge when it was time for him to take his seat. The twelve jurors hustled quickly past the families and the reporters as they headed for the jury room, next to that same doorway. Cameramen were told they could only record the procession as Wood walked down the hall and entered the courtroom: they were not to get between him and the door, and they were not to follow him inside. By the third day of the trial, those restrictions would be lifted.

As I waited for Wood to arrive, I tried to build on my earlier contact with the victims' families. I had managed to persuade two of Neil Burroughs' brothers to talk to me during the preliminary hearings, several months earlier; maybe the others would be more forthcoming now. But it wasn't going to happen, at least not yet. They still reject-ed the idea of speaking to a reporter; heeding the advice of the Crown and the RCMP, they wanted to avoid saying anything that could cause problems in the courtroom. As I stood drinking a coffee across the hall from Olive Warren, Donna's mother, an elderly woman at her side began pointing at me, obviously distressed. The woman, who turned out to be Olive's mother, explained later that she had mistak-en me for Derek Wood—she had seen him on the news and somehow confused the two of us—and couldn't understand why I was being al-lowed to wander in the hall so close to her. Donna Warren's grand-mother was very nervous that morning, but she wasn't the only one.

For those of us covering the trial, the biggest concern was how much would we be able to report. The Crown had applied for a pub-lication ban, arguing that potential jurors for the Muise and MacNeil trials must not be unduly influenced. The CBC and the *Cape Breton Post* had hired lawyers to argue against the ban, and Justice Tiddman would make a decision before the trial started. For me, this was an is-sue that went way beyond getting a good story. Prosecutors and po-lice officers have sometimes argued that the media have no legal status before the courts, and that arguments about access unnecessar-ily drag out a trial. In fact, open access to the courts is one of the tenets of our justice system, and since most Canadians do not have time to attend trials, their only access is through media reports. I have even covered trials during which Supreme Court justices have taken time to thank journalists for helping keep the process open. Fictional accounts of reporters fighting for the public's "right to know" have given the issue an undertone of cliché that even embarrasses re-porters, but the fact remains that a closed and secretive court process is a threat to every citizen.

The prosecutors involved in the McDonald's murder cases argued that the information would still become public; it was simply a mat-ter of waiting until the final trial ended. But media lawyers argued that that wasn't the point. Banning publication or broadcast of testi-mony is just the first step, they said—what about extending the ban to the identity of someone who is acquitted? That would not be in the public interest: people need to know that everyone is treated equally before the courts, and judges must be subject to close public scrutiny, so they cannot succumb to the temptation to abuse their power by showing favouritism to friends.

Shortly after nine-thirty, the families of the victims settled into their reserved seats at the centre of the courtroom, with reporters on their left and members of the public occupying the remaining seats. Front row centre was reserved for security personnel, who sat just behind a metal bar that divided the room in half and kept Derek Wood sequestered in an area off limits to everyone except court officers and lawyers. The effect was of a room split down the middle by a picket fence, topped by a dull grey railing in which two openings had been cut—these were to allow lawyers and witnesses to come and go.

Just beyond the railing were the chairs in which Wood and a contingent of security officers would sit during the trial. In front of these chairs, dominating the centre of the room, were two long tables, placed end-to-end: on one side, Ken Haley, Brian Williston, and Marc Chisholm sat huddled over their file in a flurry of last-minute preparation; at the other end, Art Mollon and Allan Nicholson also pored over their notes. Beyond the lawyers' tables sat the clerk who would swear in witnesses, roll-call the jurors, and number and label exhibits as they were introduced. And beyond the clerk's table stood a raised oak bench, which matched the panelling that covered the courtroom walls. The judge's chair was at the centre of that bench, and on either side were the doors to two private rooms—the judge's chambers and the jury room. Off to one side of the bench hung the only adornment on those dark wooden walls—a portrait of the Queen and a Canadian flag.

Before calling the jury, Justice Tiddman dealt with the preliminary issues. Visible relief illuminated the faces of the three Crown attorneys as Tiddman ruled that he would allow Derek Wood's confession. Art Mollon and his colleague Allan Nicholson were impassive; they had already decided to appeal if the ruling went against them. Next, the issue of access—and now it was our turn to be relieved. We could report on all testimony except evidence that would implicate Darren Muise and Freeman MacNeil in the crimes for which they would later stand trial.

Finally, it was time for the trial to begin, and Ken Haley stood to make his opening remarks to the jury. His tall, heavy-set body and thick, dark hair made him an imposing figure, and his comments were equally striking. Haley promised to prove that Derek Wood planned and carried out the robbery at the Sydney River McDonald's, and that during the robbery he shot Arlene MacNeil, Neil Burroughs, and Donna Warren. That simple statement began the longest three weeks of Haley's life.

As his first witness, Haley called Constable Henry Jantzen, who had been appointed exhibit man and who would present the court with all the physical evidence gathered during the investigation. When Jantzen was about to play the video tape recorded at the crime scene, Justice Tiddman issued a warning to the victims' relatives: it was very important for the jury to see the tape all the way through, he said, so anyone who did not feel strong enough to see the disturbing, graphic images should leave the courtroom until the screening was over. Several women and a few men rose from the reserved seats and headed for the hallway; those who stayed behind regretted the decision within minutes. The lights in the courtroom were dimmed, and Henry Jantzen turned on a video projector that would display the taped images on a large screen in front of the jury box. TV monitors had also been set up so that Wood, the lawyers, and the judge could watch.

The room was silent and the tension palpable as the back of the restaurant appeared on the screen. Then, the view shifted to Ident officer James Leadbetter's video tape of the crime scene; the onlookers watched in silence as the camera slowly moved towards the spot

The courtroom was silent as the rear of McDonald's, guarded by police officers, appeared on a large screen in front of the jury box. [Print from ATV video tape.]

where Jimmy Fagan had fallen. There was nervous shuffling from Fagan's family when they saw his blue kitbag and baseball cap on the ground, and then the weeping began—the screen seemed to fill with blood as the camera panned along the section of floor inside the restaurant where ambulance attendants had worked frantically to try to save Jimmy. Tears welled in the eyes of Cathy Sellars, a sister of Neil Burroughs, and a moment later the short blonde woman gasped and forced her eyes downward, sobbing audibly. The camera had moved to the area by the sinks, where Neil Burroughs lay, face down, surrounded by a frighteningly large pool of blood. Neil's brothers also began to cry as they looked at his helpless body on the floor. Finally, the grotesquely oversized image of Donna Warren's lifeless form appeared on the enormous screen, and Olive Warren broke into tears. Fighting for control and scolding herself for staying in the room in the first place, Olive forced herself to look away from the screen. Like Cathy Sellars, she stared down at her lap, hoping no-one would see her heartbreak.

The jurors sat transfixed by the images they were seeing and the emotion they were hearing; these bloodied bodies were not actors, and this was no movie. With the painful clarity of sudden awareness, the jurors realized that they were the ones responsible for passing judgment on the man believed responsible for the horror they were witnessing. The two women on the jury covered their mouths with their hands as they forced themselves to watch. An elderly man in the front row, who had spent much of the screening in a state of shock, went scarlet with outrage and empathy as the cries from the victims' relatives reached him. The cries were not loud, but in the shocked silence of the courtroom, they were impossible to miss. Meanwhile, Derek Wood sat between two guards with his head down and his eyes closed. He had already seen the tape in jail, at his lawyers' insistence, and now he showed no reaction to it—or to the sounds of grief behind him. Later, he told the guards he had drifted off to sleep while the tape was being played in court; they said they didn't believe him.

Two final images, poignant and horrible, awaited those in the courtroom. There, in a pool of blood, were the wooden sticks Arlene MacNeil had been sorting for a child's birthday party. And there was the image that had haunted Kevin Cleary ever since the early-morning hours of May 7, as he picked his way through the restaurant kitchen—an open safe and the floor beneath it, strewn with blood-soaked money.

I later asked Haley why he had chosen such a graphic record of the crime scene; weren't there photographs of the crime scene that would have shown the extent of the crime without subjecting the victims' relatives to the unforgettable impact of big-screen images? Haley said he agreed with my point, and explained that he had been against screening the tape; it was the defence team that had insisted on it being presented to the jury.

Allan Nicholson, the flamboyant associate of Art Mollon, explained this perplexing request as he chatted with reporters in the hall during a break. If he didn't have preparations to make for the next witness, Nicholson often met with reporters during the recesses; he would lean against the railing of the stairs to the lower level of the building and sip from a can of Diet Coke, his beverage of choice while on the job. To see him standing there considering an answer to one of our questions—sipping his soft drink or running a hand through his thick grey goatee or his long grey hair—one might have been tempted to write him off as an eccentric. But that would have been a mistake. His answers were anything but erratic. On this occasion, explaining why he thought the video tape was crucial evidence, he told us that when Derek Wood was first taken into custody, only hours after the murder, there was no blood on his clothing or his sneakers, which were taken from him by police right then and there. Nicholson and Mollon wanted the jury to wonder how anyone who was responsible for spilling so much blood could walk away without being covered in it.

After the video-tape screening, and after Henry Jantzen's detailed account of what he had found when he got to the restaurant, the rest of the first day of testimony proved a little easier for the victims' relatives to sit through; Daniel MacVicar and the other cab drivers gave their evidence, and so did the ambulance attendants. Outside, most of the family members who would speak to me said they felt the trial was proceeding well, but wondered why the defence lawyers kept questioning witnesses about the exact time of everything. Joey Burroughs, Neil's brother, even approached me to ask why so much emphasis was being placed on time—what time the ambulance company received its call, what time the taxi drivers heard MacVicar's distress call, what time Henry Jantzen was first contacted by the RCMP dispatcher. To Joey Burroughs, all that mattered was what had happened to his brother, and to Jimmy Fagan, Donna Warren, and Arlene Mac-Neil. I explained that lawyers on both sides were responsible for making sure that every detail was brought before the jury, and that the de-fence attorney's reasons for making an issue out of the exact times would be made clear when they presented their evidence. After Joey Burroughs sought me out that way, there was a thaw in some of the other families' attitudes towards me. I could feel they were slowly be-ginning to trust me; although they still refused to grant an on-camera interview, they did get into the habit of talking to me every day, be-fore and after court. Sometimes the conversations were brief—a com-ment on the number of people lined up each morning to watch the trial, for example. The size of the crowd varied, but the victims' rela-tives, like reporters and deputy sheriffs securing the building, noticed a disturbing trend as the trial continued. Whenever an evening news report described a day of testimony characterized by particularly graphic details, a large crowd would appear the following morning, hoping to hear more.

The second full day of testimony was a case in point. Dr. Dan Glas-gow, the pathologist who had conducted autopsies on Neil Burroughs, Donna Warren, and James Fagan, told the jury how each victim had died. Nervously adjusting his glasses as he spoke, the heavy-set, fair-haired doctor struggled to calmly describe what had happened to the victims after the bullets were fired. The Crown had provided a head-and-shoulders mannequin, from a clothing store, and a long wooden pointer, to help the doctor with his testimony. Dr. Glasgow began with Donna Warren: "There were two firearm injuries to Donna War-ren's head, one with an entrance wound behind the top of the left ear," he said, gesturing with the pointer, then shifting it around to the mannequin's eye to show where another bullet had struck. As he spoke, there were gasps and cries from the centre of the courtroom: the sight of the mannequin was too much for Donna's mother and grandmother. But they tried their best to control themselves. "The en-trance wounds were compatible with a low-calibre, low-velocity weapon," Dr. Glasgow continued. "There are no exit wounds, and as a result all bullet fragments were retained within the head."

Ken Haley walked forward and handed the doctor one of the ex-hibits that had been introduced the previous day by Henry Jantzen—a small plastic pill bottle. There was a clicking noise as something inside the bottle tumbled about. "Yes, these are the bullet fragments taken from Donna Warren's body during an autopsy I performed," Dr. Glas-gow said. "The fragments were placed in this bottle by me, initialled, and handed to Constable Jantzen, who was present at the time." With that, the muffled sobs grew louder, as Donna's relatives tried hard to erase the image the pathologist had just presented of the pretty, energetic young woman lying on an autopsy table. And it only got worse. The emotion and the stifled cries echoed throughout the courtroom with each excruciating detail of the wounds suffered by Donna Warren. The shot through her eye, which had been such a shock to everyone watching the crime-scene video, probably didn't kill her, the doctor haltingly explained; the bullet had hit the bone behind her eye socket and deflected downward, coming to rest at the back of her throat and avoiding any damage to the brain. But the second shot, which entered the back of Donna's head and travelled through her brain to lodge against the front wall of her inner skull, was fatal.

Dr. Glasgow, clearly moved by the anguish his words were eliciting, went on to discuss Neil Burroughs's ordeal. His testimony confirmed for the Burroughs family what they had feared all along: Neil had died a long and horrible death. Weeping filled the room again, as the doctor talked about the gunshots—how the bullet fired into Neil's ear travelled down into his mouth and caused no damage to his brain; how the shot through his forehead killed him, but possibly not right away; how the skin on his skull was torn away by gas blowing from the wound to the back of his head; how the weapon was pressed against his head when it was discharged. Then Dr. Glasgow described the knife wounds—how deeply and at what angle they penetrated Burroughs's neck, and the extent of what he called "blunt trauma" to the victim's forehead and nose. Because Derek Wood was not charged with Jimmy Fagan's murder, the Fagan family was spared the gruesome details of the manner of his death; but for the Warren and Burroughs families, the cross-examination, towards the end of the day's testimony, offered an even grimmer view of what had happened to Donna and Neil. Allan Nicholson asked Dr. Glasgow how much blood was likely to have splashed onto a person putting a gun so close to a victim and then firing. Clearly annoyed by this approach, Joey Burroughs marched out of the courtroom, muttering about Allan Nicholson and his questions. Olive Warren and her mother walked slowly down the stairs, comforting each other, their pain obvious to anyone who saw those quiet, deliberate movements.

By the third day of the trial, Joey Burroughs's slowly building anger was beginning to spread to the other members of the victims' families, who finally decided to start talking to reporters. What got them started was the testimony of Greg Lawrence: for the first time, they learned that Lawrence—and others—knew about the planned robbery weeks before the killings. Why had Lawrence not been charged? Had a deal been made to protect him from prosecution? How could Lawrence possibly have believed, as he said in court, that the robbery plan was not to be taken seriously? The victims' relatives were disgusted when they found out that nothing in the Criminal Code compels people to come forward if they know a crime is about to be committed; that meant Greg Lawrence was entirely within his rights to withhold information, even if he did take the plan seriously. The anger brought on by the Lawrence's testimony was in part directed towards the defence lawyers. After only three days of testimony, Joey Burroughs and his brothers, John and Brian, were afraid that Mollon and Nicholson would confuse the jury with questions the young men considered irrelevant, such as what time police officers arrived at the scene and how much information they gave Derek Wood the first night he was questioned. To them, the issue was simple: Derek Wood had confessed to killing their brother, and that was that.

For the team of Nicholson and Mollon, it was an altogether different matter. Both lawyers had handled more than an average share of

Art Mollon, left, and Allan Nicholson during a break in their client Derek Wood's trial.
[Print from ATV video-tape.]

The backpack marked escape, which Derek Wood forgot when he and the other killers fled McDonald's. His nametag, which was in the pack when police found it, was identified in court by a restaurant manager. [RCMP crime scene photo.]

murder cases, and they had their own agenda and their own sense of courtroom style—no small aspect of any defence attorney's effectiveness. Allan Nicholson's almost-theatrical manner was enhanced by his long, greying hair and Old West–style goatee, and by the cowboy boots visible beneath his staid black-and-white court robes. A free spirit who loved to champion the cause of the underdog, Nicholson was perfectly suited to Legal Aid work. He also had a gift for hypothesis, which he occasionally tried out on reporters before presenting it to the jury. Overly zealous police methods were a favourite theory: everyone knew the police still used harsh methods to get the innocent to confess; police officers were just better at hiding it now. And emphasizing his version of police interrogation techniques for the benefit of the jury was a specialty of Nicholson's. In contrast to his partner's sometimes confrontational style, Art Mollon befriended witnesses and frequently capitulated to requests from the prosecutors. During questioning, his gaze would shift from his notes, to the witness, back to his notes, and then to the jury, his expression conveying the serious concern of a man who had to be sure that the facts were clear. He would frequently run a hand through his thick, greying hair, flicking the long wisps that were always falling in front of his eyes—the picture of a hard-working, determined attorney, who, like the Crown, just wanted to get to the truth here. If the prosecutors were a little off the mark in their charges against his client, well, he would help bring them around.

The final witness on the third day of the trial, May 12, was Mc-Donald's manager Phyllis Kowalczyk. Her testimony, too, was difficult for the victims' relatives to hear, because it brought home in stark terms what they already knew—that all four victims could, and should, have been somewhere else when the robbery occured. Jimmy Fagan would have been on the witness stand, not in a grave, if he had come to work on time instead of an hour early. Neil Burroughs, who had been off work for more than two months after injuring his back in a car accident, could have stayed away a little longer, but instead traded shifts with Jimmy and took the easier workload. Arlene Mac-Neil had finished her work, and should have left at the same time as Derek Wood and the other evening-shift employees. And Donna Warren, who was scheduled for the day shift, took the swing shift for another manager.

For Derek Wood, the fifth day of his murder trial marked the end of his teenage years. Wood's lawyers brought a birthday cake to the courthouse so their client could celebrate his twentieth birthday over lunch. It was a birthday he also shared with his father, a quiet, dark-haired man in his forties, who had been sitting in the hall outside the courtroom since the beginning of the trial. The short, shy-looking George Wood had asked to be near his son during the trial, but the defence team said no. Apparently, Derek didn't want his father to hear the testimony against him. For the first couple of days, Mr. Wood's presence had pretty much gone unnoticed by the victims' relatives and the reporters; however, it wasn't long before we discovered the identity of the gentleman in the grey leather jacket, who was always leaning forward on a bench and staring at the floor. The sheriff's deputies told us who he was when we asked if he was a witness, and they also identified the woman who joined him one day—Derek's stepmother. The couple sat quietly, listening to the conversation swirling around them—all about what a frightening monster their son was supposed to be. George Wood knew all too well about the pain and outrage being felt in the community, especially in the area around the Sydney River McDonald's; he worked in a grocery store less than a block away, and was constantly reminded of the terrible crime. The pain George Wood felt was as obvious in his posture and his sad eyes as it was in the expressions of the victims' parents. He too had lost a child.

Emotions ran high again on the afternoon of Derek Wood's birthday, as Kevin Cleary took the stand, using a pointer and an architectural model of McDonald's to describe the scene he found on the morning of May 7, 1992. The $15,000 scale model had been built for the three trials to help witnesses with their testimony, but its presence didn't make Cleary's job easier on him emotionally. Cleary wanted to provide the jury with a clear picture of what had happened, but as he talked of finding the bodies inside, he could hear the relatives of the victims crying in the gallery. Each sniffle or quiet moan sent a chill down the officer's spine, but he forced himself to continue, aware that the families wanted justice and certain he could only help them by being as detailed as possible in his testimony, regardless of the effect.

By the fifth day of the trial, I had worked out my routine for this trial and the two that would follow. Early each morning, camera operator Gary Mansfield and I arrived at the courthouse to get a new shot of the suspect arriving. At the noon break, we rushed back to the station to do a live report on the 1:00 p.m. news. Then, back to court, where I would try to persuade one of the Crown or defence attorneys to make a comment on the morning session. I needed a fresh on-camera comment each day, and the victims' relatives were still rejecting requests for interviews. At 4:30 p.m., it was back to the station again, to pull together a two-minute report on the day's testimony, including the reactions of the spectators. The schedule kept us running and, unfortunately, prevented me from getting as close to the relatives of the victims or of Derek Wood as I would have liked. It seemed that every time there was a break, I was running for a phone or racing towards the truck to get back to the station.

Still, I was getting in some brief chats with Olive Warren, a very friendly woman who happened to know Gary; the cameraman grew up with Donna in the industrial suburbs of Sydney. Olive had wispy fine hair, glasses, and an expression that varied from a bright smile to deep sorrow, depending on the day and the testimony. She always wore a bright purple jacket with a faded ribbon pinned to the lapel— a tribute to Arlene MacNeil. The committee raising money for Arlene's rehabilitation had given out the ribbons months before, and Olive continued to wear hers; she told me she would only remove it when Arlene was well enough to come home. Each morning as we arrived, Olive would come over and ask Gary if he had managed to get a good shot of Wood being led from the prison van. He couldn't appear before the camera too often, as far as she was concerned.

While Olive would not yet agree to give me an interview, she did talk privately about her concerns and fears—and began to include me in a morning ritual of hers. Every day, before the doors opened, Olive would make the rounds of all the victims' families, handing out peppermints from an apparently endless supply she kept in her purse. The mints were also offered to security officers, and now Gary and I were on her treat list. When I realized that Olive was also giving candies to the prosecutors each morning, I began to tease her. She had often told me that she'd welcome the chance to get Derek Wood alone and teach him a lesson about what he had done, so one time I told her I knew what she was really up to: "I know what you're doing," I said. "When the final day of this trial comes around, you're going to slip everyone a knockout pill instead of a candy." Olive smiled conspiratorially. "Don't tell on me," she said, "and I'll keep you awake."

After my morning visit with Olive, I would try to chat up the other relatives. Al and Theresa Fagan were very friendly, and apologized for their reluctance to agree to an interview; they did not want to be rude, but they had been advised not to talk to the media. The morning also offered a few minutes to ask Ken Haley about his plans for the day—the witnesses he intended to call, and the insights he hoped to reveal through their testimony. To my sorrow, I learned that Haley had more than the trial on his mind as he arrived each day. He was spending his evenings at the home of his father, a well-respected and hard-working community volunteer who was fighting a losing battle with cancer.

On the sixth day of the trial, the jury heard from Corporal Leadbetter, who provided one of only two pieces of physical evidence linking Wood to the crime—the first being the kitbag found propping open the basement door. Leadbetter said the footprints from that door into the restaurant matched impressions made by the sneakers Wood wore that night. It was a tiny chink in the armour Derek Wood had worn since the trial began—the well-dressed, clean-cut young man, chatting quietly with his lawyers or with the guards beside him. It was difficult to believe that he was responsible for the horrific crime being re-created in gory detail for the jury. Whenever he entered or left the courtroom, he kept his head down and his face expressionless; even the jurors who watched the evening news saw only a subdued-looking, quiet young person. But when the jury was out for a break, and Wood was talking with his lawyers, he showed a little more emotion, even laughing at times. This irked Gary Mansfield, who took a great deal of pride in his work and was becoming more and more frustrated with the ever-present image of Wood with his head bowed in apparent sorrow. He wanted people to see Wood's face clearly—to see his eyes.

"As soon as I put the camera down, he comes to life," Gary told me one day. "Maybe if you stand in front of me, and I shoot over your shoulder, he won't notice." We both laughed at the suggestion. More than six feet tall, Gary packed about 225 pounds of solid muscle developed over many long hours in the gym. At five-nine and 145

A hint of a smile compromises the serious look Derek Wood assumed for most of his trial. One of his lawyers, Allan Nicholson, is behind him. [Print from ATV video tape.]

pounds, I was hardly the one to block Gary Mansfield from anyone's view—especially when he had a TV camera on one shoulder and a large video-recorder on the other. "Fine," said Gary, "but I'll get the shot even if I have to find a full-grown reporter somewhere else." Mansfield did get his shot that day, while Wood was talking with his lawyers during a break. He didn't get anyone to block for him, though; he simply adjusted his camera for available light, quickly moved into the doorway, and aimed the lens into the courtroom. He managed to catch a few seconds of the smile on Derek Wood's face before Wood saw the camera, at which point his face went blank and his head lowered. It was another chink in the armour; Derek Wood wanted to be seen as a quiet and serious young man, and his efforts had been thwarted.

On May 18 and 19, the jury also saw a very different Derek Wood, as they watched the video tape of his interrogation. This was a defiant Wood, arguing with and scoffing at Constables Wilson and Mahoney as they tried to persuade him to confess. They could also see a clear change in the young man's demeanour when he did confess—from an angry teen with an attitude, to someone clearly enjoying his conversations with police. The big-screen confession was the most telling evidence in the case, and Art Mollon and Allan Nicholson promptly set out to discredit it. In cross-examining the officers who had interrogated Wood, they showed that many details of the crime had first been revealed by the police, not Wood. For their part, the officers insisted they were trying to convince Wood that they knew what had happened, and that it was in his best interest to cooperate. But the defence team argued that the details police provided, coupled with Wood's obvious concern for the incarcerated Mike Campbell, could have prompted him to invent a confession that would help his friend. In his effort to create reasonable doubt—did Wood commit the crime or did he just repeat what police had described to him?—Allan Nicholson spent hours questioning Jim Wilson. The big, friendly constable shifted uncomfortably in the witness chair as he lived through every police officer's nightmare—a defence attorney who will not let you off the stand. The heat and humidity in the crowded courtroom added to Wilson's obvious discomfort; still, he handled the questions well, insisting he was certain that Derek Wood confessed because he was guilty. The cross-examination also gave Wilson a chance to say in public how he really felt about Wood. He may have been the one befriending the suspect in the interrogation room, but that didn't mean he was a member of the Derek Wood fan club. When Nicholson suggested that Wood responded to officers' appeals to his conscience by admitting to more than the minor role he played, Wilson flatly rejected this image of a guilt-ridden teenager. "I don't feel he has a conscience," the officer said. "When he finished his statement, he says he's sorry. That's about the only conscience he has."

Wilson spent the better part of two days on the witness stand, and near the end of his cross-examination, Neil Burroughs's sister Francine began crying quietly in the courtroom. I asked her later if she was upset because she felt the jury now believed Wood was innocent. But her concern was for Jim Wilson. "I just feel so bad for him," she said. "It's not fair for them to treat him like that. I just wanted to run up to the stand and give him a big hug."

The Crown rested its case after calling the police witnesses, and Art Mollon took over. Like many defence lawyers, Mollon doesn't give an opening statement, preferring to save his arguments for the summation. He began by calling four people to testify on behalf of Derek Wood. These witnesses came to Mollon's attention about halfway through the trial, when he received a phone call from a young woman who had been at Kings Convenience with her boyfriend on the morning of the murders. She remembered Derek Wood running into the store, and after hearing reports from the trial indicating that the time he arrived at the store was at issue, she felt compelled to call.

In early testimony, the convenience-store clerk who dialled the police for Wood just after the shootings insisted that he called the RCMP, and not the ambulance company, as the defence suggested. It made a big difference. If the first call was made to the RCMP, then Wood arrived at the store at 1:20 a.m., the time the RCMP logged the call. But if the clerk dialled the ambulance first, then Wood could have been at the store as much as fifteen minutes earlier, a point that was crucial to Nicholson's and Mollon's case. And Mollon's witness was sure that Wood had arrived before 1:15; her boyfriend agreed, as did his mother and sister, who remembered exactly what time the couple returned from Kings to tell them about the young man who reported a shooting.

The fifth defence witness, Russell Deveaux, was a guard at Cape Breton County Correctional Centre who had befriended Derek Wood during his preliminary hearing in October 1992 and had listened to Wood talk about the case several times since. But when Deveaux was called to the stand, Ken Haley objected; he wanted to discuss the admissibility of the guard's evidence. The judge had a chance to hear Deveaux's testimony while the jurors were out of the room. According to the guard, Wood talked in hypothetical terms about being in the restaurant—what if I were there but didn't shoot anyone?—and indicated that he saw Arlene MacNeil shot and tried to help Donna Warren but was prevented from doing so. He felt he could have saved Donna, and Jimmy Fagan, but instead he ran away. The statements came in bits and pieces, not as one cohesive explanation, Deveaux said, adding that he encouraged Wood to talk when he appeared to be upset during the trial.

The guard also tried to persuade Wood to testify, which, he said, Wood told him his lawyers were also trying to do. Someday, Wood told Deveaux, he would make sure the victims' families heard the whole story. But he did not feel he could testify while they were in the courtroom. The guard also insisted that Wood told him not to testify about their conversations, but Ken Haley argued that Wood was using Deveaux to get a new version of his story before the jury without having to undergo cross-examination to do it. And despite defence arguments that the Crown had been allowed to call a guard to testify about incriminating remarks by Wood made while he was in custody, Justice Tiddman ruled that Deveaux's testimony would not be allowed. The jury would not hear what the guard had to say.

Art Mollon then turned in his chair and asked his client a question; he replied, "No." Mollon never did reveal what the question was, but he had made it clear to reporters throughout the trial that Derek Wood could make his lawyer's job a lot easier by testifying on his own behalf. Whatever he had asked Mollon rested the case for the defence after Wood's reply. On the morning of May 27, the thirteenth day of the Wood trial, Art Mollon was ready to deliver his summation to the jury. "While this is one of the most brutal and senseless crimes in Nova Scotia, or even Canada, we must determine what the facts are," he said. "I believe the evidence indicates he did not do it.

"Let's look at the times," he continued. "They are critical." And Mollon slowly outlined for the jury why the timing of key events after the crime made it impossible for his client to have been at McDonald's when the murders occurred. "We have documented times," he said. "The RCMP received the call from City Wide Taxi at 1:09—that was the first call to police. At 1:20, Derek Wood phoned police." Facing the jury, a portable podium beside him to hold his notes, Mollon spoke with compassion as he outlined the tough role jurors must play. The only evidence of the anxiety the lawyer was feeling was his voice; it was a little louder and a little higher than it had been for the rest of the trial. Then his expression turned to deep concern. That call, he said—Wood's call to police *had* to be the young man's second attempt to notify authorities about the crimes. And the first call *had* to be to the ambulance company. Wood had told police the morning of the crime that he thought his first call had been to an ambulance company, and the ambulance dispatcher had told the jury he received two back-to-back calls reporting the crime at about 1:08, one from the taxi dispatcher and the other from an unidentified male calling from Kings. Mollon asked the jurors, who were from the Sydney area and knew the distances involved, if his client could have been at McDonald's at 1:05—when the taxi arrived with Jimmy Fagan—and still have been able to run to Kings to make a phone call at 1:08. "Derek was at Kings when Jimmy Fagan was shot," Mollon said. "He was a terrified young man who was involved in a plan to rob his employer. When the horror started, he ran for help."

Derek Wood's second statement to Constable Brian Stoyek on May 7 was credible, Mollon argued; the young man was in the restaurant when the first shot was fired, but he ran back out the door and headed for Kings. As for the confession, Mollon told the jury his client wanted to protect Mike Campbell, and felt he was to blame because he helped plan the robbery and let MacNeil and Muise into the restaurant. Mollon emphasized that Wood did not take any money: "Who was in control of the money? Freeman. Wood did not want any."

As he took his seat after almost ninety minutes, Art Mollon realized that his job was done—all he could do now was wait for the jurors to do theirs. While his arguments were strong, the jury still had to hear from Ken Haley, who had spent a long night preparing his address to the jury, working at his kitchen table and pausing every once in a while to think about his father. How proud he had been, only weeks before, when his son was appointed regional Crown prosecutor for Cape Breton, and how happy he would be if Haley won this very important case. The prosecutor began simply by asking the jury to consider all the evidence. Derek Wood acknowledged his true involvement in the crime, he said, reminding the court of the way Wood chose to confess. Haley asked the jury to consider the video-taped interrogation when they assessed Wood's character: was this the portrait of a terrified teenager or a cold-blood killer? Rather than admit to everything, in an attempt to satisfy police and help Mike Campbell, Wood picked up the list of charges and specified the ones for which he claimed guilt. As for the timing of Wood's calls from Kings, Haley wondered just how accurately people keep track of time; wasn't it common for people to differ by ten or fifteen minutes? Slowly building his argument, Haley questioned Wood's actions after the crime. Why didn't he tell police he was walking to Freeman MacNeil's house? Because he knew MacNeil was involved? And if he was so terrified that he took off after hearing shots, why didn't he tell police about the maniacs who went crazy with the gun? As Haley continued to summarize the evidence, the victims' relatives began to relax. Mollon's summation had them worried, but now they could feel the tide changing in their favour; "their lawyer," as they later referred to Haley, was doing a good job.

In front of the jury box, Haley paced slowly, emphasizing that what happened at McDonald's was no accident. "They talked about shooting the employees if they had trouble inside....They planned the robbery, and when things went bad they fell back on what they had talked about. Our ally is force, our ally silence. No one can tell. Eliminate witnesses." Then, for the final time, he took the jury through the crime scene, describing in detail what had happened, what Derek Wood had done. Once again, Neil Burroughs's sisters wept to hear the heartbreaking account of their brother's violent death.

In an appeal filed a week later, the defence accused Haley of being inflammatory in his ninety-minute summation—a complaint that caused a good deal of concern on the prosecuting team. Haley became quite upset about the accusation. He was certain that he had been fair and had in no way inflamed the jurors. Williston and Chishom advised him to ignore the complaint; after all, there were several reasons cited for the appeal, and they didn't agree with any of them. Finally, Haley's colleagues began to worry about his reaction; they didn't want him to lose his focus, not with two trials still ahead of them. They decided to try humour, and bestowed on him the nickname "Flames," which stuck for the duration of the McDonald's trials. To his credit, "Flames" did learn to laugh at the whole situation, and he set aside his concerns about the appeal until a more appropriate time.

With Haley's arguments over, the jurors were sent home for the long weekend. On the morning of June 1, the fourteenth day of the trial, Justice Tiddman undertook his charge to the jury, an explanation of the points of law related to the charges and evidence of the case. Tiddman's intention was to clearly and simply outline the relevant Criminal Code provisions. Making legal language understandable is a challenging task, but Tiddman was up to the challenge, and was well aware of the hazards that faced him. Many appeals have been won by defence lawyers who argued that a judge did not properly charge the jury.

Tiddman began with a caution to the jury. "It is hard to imagine crimes more horrendous. These killings understandably upset the community," he said. "Separate yourself from those emotions, and make your decision on the evidence. It is not for you to determine the seriousness of the crime, but you must decide if this accused committed all or any of the offences." He also advised jurors against making a decision too early, and urged them to approach their deliberation with open minds—and, especially, open ears.

With this warning out of the way, the judge explained the differences between first-degree murder and the related offences of second-degree murder and manslaughter. For a murder to be first-degree, he said, it must be planned and deliberate, or it must be committed by someone found guilty of unlawful confinement. Tiddman outlined what the law has to say about forcible confinement as the offence tied in with the case in relation to Donna Warren. A judge's charge is generally a long, drawn-out, technical affair, and observers expected this one to take most of the day. But Tiddman clearly wanted to avoid confusing the jury: in less than two-and-a-half hours, the charge was complete. ·

Then began the long wait, as relatives of the shooting victims and members of the media gathered in the hallway outside the courtroom. As the jurors pondered, the guessing game in the hall centred on how long they would be out, and what a lengthy deliberation might mean, Joey and John Burroughs came over to talk with me about their worries and their feelings. "If this goes long, those people are crazy," Joey said, his anxiety building. "The goddamned bastard confessed, didn't he?" After just over three hours, there was a brief wave of excitement in the hall, as deputies summoned the lawyers. Was it a verdict? No, just a request. The judge, the lawyers, the accused, the relatives, and the reporters all crowded back into the courtroom to learn that the jurors wanted a transcript of the testimony of Corporal Brian Stoyek, the first officer to come in contact with Derek Wood. The judge told them that the transcript wasn't ready yet, but he could replay the audio tape of the officer's testimony. Of course, that would mean the jury would be spending the night in a hotel, Justice Tiddman said. The victims' relatives had been praying for a short deliberation, but now they would have to spend a night waiting and wondering.

The next day, it was back to the wait in the hallway; everyone was talking about the significance of Brian Stoyek's testimony and why the jury wanted to hear it again. Crown lawyers had pointed out that in his second statement to Stoyek on May 7, Wood claimed to have run through the restaurant and out the door after seeing two men, one wearing a mask, and said he saw a man lying in the doorway where Jimmy Fagan had fallen. He could not have known this if, as the defence insisted, he had not been at the restaurant when the last shot was fired. In his final argument, Art Mollon had challenged that information by saying that during their interrogation on May 7, Stoyek and Cleary "refused to admit" they told Wood where the body was. Mollon hoped the jurors would cling to the phrase "refused to admit" and its implications, instead of concluding that the officers had simply chosen not to give Wood any information on that first morning.

The phrase, as it happened, came from a report I had written a few years before. Before his closing arguments, Mollon took me aside and said he would be quoting me to the jury. But he would not say any more, and I just couldn't figure out what I had said or done in the weeks of the trial that could be used in arguments for either side. However, when Mollon got to the part of his argument dealing with the interrogation, and said that Stoyek and Cleary "refused to admit" giving Wood the answers—his voice rising with indignation on the word *refuse*—I started to smile. The phrase had come up when I filed a report saying that a man accused of murder had "refused to admit" his guilt when interrogated by police. The man's lawyers just happened to be Mollon and Nicholson, and they promptly let me know how outraged they were. Their client had not "refused to admit" he was guilty, they said; rather, he maintained that he was innocent! So that was the phrase they were now using to defend Derek Wood, in the hopes that jurors would believe police "refused to admit" something they in fact denied. It was a key point. If the jury was convinced that Wood knew where James Fagan had fallen when he talked to police on May 7, then they could draw only two conclusions: either the RCMP told him, or he was at the restaurant after Jimmy Fagan was shot—in which case the arguments about time were no longer an issue.

As we all waited, Derek Wood spent the day pacing, sitting, or lying down in the tiny holding cell in the courthouse basement. I made several trips to the sheriff's office in the basement to watch Wood on the video monitor, and was surprised to see that at one point, the young man whose freedom was on the line appeared to be sleeping. I asked if I could go into the holding area to talk with Wood, but Sheriff Magee would not allow it. Nor could I find Derek Wood's father; the defence lawyers had made arrangements for a room to be set aside for him to await the verdicts.

At 2:26 p.m., the jury foreman sent a note to the deputy guarding the jury-room door. They were ready.

If the metal-detector searches and the secured second floor had seemed extreme to those attending the trial, the security in place for the reading of the verdicts was unprecedented. Thirteen law-enforcement officers crowded into the courtroom, most of them standing shoulder-to-shoulder to form a human wall between the gallery and the accused, who was flanked by guards. The RCMP and deputies knew that the emotions could run high at such times, and they wanted to keep the courtroom under control by making an intimidating show of force. For Joey Burroughs, it was indeed a time of great turmoil. Neil's brother had been half-joking with me for weeks about making a run for the accused when the trial was over. It was something he wanted to do with every muscle in his body. Short and stocky and very angry, Joey was boxed in, seated in the middle of the second row. The front row was empty, but there was a wall of men between him and Derek Wood. As he waited for the jury to return, the anger continued to build and Joey began to turn red, thinking of the grisly testimony from the pathologist, of the video tape, and, most of all, of how Derek Wood had come to court every day and shown no sign of remorse. Joey gripped the back of the wooden seat in front of him as the jurors finally took their places.

Before asking for the verdicts, Justice Tiddman addressed Joey Burroughs and the other anxious relatives of the McDonald's victims, commending them for showing strength throughout the trial, but warning them that he would not tolerate any outburst. Those who felt they could not control themselves should leave, he said.

He then asked for the verdicts on a count-by-count basis: "On count one, the attempted murder of Joan Arlene MacNeil, how do you find?"

"Guilty." As the foreman spoke, a stifled cry from Arlene's mother could be heard, and Joey Burroughs pulled slightly on the back of the chair he was still gripping. Derek Wood looked pale, and lowered his head as he stood beside his lawyer.

"On count two, the unlawful confinement of Donna Alecia Warren, how do you find?"

"Guilty." A louder cry from the gallery, and a firmer pull from the white-knuckled Joey Burroughs. Wood did not move.

"On count three, the first-degree murder of Donna Alecia Warren, how do you find?"

"Guilty." Now a cheer—and the relatives quickly restrained themselves, grabbing each other by the arms and crying. There were tears of release. But Joey Burroughs still sat with his head bowed, both hands gripping the chair. And Derek Wood remained motionless.

"On count four, the first-degree murder of Neil Francis Burroughs, how do you find?"

"Guilty." More crying, more hugging, and further attempts at self-control. Joey Burroughs pulled so hard on the wooden chair that it rocked backwards, straining at the ageing bolts that held it to the courtroom floor. If Derek Wood felt anything, he did not show it.

"On count five, the armed robbery..."

"Guilty." A louder cheer echoed through the room, and the relatives hugged each other wildly before Justice Tiddman shot a stern look in the direction of the overwhelmed family members.

The judge then asked Derek Wood if he wished to speak before sentence was passed.

"No, my lord." Wood's voice was strained, but he maintained control. Justice Tiddman sentenced Wood to two terms of life imprisonment with no parole for twenty-five years on the first-degree murder counts, a term of life imprisonment on the attempted murder charge, and two terms of ten years for the robbery and unlawful confinement. They were long sentences, but they would not be served consecutively. In Canadian law, a life sentence is a life sentence, and once it is imposed, no term can be added to it. There is no such thing as a multiple life term, or a consecutive parole-eligibility restriction.

As the sentences were handed down, Joey Burroughs bolted from the courtroom. He wasn't going to attack Wood, but he was too angry to allow him to leave without response. The prisoners entrance at the courthouse is located below a cement wall that borders an upper parking area. Burroughs ran to that wall and waited for Derek Wood to be taken to the waiting van. Others gathered and began to shout obscenities and threats at the young man as he was led to the van amid tight security. Joey Burroughs gripped the cement wall, his angry voice rising above the rest: "May you choke on every cock you suck from now on, you fucking prick!" he shouted, hoping everything he'd heard about prison was true. The other onlookers picked up the theme, shouting at the departing prison van. The verdicts had been a victory, but it was a hollow one; it could not restore the lives that had been lost or shattered. Their outburst at least relieved the tension of the three gruelling weeks of testimony.

After the release of frustration, those who had ventured outside returned to the courthouse, where the mothers, sisters, brothers, fa-

Relatives of the McDonald's murder victims weep and embrace in the hallway of the Sydney courthouse after Derek Wood is found guilty of all charges against him.
[Print from ATV video tape.]

thers, and cousins of Arlene MacNeil, Donna Warren, Neil Burroughs, and Jimmy Fagan hugged, kissed, and cried in front of the television cameras. I rushed from one emotional relative to another, asking how they felt, getting their comments and tears on camera. Julia Burroughs sat crying on a bench, repeating the phrase: "You'll never know. No-one will ever know." Germaine MacNeil was overwhelmed with emotion. Earlier in the day, as we waited for the verdicts, she told me Arlene would be arriving from Halifax the following day; she was being transferred to a hospital closer to home. Now I asked her to tell me the good news in front of a TV camera. She cried and gasped as she spoke: "Arlene…is…finally…coming home." It was all Germaine could manage. Then I saw Joey Burroughs, still fuming; Gary and I went over to him. He too tried to express what he was feeling, but he was too emotionally spent to do much but cry. Al Fagan reluctantly agreed to make a brief comment on behalf of his family, saying only that he was relieved by the verdict. He was still worried that emotional comments from victims' relatives could threaten the trials of Darren Muise and Freeman MacNeil, who were charged with Jimmy's murder. I turned away from Mr. Fagan and saw Carmel Burroughs standing in the hall. Neil Burroughs's mother had been at home for most of the trial, but sometimes called me in the evenings after my news reports; her kids always told her what had been said in court, but she wanted to talk with someone who had been through murder trials before. When I asked Carmel for her reaction, she gave a very short comment about her feelings of relief, then pushed the microphone aside, wrapped her arms around my neck, and gave me a hug. Nearby stood Olive Warren, who was crying too hard to say much; she too pushed past the microphone and hugged me.

Just down the hall, in a closed office, another emotional scene was being played out, far away from the prying eyes of the cameras. After the verdicts were read and the weeping of the relatives spilled out into the hallway, a wave of emotion swept over the prosecuting team. At first, the lawyers joined the families in the hallway, but soon Ken Haley and Brian Williston realized that they couldn't remain— their eyes were filling with tears, and they needed time to regain control. Marc Chisholm also felt the force of the emotion being expressed, but he knew his colleagues from Sydney were under more strain than he was. They lived here, and they felt a particular pressure to successfully prosecute the case that had so dramatically changed their home town. After regaining their composure, the lawyers went

back out in the hallway, where Haley took a few questions from reporters before returning to the office with his partners to begin working on the next trial.

Once we had something on camera from all four families, I took
one last look around for Derek Wood's father, but could not find him.
Gary and I headed back to the station to prepare our report, and afterwards I sat in the newsroom and began to wonder about the way
Carmel Burroughs and Olive Warren had reacted. I had befriended
both women during the trial—they were friendly people, and it would
have been hard not to do so—but I didn't want to become emotionally involved in the story, nor did I want them to think of me as being "on their side." Providing information about the legal process was
something I did for many people in the community who approached
me with questions during the trials. Television viewers often feel free
to walk up to a reporter they watch at home each night, and talk as
though they knew you well, and I always take time to answer their
questions or just say hello. I decided that Olive and Carmel just felt
overwhelmed after the verdicts, and expressed their thanks in a more-
emotional way than they otherwise would have. Besides, like all the
victims' relatives, they were facing another roller-coaster ride starting
the very next day. The trial of Darren Muise was about to begin. And
these overwrought people could use some understanding.

fourteen

THE DARREN MUISE TRIAL was a very different experience for the victims' relatives, despite their feelings that they were now wise to the ways of the courtroom. Justice William Kelly, who was hearing his case, agreed that the publicity surrounding the Wood trial could make it difficult to find an impartial jury for Muise, and allowed the murder trial to proceed in front of a judge alone. Another difference between the two trials was the defence. The victims' families had been angered and frightened by some of the questions raised by Art Mollon and Allan Nicholson—the insistence on knowing how much blood was spilled during the murders; the preoccupation with the time Derek Wood made his phone calls. But Muise's lawyer, Joel Pink, was someone to fear even before they saw him in court. The well-known Halifax defence lawyer had been involved in some high-profile cases, and there was speculation about the prosecuting team being up to the clash. But perhaps the most striking difference between the two trials was the demeanour of the two accused men. Where Wood had avoided eye contact and kept his head bowed, Muise held his head high, looking directly into the cameras and the at people gathered in the courtroom as he was led to the chair where Wood had spent the past three weeks. Muise's tendency to swagger when he walked quickly annoyed the relatives, who wanted him to look frightened and overwhelmed, not confident and self-assured.

The first day of Muise's trial offered little more than an opportunity for reporters and the angry relatives of the shooting victims to take a look at the second suspect. Marc Chisholm, who was prosecuting the case, asked Justice Kelly for a few days to gather the exhibits from the Wood trial and have them released by Justice Tiddman. Many of the exhibits were common to all three cases, and the prosecutors had expected an interval of several days—not eighteen hours—between the end of the Wood trial and the beginning of the Muise trial. A new starting date was set: on Monday, June 7, the crown would begin its case against Muise.

Chisholm knew that to win the case, it was absolutely imperative for him to win the pretrial argument over the admissibility of Muise's confession. He would have to convince Justice Kelly to listen not only to the confession, but also to the prolonged interrogation that preceded it. Joel Pink had carefully prepared his arguments against allowing the confession. A psychiatric specialist had seen the video tapes of the police and Muise in the RCMP detachment and read all the written statements, and he was prepared to testify that Darren Muise did not confess with an "operating" mind—one of the legal criteria governing the admissibility of an accused person's statement to police. The doctor's opinion was that the long interrogation and the techniques used by the police had somehow robbed Muise of his faculties. But the prosecutors weren't so much worried about defence arguments as they were about Kelly's practice of hearing only one side of a statement.

Some judges prefer to hear both the police's questions and answers given by the accused, in the belief that the answers offer insight into a suspect's state of mind at the time. Others—and the prosecutors thought Justice Kelly was among them—prefer only to hear the questions, which they believe will reveal any threats, promises, or inducements on the part of the police, these actions being the other means by which a statement is judged admissible. Marc Chisholm and Joel Pink were preparing to go head-to-head on June 7, but the first day of the trial was taken up by other arguments. Art Mollon, Derek Wood's lawyer, had applied for a ban on evidence implicating Wood, arguing that any new trial ordered as a result of this client's appeal could be prejudiced. Justice Kelly dismissed that implication, but he did decide to follow the pattern established in the first trial by banning media reports on evidence that implicated Freeman MacNeil.

On June 8, the admissibility issue was finally considered. Chisholm urged the judge to listen to both sides of the conversations between police and Muise in order to get a clear picture of the accused's state of mind, while Pink argued that the police's behaviour during the discussions would show whether or not his client's rights had been violated and his mental state affected. Kelly reserved decision, saying he would deal with the issue when the evidence was presented. This left the door ajar, but the Crown attorneys realized there was a very real chance they could lose the argument. The brief encounter between Darren Muise and Brian Stoyek would be a problem if Kelly heard only what the officer had to say; a man the size of Stoyek calling an average-size eighteen-year-old a cold-blooded killer certainly sounded like a case of intimidation. Without considering Muise's reactions to Stoyek and the other officers, the judge might well rule that his confession was illegally obtained—and that would effectively destroy the Crown's case, because Freeman MacNeil and Derek Wood were not willing to testify against Muise. But the Crown would try its best. The prosecutors began the *voir dire* hearing with testimony from the RCMP's Glen Lambe and Phil Scharf, who described their frustrating conversations with Muise on May 13, 1992; and continued with a screening of the video-taped debate between Muise and Scharf over the polygraph test. That was as far as they got that day. As Muise stood to leave with the deputies, the victims' relatives glared at him from the gallery. They then filed out of the courtoom, only to be asked to stay a while longer. The RCMP had requested a meeting.

Ken Haley, Marc Chisholm, and Brian Williston walked across the courthouse parking lot to the prosecutor's office. They had been told that a meeting was being set up, but they wanted to get some work done before heading back to the courthouse. They had an idea what the meeting would be about, and decided to attend but remain quiet and listen to what the others had to say. A short time later, they were called back to the courthouse. The courtroom was packed with representatives of the victims' families and some of the highest-ranking officers involved in the RCMP investigation of the McDonald's murders.

Phil Scharf did most of the talking, but other officers had a chance to say their piece, too. The police knew that there had been a new offer from Darren Muise's attorney—Muise was willing to plead guilty to the second-degree murder of Neil Burroughs and to the robbery, if the Crown agreed not to offer evidence on the unlawful confinement charge and the murder of Jimmy Fagan. The victims' families were also aware of the offer; the prosecutors had told them about it before the trial, but said at the time that they intended to fight for first-degree convictions. Since then, however, the police had become concerned about that decision, afraid that it might cost them a victory. Scharf explained to Fagan's relatives that there was a wealth of experience on this investigating team, and that experience told the officers that it was unlikely Muise would be convicted of Fagan's murder. The only way to prove that Darren Muise handed Freeman MacNeil the gun would be to call MacNeil to the stand—and they were certain that MacNeil would not cooperate. Police also wanted the family of Neil Burroughs to accept that a second-degree murder conviction would be a lot better than having to see Darren Muise on the street. They explained that the judge might not agree to listen to Darren Muise's responses to the comments investigators had made to him, and that the confession might never be heard.

At first, the victims' relatives were angry; Joey Burroughs said he thought it would be just fine if Muise wanted to walk out of the court-house and deal with him and his brothers. But the mood changed, slowly. In an emotionally charged moment during the meeting, Brian Stoyek stepped forward and explained that he knew what the victims' families were going through. Tears welled in his eyes as he talked about the assault on his wife, and the feeling of powerlessness that he was left with. By the end of the meeting, the consensus was that the prosecutors should accept the offer and fight for a lengthy sentence. Haley, Williston, and Chisholm explained that they would have to discuss the issue among themselves, and they returned to the prose-cutor's office. Finally, they reached a decision: they would not take the chance of losing this one on technicalities. The promise made by Frank Edwards would not be kept. And the third member of the Crown team would get his nickname: Haley and Williston settled on "Deuce"—referring to the second trial, and the two charges to which Muise would plead guilty, one of them being the second-degree mur-der charge. Chisholm didn't like the name any more than Haley or Williston had welcomed theirs.

On June 9, the victims' families arrived at the courthouse dis-heartened. Darren Muise had confessed to being in the restaurant and using a knife on Neil Burroughs, and now the courts were hung up on the niceties surrounding the police interview. For those who had seen the video-taped image of Neil Burroughs's corpse, and heard the pathologist describe his wounds, the plea bargain still seemed to be a terrible deal. What the hell were the courts for, Joey Burroughs won-dered, if not to see justice done. He could find nothing just in the deal. As Justice Kelly reopened the *voir dire,* Joel Pink interrupted, and asked the judge to reread the second and fourth counts from the in-dictment. Before reading the charges, Kelly asked Darren Muise if he was aware that the judge had played no part in any agreements be-tween counsel. Muise told the judge he understood, then pleaded not guilty to the first-degree murder of Neil Burroughs, but guilty to the included offence of second-degree murder, and to the robbery. The other charges were dismissed after Marc Chisholm said he would call no more evidence. Kelly set June 24 and 25 as the dates he would hear arguments from Marc Chisholm and Joel Pink on how long Darren Muise should remain in jail before applying for parole. First-degree murder carries a mandatory life sentence with no parole for twenty-five years; a life sentence is also mandatory for second-degree murder, but the parole issue is open.

June passed quickly as the lawyers scoured their books in search of convincing arguments for and against a longer than usual parole restriction for Muise. On June 24, Marc Chisholm opened the proceedings by describing Muise's role in the McDonald's murders; the judge needed this information before he could sentence the young man. What took weeks to reveal during Derek Wood's trial was compressed into a single day. Chisholm walked the judge through the crime scene, using the scale model of the restaurant, which dominated the front of the courtroom. Constable Henry Jantzen removed the roof from the model, then lifted out the first floor to expose the basement area, as the young prosecutor took a pointer and retraced the steps of Wood, Muise, and MacNeil through each room. Chisholm's show-and-tell took everyone through the nightmare one more time, as he described how the victims were found and how ambulance attendants tried to help them.

"Donna Warren was moved from the small manager's office...she was pulseless. When her chest was pushed, blood came out of her mouth. There was blood and cerebral spinal fluid coming from her left ear." Olive Warren wept as the image of her helpless daughter returned; Darren Muise showed no reaction. "Neil Burroughs was checked by two ambulance attendants. His throat had been slit and gunshot wounds to the head were noted. He was lying in a large pool of blood. He was pronounced dead at the scene." Julia Burroughs kept a tissue pressed to her nose and mouth as she cried, remembering her husband. "Arlene MacNeil...lying on her stomach holding a handful of straws. Her head was in a pool of blood. She was unconscious...bleeding from the nose and mouth...gasping, barely breathing." Chisholm circled the model, moving his pointer from one area to the next as he identified the location of each victim. "James Fagan...in a pool of blood...his teeth clenched in pain. He was still alive."

Justice Kelly left his seat at the centre of the raised bench and walked over to the witness chair to get a better view of the model.

Chisholm also presented the judge with the crime scene photos as he told his story. Walking about the courtroom with his wooden pointer, his posture extraordinarily erect, Chisholm looked for all the world like a strict schoolmaster—a demeanour appropriate for a man advocating severe punishment. The silver-haired judge appeared to be a particularly good student: Kelly hung on every word, occasionally looking at the book of photographs of the crime scene, or walking towards the witness chair to get a better view of the scale model. Darren Muise sat in the prisoner's chair, at times leaning forward to offer a comment to his lawyer, and at times staring at the floor in apparent boredom.

Chisholm soldiered on, making every effort to convey the terror, pain, and senseless death for which Muise was partly responsible. He emphasized Muise's actions in the days following the killings, portraying the eighteen-year-old as a cunning, calculating, uncaring criminal who benefited from the proceeds of the robbery—"blood money, which is freely and without conscience spent." Like Kevin Cleary, who had found himself deeply affected by the reactions of the victims' relatives to his testimony at the Wood trial, Chisholm knew how hard it was for the families to hear what he had to say. Yet he had to continue, leaving out no detail, no matter how painful. His presentation to the judge would be a determining factor in how much time Muise spent behind bars.

When Chisholm finished the outline of Muise's part in the crime, he said the Crown was ready to move on to the victim impact statements—comments from those affected by a crime that are used in determining the sentence an accused person will face. Joel Pink had an objection; he did not feel impact statements from the MacNeil, Fagan, or Warren families should be permitted. His client had pleaded guilty to killing Neil Burroughs, and he was being sentenced for that crime alone. Justice Kelly agreed, and apologized to the three families. The judge also ruled that the statements from the Burroughs family would have to be read into the record by the prosecutor; he could not call the relatives to testify.

Cathy Sellars stood up and stalked out of the courtroom, her eyes filling with tears as anger began to bubble up towards the surface. All she could think about was her brother Neil, lying in a pool of blood. In the hallway, she came face-to-face with the television cameras. Cathy had never objected to the unrelenting television coverage of the case—in fact, she hoped it would show the public how terrible the crime was—but this time she had no patience for the media or for anyone else. The outraged young woman wheeled around and headed towards the bar that kept her family separate from Muise, the judge, and the lawyers. Justice Kelly had already left the bench and walked out the back door of the courtroom, and guards had escorted Muise out through another rear exit; only the lawyers remained. Marc Chisholm, who had spent his day working desperately to persuade the judge to use his power to lock Darren Muise up for the maximum term, was suddenly confronted with the full force of grief turned to fury, a powerful feeling shared by many of the victims' relatives, who could no longer abide the civilized atmosphere that surrounded the court proceedings.

Red-faced and shaking, Sellars shouted at Chisholm, her voice distorted with hysterical anger, her words almost unintelligible. The prosecutor stared blankly at the small, angry woman, who screamed for vengeance, sick of a justice system that she saw as protecting the guilty at the expense of the innocent. Tears filled her eyes, and other family members in the hallway hugged each other and wept to hear her echo their own feelings: "Day after day, we have to listen to this— how he was shot and stabbed and hit. Well, no more! No more waiting for you to do your job. An eye for an eye!" Marc Chishom knew the anger was directed at the system and not at him. His first thought was to turn and walk away, but he realized that would insult her, so he just stood and listened as she vented her fury.

Her outburst over, she marched out of the room again. Carmel Burroughs, Cathy's mother, had returned to try to calm her daughter but instead found herself caught up in the same emotional tide. The quiet, white-haired woman turned on Joel Pink; wasn't he the man who had besmirched her son's memory by seeing to it that Darren Muise was being sentenced on a reduced charge? "That's our son you're talking about, and he got it worse than all of them!" she shouted at Pink. "That bastard took our boy away, and now he has all the rights!" As the elderly woman was led from the room, one of Neil Burroughs's nephews screamed that he would get Muise at the correctional centre.

Those of us covering the trials were not surprised by the outburst. The constant strain on these families had not let up for a moment, and many had already expressed their dissatisfaction with the justice system. Dry legal arguments did little to ease their pain, and their longing for something—anything—that would mitigate their loss. As the shouting broke out in the crowd, I concentrated on what Gary was recording and took notes on what was happening out of the camera's reach. There would be very little time to edit all this into a report that showed not only the storm of emotion that had surfaced in the courtroom, but also the events preceding the outburst. Like the other reporters who were covering the trial, I tried not to dwell on the pain itself, just focus on what was being said and by whom. The daily grind of compressing hours of testimony and emotional anguish into a two-minute report was difficult enough; there was no time to stop and consider all the implications of the human drama that was unfolding.

Earlier in the day, one of Neil Burroughs's sisters had given me a poem that showed how deeply the victims' relatives were being scarred by their exposure to the court system. The poem was by Al Fagan, the retired steelworker and the father of Jimmy Fagan. I wanted to include it in my report, but I knew that the time constraints of television news would not allow it. Still, the words of the grieving father told the story better than I could, and I read it again, as we raced back to the station, our deadline less than an hour away.

> Three punks came in with a lust to kill,
> The sorrow they brought is with us still.
> Shot in the head, four people were down,
> Slaughtered and crippled by murderous clowns.
>
> In the midst of our sorrow we have to smile,
> Then carry our cross just one more mile.
> There never seems to be an end,
> Good news, they say, is round the bend.
>
> We talk, we grieve, in a continual rage,
> The prosecutor turns another page.
> We sit in silence week after week,
> For we are the parents, we cannot speak.
>
> What will we have when the trial is done,
> To repair the damage from one small gun?
> We sit and we ponder, my wife and myself,
> About what can replace a human life.

Reports of the emotional scene in the court reinforced the decision Sandy and Gail Muise had made to stay away. They were glad their son had admitted his guilt, and they would continue to support him as best they could. But the Muises just weren't able to cope with what he was going through; they couldn't sit there in court and listen to what had to be said.

The second day of the hearing proved to be as emotional as the first. Before opening the session, Justice Kelly told the families of the victims that he understood the feelings that prompted the events of the previous afternoon, but he warned them that it was his job to maintain order in the courtroom. It fell to Brian Williston to read the victim impact statements into the court record. There were two—the first by Anne Marie Fletcher, a sister of Neil Burroughs, and the other by his young widow, Julia. In her three-page letter, Mrs. Fletcher talked about how Neil's death had affected his family, and described the anger and frustration produced by some aspects of the criminal justice system. After he finished reading, Brian Williston took a deep breath as he turned to Julia Burroughs's letter; he had already read it to himself, and he knew it was powerful. Williston had dealt with pain and sorrow for much of his adult life, but for some reason he felt particularly uncomfortable as he lifted the pages from the podium and began to read.

On May 7, 1992 my husband Neil was brutally murdered by Darren Muise. For the past year we have heard about Darren Muise's rights. All rights my husband had were taken away from him that night so violently that it is hard to imagine what he went through in the last moments of his life.

Over the past year I have suffered many lonely and sleepless nights. The nights seem to go on forever after I put our son to bed. Neil was always there for me, and the longing for him to be by my side once again sometimes is unbearable.

I not only lost my husband, but I lost my best friend. Neil was

Darren Muise's lawyer, Joel Pink, and his associate Heather MacKay talk to the author and other reporters during the sentencing hearing for Muise. [Print from ATV video tape.]

*a hard-working, loving family man, who I planned on spending the rest of
my life with.*

*On December 10, 1988, our son Justin was born. I can honestly say it
was the happiest day of our lives. Neil was not only Justin's daddy, but his
buddy. They went everywhere together. Justin was Neil's shadow. Neil would
could home from the back shift and care for Justin while I worked during the
day. He did not want to miss a moment of Justin's life. Neil was there when
Justin said his first word and took his first step, but sadly, over the past year
he missed Justin catching his first fish, skating on his own, and receiving a
trophy at his Kinderbowl banquet. Many nights Justin will cry himself to
sleep, wanting his daddy back.*

Brian Williston's voice wavered as he became choked by emotion.
Many of the relatives of the four victims wept openly but quietly in
the court as they listened to Julia's letter. Their hearts went out to the
fatherless boy and the young mother.

*Justin knows how his father was killed and that he is in heaven. It is
very difficult to explain to a four-year-old what heaven is. He asks questions
like, 'Does Daddy sleep in a bed? Is he hungry? What does he wear?' My
heart breaks, every time he asks one of these questions. Very often Justin has
to be reassured that the "bad men" that killed Daddy are in jail, and the police threw away the key so they cannot get out. I am sure he is afraid they
will hurt or kill us.*

*On June 20 of this year, while most young women with small children
took their husbands out to dinner for Father's Day, Justin and I went to
Neil's grave and placed flowers.*

*Neil's death was so senseless, and when he died part of us died with
him. The pain of losing a loved one to such a violent death will remain with
us forever.*

*Neil's plans and dreams for a long happy life ended at the hands of Dar-
ren Muise....Darren Muise has admitted to murdering Neil, and now it is
time for him to pay for what he did.*

Julia concluded her letter by asking Justice Kelly to impose the maximum sentence—no parole for twenty-five years—and Marc Chisholm
echoed the sentiment as he began his final arguments. He said Muise
committed the crime for the simple pleasure of doing it, and described the eighteen-year-old killer as a self-centred, shallow, spoiled,
and greedy individual, who first told lies, and then tried to create

sympathy for himself. The prosecutor quoted from a presentence report in which Muise told a social worker that he longed to wake up in
a "normal," rich family with "normal" problems. Chisholm pointed
out how loving and supportive Muise's parents were, and questioned
how the young man could claim his problems were in part a product
of the family's financial difficulties—or, as Muise suggested in the report, the result of all the time he spent at the pool hall with what he
described as a less-than-enlightened crowd. Chisholm told the judge
that when Muise cut Neil Burroughs's throat, he committed a crime
that was even more heinous than shooting someone. He ended his
summation by asking the judge to impose the maximum term on a
second-degree murder conviction—life with no parole for twenty-five
years. If Kelly agreed, he would become only the second judge in
Canadian history to impose such a term.

I returned to the station to do a live update on the one o'clock
news. As I quoted from Julia Burroughs's statement, and got to the
part where her son began asking those heartbreaking questions about
his father, I had to stop talking. The camera was a metre away, and
could not pick up the tears in my eyes; and the anchor in Halifax took
the pause as his opportunity to ask me about the issues being debated
in court. It was a good thing that he asked that question, because it allowed me to compose myself. That was the first time in my thirteen
years as a reporter that I had succumbed to emotion while doing my
job. But the image of the innocent child asking if his daddy had a bed
in heaven was simply too powerful. Neil Burroughs was only a few
years younger than me, and we both had young families. From the
moment he was identified as a victim, and I learned he had a child, I
felt a connection to him. I don't think the knowledge influenced my
reporting—at least, not until that news broadcast—but I have to admit that it played on my mind from time to time. It was difficult to
understand how a young man trying to support his family could be
gunned down for no reason. I knew why Justin Burroughs's question
had upset me, but I was angry with myself for letting it happen, and
promised myself to remain focused as I continued to cover the story.

It would not be easy: Gary and I returned to court only to be met
by yet another intensely emotional situation. In the days between the
Wood trial and the Muise sentencing, Arlene MacNeil had been transferred from Halifax to a hospital in Cape Breton, not far from her
home. When we walked back into the courthouse, there was Arlene in
the hallway, sitting in a wheelchair beside her mother. Germaine

MacNeil called me over; we had become friendly during the Wood trial, when I tried to answer her questions about the legal process, and now she wanted me to meet her daughter. In the year since the shootings, I had often looked at the photographs of the four shooting victims—but now I saw a very different Arlene MacNeil. The stunning beauty with the brilliant smile, whose graduation picture I had shown on TV countless times, had been replaced by a disabled and disfigured young woman, her head shorn of the long black curls that gave her such a confident appearance in her school photo. Arlene's speech was laboured and difficult to understand, but that I could make out what she was saying was in itself a miracle. She was alive, and she could speak. I knelt beside her wheelchair and took hold of the hand she offered as she greeted me: "Hi, how are you?"

"I'm fine, Arlene, how are you?" One side of her face was now contorted in a grimace; one eye drifted slightly; and her close-cropped hair was silent testimony to the brain surgery she had undergone. Yet Arlene MacNeil was truly beautiful; she radiated strength and purity, and the innocence of a child. Clinging to my hand, she smiled, looking from her mother to this stranger her mom said she had been watching on TV. Then she released her grip and gave me the thumbs-up signal, which was captured by the cameras—an eloquent image of the courage and determination that kept Arlene fighting to regain

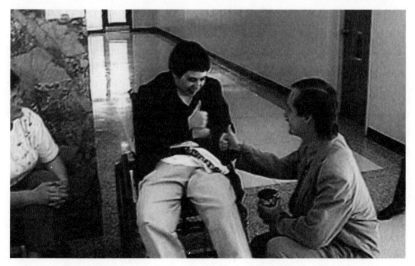

Arlene MacNeil and the author exchange a thumbs-up signal outside the courtroom during the sentencing hearing for Darren Muise. [Print from ATV video tape.]

more of her life each and every day. Seeing Arlene and listening to the painful letter written by Julia Burroughs drove home a powerful message: the victims of this crime were innocent people who had done nothing to deserve the pain that had been brought into their lives.

Arlene was rolled into the courtroom, and when Joel Pink came in and saw her, his expression changed from a cheerful grin to a look of concern; he turned and left the room. Was he going to ask that Arlene MacNeil be removed from the courtroom? It is highly unlikely that he would even have contemplated making such a request, but it is almost certain that he prepared his client for her presence. Since the courtroom door was being kept open because of the heat and humidity, I asked Gary to record the procession of officers leading Muise to his seat, and to include Arlene in the shot. Her wheelchair was placed near the door between the camera and the seat Muise would occupy, and I wanted to know how he would react to seeing her. But it never happened. Darren Muise, who had been walking so tall, and staring out into the gallery each time he entered the courtroom, now lowered his head as he followed the deputies to the prisoner's bench. He did not see Arlene MacNeil, and shortly afterwards her mother rolled her back to the hallway, where her father was waiting to take her back to the hospital.

Like the prosecutor, Joel Pink had to ignore the emotions in the room in order to do his job effectively. And he did, painting a picture of his client that sharply contrasted with the image created by Marc Chisholm. Even their physical impact was a contrast—the tall, slender prosecutor and the short, stocky defence attorney, leaning forward slightly, his left hand against his hip. Pink's right hand was always moving, as he picked up a piece of paper from the table in front of him and stabbed the air with it for emphasis, then dropped the page back on the table and ran his hand over his bald head, exaggerating the deep-set lines in his brow. Muise's lawyer pointed to his client's youth, and the likelihood that he could turn himself around; he insisted Muise had intended to rob, not to kill; he even downplayed the knife wound, telling the judge his client had only inflicted slight cuts on the side of the victim's neck. Pink drew no sympathy from the gallery when he told the judge how his client had cried during sessions with a forensic psychiatrist at the correctional centre in Halifax; nor when he informed the court that as Darren Muise sat in a courtroom, his former girlfriend was preparing for her graduation prom. The relatives of the victim were shocked to hear the lawyer list case after case of brutal murders for which criminals had received jail terms of life with parole after twelve or fifteen years. Could the courts be that lenient? By the time the defence lawyer had finished, many in the courtroom were sure that Muise would get a parole eligibility term ranging from ten to fifteen years—nowhere near the maximum. And this despite the Crown's convincing arguments that each case must be judged on merit, that Darren Muise must be sentenced for what he did.

With the legal arguments complete, Justice Kelly asked Darren Muise if he had anything to say on his own behalf. Unlike Wood, he did: Muise had stayed awake in his cell the night before, writing a letter expressing his feelings, and even practising it on the guard. Now he had his chance to tell the court how he felt. Members of the victims' families leaned forward to listen, as the clean-cut young man stood to speak. Muise faced Justice Kelly, but his words were for those seated behind him in the court. His voice did not quaver, and while he sounded rehearsed, he also sounded as though he meant what he was saying: "I would like to express sympathy to Julia and Justin Burroughs…I pray the hurt may subside. I know nothing I say or do can make that happen. I accept responsibility for what I did and understand your hatred. I am not a callous murderer and not without conscience. I have made a grave mistake and I will pay. I wish I could take his place. I did not want anyone to get hurt." Although he was not being sentenced for the shootings of the three other victims, Muise also spoke to their families, but without implicating himself. "What they did was wrong," he said. "I pray for Arlene and offer sympathy to the others. I would like to say I'm sorry to my family and friends. I am not the person painted to you by the Crown. I have cried not because of my predicament, but for the sorrow I have caused."

Muise's comments marked the end of the hearing. Justice Kelly needed time to make his decision, but he didn't want to make things harder on anyone by delaying the sentencing, so he took the unusual step of scheduling a court session for Saturday morning. That way he could spend the night writing out the reasons for his decision, but not put the families of the victims through a weekend of wondering and second-guessing. Julia Burroughs stopped me as I walked out of the courthouse. "What did you think of that?" she asked.

"Of what he had to say?"

"Yes, do you think the judge will believe that?"

"Did you?"

"No, it was nothing but bullshit. He's just trying to make himself look good."

"I guess I can say you don't accept his apology?" Julia stepped a little closer, putting her hand on my arm and lowering her voice to a conspiratorial tone. "If you want to make me happy, you can say he's a bullshitter and a bastard. Just don't say I said it."

"I'll paraphrase that. See you in the morning." At the close of my report that night, I told the audience that the widow of Neil Burroughs did not accept the apology offered by Darren Muise, and that she considered it contrived and self-serving. Julia later said she appreciated the diplomatic translation.

Saturday, June 26, was a sunny, warm day, but the weather did nothing to reduce the stress that Julia and the other relatives were feeling as they entered the Cape Breton County Courthouse yet again. Nor did the mood improve when they were greeted by yet another display of intense courtroom security. The outburst two days before had convinced court officers that emotions at this hearing were running a little too high and that extreme measures would be needed at the moment of sentencing. The sheriff's deputies had become friendly with many of the victims' relatives over the past weeks, and these officers were quite aware that many of the relatives were still angry about Muise's deal. If he also was given a light parole-eligibility term, this would likely bring on another outcry, perhaps even a physical confrontation. Gary and I stood chatting with guards downstairs at the prisoners entrance, waiting for the van from the correctional centre. The guards were speculating on what term the judge might impose, and they hoped it would be a long one; they did not want to have to restrain anyone.

As Justice Kelly took his seat, a deputy stood near the bench; two others sat with Darren Muise; and eight officers, mostly RCMP, lined the front row of the public gallery. Meanwhile, Sydney police were in place outside the court to ensure that the prisoner would leave without incident. These measures annoyed the law-abiding citizens who were there to hear the sentencing of the criminal who had deeply affected their lives. "What are they expecting, some kind of attack?" Al Fagan asked, pointing out the extra precautions. "This is ridiculous." The victims' relatives knew the security was in place to keep them away from Muise, and it made them feel dirty—they felt they were being treated as though they were a danger to society, although they had done nothing to break the law. The tension in the courtroom was high as the judge began to read his decision. Like most judges, Justice Kelly took a fair amount of time to outline the factors influencing his

decision. Many in the court fid-
geted and shifted in the uncomfortable wooden chairs as
they tried to see where the
judge was headed with his dis-
sertation. At times, the victims'
relatives would stare at each
other in disbelief as the judge
appeared to be leaning towards
a light sentence. At one point,
he described Muise as "an undi-
rected teen hanging out at a
pool hall, playing games. [It
was] an aimless, pointless existence, but not a problem to the
community. His actions were
out of character." Then, the relatives would see a glimmer of
hope: "His actions before dur-
ing and after the crime show a high degree of criminality."

Darren Muise, looking clean-cut in a fashion-
able suit, arrives in court to face his sentencing. [Print from ATV video tape.]

Justice Kelly made it clear he did not accept the statement Muise
made in his confession—that he had cut Neil Burroughs's throat to
help him by causing a quick death. Instead the judge called the action
"a cold, calculated, extremely brutal act, exposing a personality without conscience, or out of touch—either way a danger to society." The
judge pointed to the moment when Derek Wood shot Arlene Mac-
Neil, saying that Muise could have tried to stop Wood; or he could
have helped Donna Warren escape when Wood ran upstairs. He said
Muise expected violence and was prepared to use it when he entered
the restaurant. But then, Justice Kelly outlined the legal factors he had
to consider, and Neil Burroughs's relatives began to despair again. The
judge said he found only one case of second-degree murder that carried a parole eligibility restriction of more than twenty years, and that
restrictions of more than seventeen years involved criminals with extensive histories of recidivism.

By the time the judge neared the end of his prepared statement,
sixteen court- and police officers had filed into the room. Justice Kelly told Darren Muise to stand, and ordered him to be held in prison
for life, without parole eligibility for twenty years. Muise was led away
as the victims' relatives crowded into the hallway, tired and a little

baffled. They had wanted a twenty-five year term but were left feeling grateful for the twenty-year sentence. There was none of the spontaneous joy that had erupted when the verdicts were read in the Wood trial, but there was a similar display of anger; a few people gathered outside to yell at Muise as he was led to the waiting prison van. Among them was Julia Burroughs, who shouted "Bastard!" as the vehicle pulled away from the court. She wanted to do more, say more, but she felt helpless. And the van was gone.

Fifteen

AS DARREN MUISE was on his way to prison that sunny Saturday afternoon, the victims' relatives gathered in the courthouse parking lot to discuss the final court case. They would all be coming back in September to attend the trial of Freeman MacNeil, and they hoped no deals would be made in the weeks ahead to allow MacNeil to avoid a first-degree murder conviction. That didn't happen, but something almost as frustrating did. At the conclusion of the Wood and Muise trials, and in the wake of the intense publicity that surrounded them, MacNeil's lawyer, Kevin Coady, applied for a change of venue. Ken Haley told me privately that he thought the application would probably succeed. When William Kelly agreed to hear the Muise case with no jury, he pretty much tied the hands of Justice David Gruchey, who would preside over the MacNeil trial. It would be tough for the new judge to say that MacNeil could find an impartial jury in Cape Breton after Justice Kelly had found that Muise probably could not have. In fact, Gruchey did order the change of venue: MacNeil's trial would be held in Halifax. This outraged the MacNeil, Warren, Burroughs, and Fagan families. Why should they have to leave home for weeks in order to see justice done for their loved ones? A few philanthropic Nova Scotia corporations agreed, and offers of free accommodations and air fare were soon made; the provincial attorney-general's department also gave some assistance by coordinating a program designed to make the change of venue easier on the families from Cape Breton.

For me, Justice Gruchey's decision proved to be an ironic coincidence. After the Muise trial, I was asked by the network to accept a new posting in Halifax, and although that meant I would not be covering the McDonald's story, I accepted the transfer. In August, my wife and I were driving along a highway outside Halifax, on a house-hunting expedition, when a radio newscast reported the change of venue in MacNeil's forthcoming trial. I looked at my wife and smiled as the announcer said that the trial would begin September 8—the same day I was to begin working in the Halifax newsroom.

The building that houses Halifax County and Supreme Court is located on Upper Water Street, in the heart of the city. Courtrooms, judges' chambers, and associated offices occupy much of the large building, and the business of justice keeps the place buzzing year-round. To facilitate security for the MacNeil trial, it was scheduled for Courtroom Three, which has a side door leading to a hallway away

Kevin Coady and his colleague Marguerite MacNeil work on their arguments in favour of having Freeman MacNeil's trial moved to Halifax. They won that battle. [Print from ATV video tape.]

from the public area, enabling sheriff's officers to move a prisoner in and out of the room without interference. On the first day of his trial, MacNeil arrived in a prison van, which passed through the underground parking garage to a second, more secure, garage beyond a large motorized door—and that door was lowered before MacNeil was taken from the van to the holding area. Since there was no camera access to him in this building, we would use tapes recorded during MacNeil's court appearances in Sydney, the best of which came from the hearing for his change of venue—he was led directly in front of the television cameras and into a makeshift courtroom that was being used while the provincial government decided what to do about air-quality problems in the old Sydney courthouse. MacNeil looked right into the cameras that day, and the ATV editors used slow-motion and freeze-frame technology to capture the moment when his eyes met those of the viewer. This was the image we used throughout the trial.

The jury-selection process that began MacNeil's trial was similar to the one for the Wood trial, although there were fewer potential jurors. By the second day, six men and six women had been selected to hear the case; but their job would not start until after the *voir dire* hearing into the admissibility of MacNeil's statements to police. This time, the prosecutors were much more confident of victory. Brian Williston, who was prosecuting the case, had thought of little else over the summer; in fact, he took the bulging MacNeil file along with him on what was supposed to be a family vacation, in Prince Edward Island. One day he even hauled the file to the bank of pay phones near the paddle-boat pond at Rainbow Valley tourist park; while his wife and children enjoyed the park's many attraction, Williston spent more than two hours on the telephone to Ken Haley back in Sydney. He was more than ready for this hearing, and he was gratified to see Al and Theresa Fagan seated in the courtroom; more than in any murder case he had ever handled, Williston felt a strong sense of connection to the victims in this case.

The other victims' relatives were back in Cape Breton waiting for the scheduled start of testimony on September 21, but the Fagans had decided they would not miss a moment of the trial. Freeman MacNeil had confessed to shooting their boy, and these proceedings would determine if that confession could be used in the trial. They had to be there.

For the first day of the hearing, MacNeil wore a conservative grey suit, white shirt, and dark tie; his glasses and clean-cut appearance,

Freeman MacNeil fixes the camera with an icy stare as he enters the courtroom for his change-of-venue hearing. The image was used by ATV throughout his trial. [Print from ATV video tape.]

and the way he talked with his lawyer—confidently, but with respect —suggested a university student on his first job interview, not a killer on trial. MacNeil's lawyer, Kevin Coady, sat near his client, his greying hair and thick moustache adding to his look of concern. Although the victims' families saw him as just another Halifax lawyer, Coady was in fact a Cape Bretoner. He had grown up in the Margaree Valley, one of Cape Breton's most-scenic communities, but not one that required the talents of a trial attorney on a regular basis. Coady could make a better living working in the Nova Scotia capital, where he now prepared to fight one of the toughest battles of his career.

As the police officers sat in the hallway waiting to be called as witnesses, Kevin Cleary and I discussed how he and the others were feeling as the officers' actions were being picked apart inside the court. They just wondered, he said, why no-one seemed to worry about a policeman's state of mind during an interrogation. That weekend in May 1992, officers spent hours locked in the interrogation rooms to debate and plead with Wood, Muise, and MacNeil, only to give up in utter frustration as their colleagues watched and hoped for success. They always left the interview room to vent their anger; some kicked over garbage cans, pounded desks, cried, and literally banged their heads against walls as they tried to understand the casual attitude the young suspects were displaying. No, the agony and frustration of the police, whose job it was to get the

From left, Ken Haley, Marc Chisholm, and Brian WIlliston at the Halifax courthouse during the trial of Freeman MacNeil. [Print from ATV video tape.]

256

much-needed confessions, was not an issue. But how much food or sleep a suspect had was critically important.

Brian Williston ran a hand through his thick, greying hair. Usually given to bright smiles and a polite but friendly tone, he was all business now, as he led the police witnesses through their dealings with MacNeil. He elicited every comment made by the officers or the accused, and finished every examination with the question: "Did you threaten Mr. MacNeil, or make any promises or inducements to him during the time you questioned him?" Each officer answered the question with a confident "No." For his part, Kevin Coady attempted to outline his client's state of mind before he confessed. Constable Rod Gillis admitted that he challenged MacNeil to come over the table and attack him, and that he called him a coward who "could walk under a snake with a top hat on." But unlike the frustrated outburst from the imposing Brian Stoyek, which had been of such concern to the Crown in the Muise case, Gillis's behaviour was less of an issue. It was clear to Justice Gruchey that Freeman MacNeil was bigger than either Gillis or his partner, Wayne MacDonald, and both officers testified that the remarks were not made in a threatening manner but were simply an expression of exasperation. What's more, the officers told MacNeil immediately afterward that they were through with him, and returned him to his cell. Pat Murphy also helped the Crown's case by presenting his detailed notes of MacNeil's May 16 confession, explaining that he left the room to get some water and found MacNeil's lawyer waiting in the hall. That MacNeil's lawyer conferred privately with him before the young man gave his second statement made it clear to the judge that MacNeil was well aware of his rights when he confessed.

To combat the convincing evidence of the police witnesses, Kevin Coady called his client to the stand. It was the only way he could hope to show the judge how MacNeil felt while confessing. Much to the disappointment of Al and Theresa Fagan, he wasn't asked about the murders; the issue was the admissibility of his statements. As he took the stand, Freeman MacNeil was the very image of a confident, intelligent, and likeable young man. He had changed from his suit to a grey herringbone blazer and pants, a white shirt, and black leather tie, and he had removed his glasses; the "university student" who had first appeared in the prisoner's bench now looked very much like another police witness.

MacNeil began with the events surrounding his lie-detector test at the North Sydney RCMP detachment. He tried to argue that he cooperated with police because he thought he had to—a point the judge did not accept after learning that MacNeil had been a security guard and even carried a card bearing the standard police warning and Charter of Rights advisory. Well, MacNeil said, maybe he just felt he would be seen in a negative light by police if he refused to take the test. Then he described his feelings after he was told he had failed the polygraph. "I thought I would be leaving after the test...I was tired and upset and wanted to go home. When Phil Scharf told me I failed, it had an impact on me. I became nervous, upset, and anxious about leaving. Sergeant Scharf moved closer to me and started asking more direct questions....His tone changed, and his facial expressions were different. I felt I could not leave; he was blocking the door."

When Scharf suggested MacNeil was involved, he said he agreed because he thought he would then be able to go home—one of many times during his testimony that the young man would imply that police were making a promise or inducement. Another point of contention was the recording of his discussions with police. MacNeil said he thought the second interview room was video- and audio-taped, as the polygraph suite had been; Sergeant Scharf said all his comments would be recorded, but no-one told him that ended when he left the polygraph suite. Then there was the matter of the written statement he gave the officers—not a transcript, he said, but a summary of his answers to their questions. MacNeil claimed it was at this point that he began to worry about his family, and that his fear arose from something his co-accused had said to him earlier. He did not elaborate on what that statement was. But Phil Scharf made it worse by saying that the other two were on the street and probably going after his family at that moment. And they kept on questioning him and questioning him: "I was tired, hungry, and anxious to leave. I was upset. They were telling me all day I could leave, and when it was time to leave, they said they had more questions." What MacNeil failed to grasp was that *he* was the reason for the prolonged interrogation; every time he changed his story, he forced police to reassess his most-recent claims and deal with any contradictions.

Then, MacNeil said, he felt betrayed by police when "they indicated they would take me for a drive on the way home," then told him he could not go home after all, but had to remain in custody because some RCMP higher-up had overruled the officers he was with. The "drive on the way home" was to enable police to observe the route he took to drive Muise away from the scene of the crime. Mac-

Neil apparently did not see the irony in his claim that police betrayed him, after he himself had betrayed Derek Wood and Darren Muise during his re-enactment of the drive with Darren Muise after the crime. Throughout the testimony, MacNeil appeared rehearsed. His answers were detailed and contained all the information calculated to convince the judge that he was cooperating with police because he had been promised a reward for doing so—the reward being his release. His only sign of nervousness was his rush to get through his long and detailed answers, as if he wanted to be through with his testimony and get back to the relative safety of his seat. Kevin Coady carefully guided his client through the police interrogation, to the moment when he confessed to Kevin Cleary and Pat Murphy. MacNeil explained that he learned after talking with his lawyer that he did not have to answer police questions, but began to lose his resolve when Pat Murphy became emotional as he read the charges and told the story of his daughter's death. "They said it would be best for me in court if I told my version," he said. "My mother would know I told the truth. This began to affect my decision to remain silent. I was emotionally upset. I was getting tearful and trying to avoid them as best I could. Cleary said 'Don't bottle yourself up.'

"Once the crying started, it is not clear after that. I remember up to when they said I cried, but not much after that. I have no recollection of what I told them after that. My recall is gone after they said I entered the restaurant with the stick. I cannot say why I answered the questions. I had no intention of talking to them."

When MacNeil had finished his testimony, Ken Haley stood to cross-examine him. As in the first two trials, the lawyers had decided to share the work in the MacNeil case, and while Brian Williston was the lead prosecutor, Ken Haley had agreed to conduct this cross-examination. His witness, the prosecutor soon discovered, knew very well how to respond to questions. As Haley tried to provoke MacNeil by pointing out the inconsistencies in his statements, he neither confirmed or denied the contents of the statements, simply agreeing that they existed. Haley was powerless as long as MacNeil continued to agree with everything he said; still, both men made it clear that a confrontation could come at any moment. Haley's voice was higher than usual, his tone angry and condescending. MacNeil got a stern look on his face and leaned forward slightly in the witness chair, his arms resting on the arms of the chair, his hands gripping the ends of the armrests. Justice Gruchey stopped Haley as he continued to work around the inconsistencies in MacNeil's statements, showing how they gradually implicated Muise and Wood and drew suspicion away from MacNeil. His questions, the judge said, were irrelevant to the issue of admissibility. But, Gruchey added, if it was Haley's intention to show that MacNeil was blaming others for the murders, this was already abundantly clear. Finally, realizing that the cross-examination would bear no fruit, Ken Haley said he had no further questions. The only opportunity the Crown had to question any of the three killers had been a non-event. But the frustration evaporated when Justice Gruchey ruled in favour of the Crown, saying he was convinced that Freeman MacNeil knew what he was doing when he confesses to shooting Jimmy Fagan. The trial could now begin.

MacNeil pleaded not guilty to the first-degree murders of Neil Burroughs and Jimmy Fagan, to the unlawful confinement of Donna Warren, and to the robbery. Brian Williston would call thirty-five witnesses as he attempted to prove his case. As in the Wood case, the jurors were led slowly through the events of May 7, 1992, then found out how police first met Freeman MacNeil, and how his role gradually changed from witness to suspect. MacNeil's friends testified about his spending spree in the days after the murders, and about his apparently normal behaviour—the only contradictory evidence coming from Greg Lawrence's girlfriend, who said he seemed pale and "spooky" the day he visited their apartment. As the witnesses gave their impressions of MacNeil's behaviour, Kevin Coady questioned them about how long, and how well, they knew him before the crime. Coady had already planned the defence he would present, and the testimony about MacNeil's behaviour after the crime would be critically important.

As the trial continued, some of the victims' relatives began to tire of the constant exposure to television cameras and reporters. There were private rooms set up for them in the courthouse, but they still had to enter the courtroom and subject themselves to searches by sheriff's deputies, standing with their arms outstretched as metal detectors were moved around their bodies. To the families, it was an insult to be shown on TV every day as dangerous people who had to be searched for weapons. At the end of a particularly emotional day of testimony, Justice Gruchey addressed their concerns. I was seated directly behind Freeman MacNeil during the trial, and the judge fixed his gaze on me as he asked the media to show some humanity in dealing with this case, then looked towards the families and apologized that he could not force the cameras to leave them alone. He asked them to let him know if there were any further problems, though, implying that he might restrict the access camera crews had in the court building.

It wasn't the first time Justice Gruchey had talked to me about what I should and should not record in and around a court. We had met months before, during the sexual-assault trial of a Roman Catholic priest. The tall, heavy-set judge became very upset when he arrived at a rural courthouse to find a TV camera waiting in the parking lot. He ordered the young cameraman to turn the camera off, then told the sheriff to bring me to his chambers, where he informed me in no uncertain terms that in his opinion, Supreme Court judges should not be highly visible. He enjoyed his private life, he said, and did not want to be recognized when he was out shopping with his wife or doing anything unrelated to his job. I didn't agree, but there was no point making an enemy of the man over such a small point. The shot of the judge arriving in his car was not that important; besides, Gruchey himself agreed to allow the camera inside the building before the jury arrived, so I could have a few shots of the old courtroom. But this time, I knew that I could not and would not agree to stop recording the proceedings outside Courtroom Three—not that I wanted to push him to the point where he would order cameras out of the building, of course. I soon found out, however, that even the victims' relatives were not in agreement on the issue. Neil Burroughs's father, for example, was very angry about the daily searches, but told me he had no problem with the cameras; it was not our fault he was being searched. One of Jimmy Fagan's brothers felt his parents should not be shown while being searched, but Al Fagan said he was not worried about it. And some actively wanted the cameras present—Cathy Sellars and her brother Joey Burroughs approached me after the comments by the judge to say they wanted people to see how they were being treated by the justice system.

This was not the only point of disagreement among the relatives. Another incident of friction arose when one of Neil Burroughs's sisters called out to Greg Lawrence as he was led from the courtroom after his testimony. Concerned for Lawrence's safety, the RCMP took Francine Fortune to a back room and kept her there until Lawrence was safely away from the court building. This infuriated the Burroughs family. They could not believe that the diminutive Francine was being detained, while the man who knew in advance that the Mc-

Donald's robbery would occur was being protected. As I walked out of the courtroom that day, I was confronted by several angry members of the family—most notably Francine herself. "Where the hell were you?" she demanded. "You're out here every day with that camera, taking pictures of us. Why weren't you chasing after him and asking him why he didn't call the police?" Her father was also upset: "God-damn it, they shouldn't treat us like this! Why can't you show how they're treating us?" It was pointless to explain that I had no idea a confrontation was occurring outside, because I had been talking with the prosecutors. All I could do was stand and listen as they vented their frustrations. Finally, as they left for lunch, I asked Joey and Brian Burroughs to return in an hour and talk on camera about what had happened. I glanced over at the cameraman assigned to work with me for the day and wondered why he had missed all the activity in the hall. Meanwhile, members of the Fagan family were also upset about the confrontation—but for entirely different reasons. They were afraid the outburst might have an impact on the trial and somehow allow Jimmy's killer to go free. The clash of opinions led to cross words between members of the two families that demonstrated the pressure the victims' relatives were under. Even within the Burroughs family, the incident caused acrimony; Neil Burroughs's widow did not care for the public outbursts of some of her in-laws. It seemed the strain of the trial and the isolation of life away from home was driving people apart—people who had once hugged each other and cried together as though they belonged to the same family.

Later in the trial, I had an entirely different kind of experience with the Burroughs family. Cathy Sellars, who had stayed in court during Derek Wood's trial to see the crime-scene video, found herself recalling that haunting image as the pathologist detailed the wounds her brother Neil had suffered. She felt her whole body weaken, and she rushed towards the exit, where she collapsed. Brian Burroughs lifted his sister in his arms and ran out of the courtroom, not at all certain where he was going. The ATV camera recorded the panicked Brian carrying Cathy, her arms and legs dangling at his side, and I used the shot in that evening's wrap on the trial. Later, as I walked to my car, I remembered the judge's lecture. Maybe he was right; maybe I had no sense of human decency. I could have filed a report without showing the tape of the unconscious Cathy Sellars, but I used it anyway. The image powerfully demonstrated the emotional turmoil these families were undergoing, but now I wondered if it would only serve to heighten their anguish. It was too late to change my mind—the report had already been aired—and I knew I would have to face Cathy and Brian in the morning. I had developed a pretty good relationship with them, but the lambasting I had taken a few days earlier made it clear that they would feel free to tear a strip off me if they were upset about the report.

The following morning, as I arrived at court, I saw Brian and Joey Burroughs standing outside, talking with Ernie Sellars, Cathy's husband. Well, here it comes, I thought, as Joey approached. "Look, we just want to thank you for last night," he said. It was not the greeting I had been expecting. "It's about time people saw what this trial is doing to us," Joey continued. "We gotta sit here and listen to this bullshit every day, while he sits there with his lawyer, making sure his rights are protected. Nobody gives a damn about our rights."

I turned to Ernie Sellars: "How'd Cathy feel about seeing it?"

"She thinks it was good, too. But she was happy you couldn't see her face."

I thanked them and hurried into the court building, wondering why I had been so worried. My instincts had been correct: the shot showed what the families were going through. But once again, I was concerned about getting too close to the people involved in this story. Many of them were beginning to treat me like a close family friend; Olive Warren had even invited me to sit in the section of the courtroom reserved for the families; she felt I belonged there. I knew it was important to develop a relationship with them in order to tell their story effectively—and this was definitely their story, not just an account of perpetrators and deceased victims. Their presence in court every day had given this trial an entirely different dynamic; most murder trials are dry, routine events, with legal issues argued by robed attorneys in front of jurors who do not know the people involved. But the McDonald's trials brought home to everyone involved that the victims were real people, who were loved and missed, and that no amount of legal debate could ease the pain felt by those left behind.

Still, the challenge was to remember that although the victims' relatives were an important part of the story, my responsibility was to cover the court cases in a balanced way. I made a point of interviewing Kevin Coady regularly and asking how MacNeil was handling the pressure. And I tried to show in my reports that MacNeil's mother was as distraught as the relatives of the victims. This was hard to accomplish, because Mrs. MacNeil tended to avoid our camera, spending most of her time in a private room, where she stayed until the court was called to order. There wasn't even much of a photo opportunity when she entered the courtroom; she was not stopped and searched at the door, because court officers logically assumed the accused's mother was not about to do him any harm. When we finally managed to record a shot of Freeman's mother and sister entering the court, it was really too brief a moment to portray much of the emotion she must have been feeling. MacNeil himself was holding up well, according to his lawyer. Coady said he was amazed at the character of the young man and his ability to deal with the trial and what it meant to his future.

Late on Thursday, September 30, Brian Williston wrapped up his case with the testimony of Kevin Cleary. The defence case began the following Monday, and it quickly became clear why Coady had asked all those questions about his client's state of mind after the crime. He hoped to convince the jury that Freeman MacNeil could not have intended to kill Neil Burroughs or James Fagan, because he was suffering from post-traumatic stress syndrome. First diagnosed in soldiers after battle, this condition can cause mental numbness and shock in a person exposed to a cataclysmic experience—extreme violence, for example, or a serious car accident. The symptoms apparently become more extreme when the sufferer is not in control of what is happening. Post-traumatic stress syndrome has been used successfully in a number of court cases as an argument for diminished capacity—a reduction in one's ability to think about an action while it is being carried out. If proved, it makes for a solid argument against a murder conviction, because to commit murder a person must form the intent to kill or to inflict severe injury that is likely to kill.

To prove his theory, Coady called Ottawa-based forensic psychiatrist Dr. John Bradford, who had visited Freeman MacNeil at the Cape Breton County Correctional Centre on August 13 and interviewed him for three to four hours. Dr. Bradford said he examined MacNeil's family background to see if he exhibited any early signs of mental illness, and although there were no such indications, he pointed out that MacNeil's father had committed suicide by shooting himself, which the psychiatrist considered significant. Dr. Bradford had been called as an expert witness in many trials, and he testified in a clear and confident tone, and made every effort to explain post-traumatic stress syndrome in an understandable way. It was his opinion that MacNeil suffered from symptoms of this condition, including vivid dreams and flashbacks related to the killings. In particular, he had told the doctor about a recurring image of Neil Burroughs after he was stabbed by Darren Muise. Apparently, the condition set in immediately after Derek Wood shot Arlene MacNeil, an act MacNeil had no control over. During his interview with the psychiatrist, MacNeil described feeling numb and confused after Arlene was shot, adding that he felt emotionally numb when he hit Neil Burroughs with the shovel handle. The doctor concluded MacNeil did not have a normal, functioning mind when he hit Burroughs or when he shot James Fagan.

Brian Williston listened attentively, taking extensive notes, then launched into a lengthy cross-examination focused on the fact that the psychiatrist had based his diagnosis on what the suspect told him; in other words, if Freeman MacNeil lied to him, the diagnosis was faulty. Couldn't the doctor have conducted tests to determine the accuracy of MacNeil's claims? Apparently so, but those tests were not administered. And Dr. Bradford had to concede that it would have been helpful for him to see the video-taped re-enactment MacNeil had conducted for police on May 15, 1992, to see how the young man had behaved at that time. As far as the victims' families could see, Williston had successively discredited the doctor's testimony. But Williston was not so confident; he intended to call psychiatric evidence on his own, on rebuttal, but first he had to wait for the defence to finish its case.

The only other defence witnesses were the mother and sister of Freeman MacNeil's girlfriend. They testified about seeing the silver gun—the gun used in the murders—and showing it to a girl who was dating Derek Wood. Margaret Chiasson said she found the gun in her husband's dresser and thought it was pretty, so she showed it to her daughter and Wood's girlfriend. That incident occurred some time before the robbery and raised the possibility that Wood might have taken the gun. If the jury would not accept the post-traumatic stress theory, they might believe MacNeil didn't know that Derek Wood had the gun that night. On cross-examination, Mrs. Chiasson said that Freeman MacNeil slept at her home on the night of the murders and that he was surprised when she woke him and told him about radio reports of the shootings. She smiled at MacNeil as she left the witness stand.

With the defence case concluded, Marc Chisholm called Dr. Syed Akhtar, the psychiatrist in charge of the Nova Scotia Hospital's forensic services unit. The prosecuting team had had a bit of a debate over

calling the psychiatrist to the stand. Haley believed Williston had successfully discredited Dr. Bradford's evidence, and wondered if the rebuttal might give jurors the impression that the doctor's evidence was
so important that it required countering. But the prosecutors finally
agreed that a second opinion was just what the jury needed. He was
right. The small, fragile-looking Dr. Akhtar not only criticized Dr.
Bradford's methods, but also strongly disagreed with the other psychiatrist's findings. Dr. Bradford should have done much more than
interview Freeman MacNeil if he wanted to make a proper assessment
of the young man's condition during the crime, he said, then went on
to mention factors which, he felt, pointed away from a finding of
post-traumatic stress; the detail of the confession, for example, and
MacNeil's actions after the crime.

In his cross-examination, Kevin Coady only succeeded in further
discrediting his own star witness and getting himself in a tangle. He
tried to persuade Dr. Akhtar to admit that, had he examined Freeman
MacNeil, he might have come to the same conclusion as Dr. Bradford.
Much to the displeasure of Justice Gruchey, the witness pointed out
that he had wanted to talk to MacNeil, but that Coady would not allow it. Coady then tried to set up a hypothetical scenario for the doctor—let's say he talked to MacNeil, and was given the same answers,
and was convinced MacNeil was being truthful. Could he have come
to the same conclusions? But Dr. Akhtar knocked that theory on the
floor. "It's highly unlikely I would come to the same conclusion that
Dr. Bradford did," he said. "I don't agree with his diagnosis. It must be
post-traumatic. You need time to develop this syndrome. At the time
of the crime, he would not have had it. He may have it now, but not
then." Brian Williston smiled as his final witness stepped down. At
4:20 p.m. on October 4, 1993, the last of the evidence in the three Mc-
Donald's murder trials was in. All that remained was for the jury to
hear arguments from the lawyers and the charge from Justice Gruchey.
They were told to get a good night's sleep and return in the morning.

In his closing arguments, Kevin Coady told the jury that things
were not always what they seemed to be. Members of the victims'
families cringed when he described the murders as a robbery gone
bad, a characterization they were tired of hearing. The defence attorney went on to point the finger of blame at Derek Wood: "It happened because Derek went nuts," he said. "Derek Wood was the
author of the carnage that took place inside that restaurant, [and
there was] no question Darren also caused injury to Burroughs."

Coady struggled to ignore the muffled reactions of the victims' relatives as he tried to downplay the role his client played in the murders, in particular the murder of Neil Burroughs. "Wood or Muise caused his death. The only thing he did was hit him with a stick. The stick did not kill Mr. Burroughs, [and it is] questionable if this hit would even knock him out. The responsibility for Burroughs's death lies with Muise and Wood." And he asked the jurors to consider Freeman MacNeil's state of mind at the time of the murders, to think about what Dr. Bradford had to say. "What made Mr. MacNeil shoot Mr. Fagan? He had not become involved in the shootings to that point. He was not able to resist the orders of the other two. He was not of an operating mind at the time." Kevin Coady finished his difficult task in thirty-seven minutes, his quiet, sombre tone perhaps disguising the anxiety he was experiencing, aware as he was that his job was to properly represent his client, but equally aware that he was the subject of the intense dislike of some of the people sitting behind him.

Brian Williston began his final remarks after the lunch break. Unlike his opponent, he had the benefit of knowing that most of the people in the room were silently cheering him on. Most, but not all: Freeman MacNeil's mother and sister sat at the side of the courtroom, farthest from the victims' relatives. The MacNeils had attended the entire trial, and now they listened quietly as Brian Williston told the jury what he believed was the impulse that led to the murders—"the thirst for money." The prosecutor went on to explore the reason for Neil Burroughs's murder, emphasizing that the blow with shovel handle was a major contributing factor in his death. "Why did he hit Neil Burroughs with the shovel handle? To assist his partners in ending the life of this man who was alive and could identify him. He was already shot and cut—then struck with the stick. This blow contributed by keeping him down and less able to resist his attackers." Williston told the jury that Freeman MacNeil killed, and watched his friends kill, but it did not play on his conscience. "Don't let him fool you. You will know the truth."

The summation took just under an hour. Afterwards, Justice Gruchey told the jurors to return the following morning—with overnight bags, in case they found themselves deliberating for more than one day. As Justice Gordon Tiddman had done in the Wood trial, Justice Gruchey began his charge the next morning by asking the jury to put aside the natural emotions stemming from this brutal crime, and to disregard the public outcry that had followed the mur-

ders. In order to find MacNeil guilty of the first-degree murder of Burroughs, he said, they would probably have to accept that the murder
had occurred during the unlawful confinement of Donna Warren,
and that MacNeil was a party to that confinement. And to find him
guilty of the first-degree murder of James Fagan, they would have to
find that the unlawful confinement was part of one continuous criminal activity—although Donna was already dead when MacNeil shot
Fagan—or that MacNeil deliberately planned to kill Fagan to eliminate him as a witness.

While the jury was sequestered, the relatives gathered in groups
and talked about the case—and anything else they could think of to
keep their minds off the slowly ticking clock. For Julia Burroughs,
spending time in Halifax for the trial meant she had to be away from
her son; she missed Justin a great deal, and knew from talking to him
on the phone that he was more than anxious for his mom to return.
But there would be no verdict that day. The jurors were taken to a hotel, and the relatives left.

Ken Haley would not be back to hear this final verdict in the Mc-
Donald's case. Early the following morning, before deliberations resumed, Haley received a call from home. His father had succumbed
after his long battle with cancer—perhaps, his son thought, he waited
until the prosecutors had finished their work and the case was in the
hands of the jury.

By about five o'clock that evening, it seemed a verdict was forthcoming. The jury asked for a little more time when the judge offered
to send them back to the hotel for the night, but half an hour later
they sent out a note, saying they had better sleep on it again. On the
morning of October 8, the large public foyer outside the courtroom
once again filled with reporters, camera operators, police officers,
sheriff's deputies, and the anxious relatives of the McDonald's victims. This time, Brian Williston joined those gathered in the common
area; he too was beginning to wonder what was keeping the jury. At
one point, Germaine MacNeil went into the room where Freeman
MacNeil's mother sat waiting with her daughter, and asked the other
Mrs. MacNeil to come and see her daughter—to see what "they" had
done to Arlene. Germaine was red-faced and crying, and sheriff's
deputies avoided a confrontation by quickly asking her to leave the
area. It was an awkward moment for those waiting in the hall; both
women were clearly victims of this crime. Throughout the trial, Freeman MacNeil's mother avoided all contact with the media, the police,

and others gathered outside Courtroom Three. She remained secluded in the small witness room set aside for her, and as she entered and left the courtroom, her head was always low. She would not show the anguish she must have felt. Freeman was her baby, and although he was still alive, there was no question she was losing him. He would not be coming back home.

Finally, at about 11 a.m., the jury sent its notice to the judge: the verdicts were ready. While intense security had become part of the routine of the trial, it somehow seemed particularly obtrusive to the victims' relatives this time. When Jimmy Fagan's brothers were asked to remove their cowboy boots so they could be searched for weapons, they joked about the process, but inside they felt humiliated. Neil Burroughs's father looked angry but remained silent as a contingent of security officers escorted Freeman MacNeil's relatives to their seats. All he could think about was that *those* people were not being harassed, but he and his family were. Inside the courtoom, the tension increased when the relatives saw that a large, heavy court table had been placed across the gate between the public area and the main court, and that the prisoner's chair had been moved several metres beyond the waist-high bar that divided the room. As well, there were twenty-five officers crowded into the court, most seated between the public gallery and the area occupied by the judge, jury, lawyers, and accused, and there were a few RCMP officers stationed at the back of the room.

Before asking the jury to come in, Justice Gruchey urged the victims' families to maintain the composure they'd shown throughout the difficult trial. "Please, when the verdict is brought in, I ask that you maintain that dignity. Any demonstrations now—any untoward action—will reflect badly on the excellent names and reputations you clearly deserve." Once again, anxiety and stress built as the relatives waited to hear what a jury of strangers had to say about one of the men responsible for taking their loved ones away. Neil Burroughs, Sr., continued to fume at the spectacle of the intense security measures court officials felt were needed to protect Freeman MacNeil. Why was MacNeil being protected, while he and his family were made to feel like criminals? The jury foreman began to read the verdicts, but unlike Justice Tiddman, who had detailed each charge against Derek Wood before asking for the verdicts, Justice Gruchey simply listed the counts by number, and the jurors responded with verdicts: count one, guilty as charged; count two, guilty as charged; count three, guilty of

second-degree murder; count four, guilty as charged. There was confusion in the courtroom, and the victims' relatives questioned each
other frantically as they tried to determine what each count meant.
The second-degree verdict had to be either for Jimmy's or Neil's murder, but for a few agonized moments no-one was sure which was
which. Finally, all became clear: the jury had found MacNeil guilty of
the first-degree murder of Neil Burroughs; Jimmy Fagan's killing was a
case of second-degree murder. In addition, MacNeil was also found
guilty of the robbery and the unlawful confinement. The verdicts
made it clear that the jury had not accepted the evidence of Dr. Bradford; had they agreed that MacNeil was suffering from post-traumatic
stress syndrome and had a diminished mental capacity, the verdicts
would have been manslaughter, not murder. Apparently, the jurors
concluded that the blow to Neil Burroughs did contribute to his
death, which occurred while MacNeil was participating in the unlawful confinement of Donna Warren. But the jurors clearly had decided
that the confinement ended with Donna's death, and thus could not
be connected to the shooting of Jimmy Fagan. They believed that
MacNeil killed Fagan, but not that he planned the murder; they must
have decided that the shooting was a spontaneous act.

Cathy Fagan could not believe it. She began to rock in her seat and
cry. Her sobs grew louder, and the others soon wept with her. Justice
Gruchey quickly sentenced MacNeil to the mandatory life term with
no parole for twenty-five years on the first-degree conviction, and
asked the jury to consider an appropriate parole eligibility on the second-degree conviction. Juries are not required to make such a recommendation, but judges must give them that opportunity. The jurors
retired to consider the issue, and Freeman MacNeil was just being escorted out of the courtroom when a flashfire of emotion and pain
burst through the courtroom. MacNeil went pale as he was hustled
away, and Justice Gruchey also left quickly. But the prosecutors and
defence lawyers remained to witness what they later called a very
painful expression of grief.

· Sixteen ·

ATHY FAGAN IGNITED the explosive build-up of tension in Courtroom Three, crying out to her brothers as Freeman MacNeil was being led from the room: "Go get him! Paul, David, go get him!" Her knees buckled as she tried to push her brothers towards the wall of security officers protecting MacNeil. Paul and David Fagan had no intention of moving in that direction; instead, they turned to help Cathy. But their anger burst through the surface as deputies roughly escorted Cathy from the courtroom. "Get your hands off her, you hear me? Don't you hurt her!" they shouted. They rushed towards the back of the room as the rear doors flew open, and the sheriff's deputies and a hysterical Cathy Fagan stumbled into the anteroom beside the courtroom. The noise attracted the attention of the camera crews outside, who began recording as Cathy struggled with the guards, screaming that she didn't want to be filmed. Her brothers tried to chase the journalists away, even pushing a guard in their direction, but that only made for more drama, and the scrum of camera operators and photographers moved in closer.

Back in the courtroom, Joey Burroughs screamed at Kevin Coady, who remained in his seat with his back to Burroughs, a hollow feeling in his heart as he listened. "You fuckin' scumbag, you don't have a heart!" howled the enraged young man. "He fuckin' murders people! Coady, you'll fry in fuckin' hell!" An angry and tearful Julia Burroughs sat on the bench she had occupied for weeks. She turned sideways and pulled her knees up, hugging them and crying, "We had no protection!" Meanwhile, her mother-in-law marched to the front of the room and began to berate Freeman MacNeil's mother: "I hope you don't get one minute of sleep, lady. We don't get a night of sleep after what they done to our kids." Edith MacNeil made no response, just kept her head down and stared at her hands, clasped tightly in her lap. Her mind filled with the jury foreman's words: "Guilty...

guilty…guilty…guilty." Her son, guilty of the most serious offences in the Canadian criminal justice system. Any hope she might have had that Kevin Coady could somehow persuade the jury to go easy on Freeman had evaporated. Edith MacNeil seemed lost in a world of her own, oblivious to the turmoil going on around her. Mrs. MacNeil's friends would later say that she had changed completely—that anguish had aged her. Once a lively, friendly woman, she had become quiet and sullen, and at times, during the trial, she looked almost like a frightened deer, frozen in the headlights of an oncoming car.

Theresa Fagan, who had remained silent for a year and a half, could not believe what was happening around her. She had done what the lawyers wanted; she had kept quiet, and her kids had stayed away from the reporters. But now, all she could think was that the verdict meant Jimmy's death wasn't as important as the others. "Jimmy never hurt a person!" she shouted to no-one in particular. "He never said a cross word to anyone!" I watched, listened, and wrote as much as I could in the pandemonium. Those relatives who weren't yelling were crying and comforting one another, or just sitting there, looking pale and confused. It wasn't supposed to end like this, I thought. Two veteran newspaper reporters stood near me, and I could see they had tears in their eyes; no-one was immune to the raw emotion being displayed around us.

As the crowd began to move out to the foyer, ATV cameraman Stuart McDougal and I followed. Outside, I grabbed a microphone and tried to record the emotions of those leaving; Stuart, his energy heightened by all the emotion, was right with me. "Joey, what can you say?" It was a stupid question, but I knew that Joey Burroughs had a lot to express and wanted the chance to speak out. Other camera crews rushed over as Joey, still running on emotion and adrenaline, began to shout into the microphone and condemn what he saw as a justice

Neil Burroughs's brother Joey vents his frustration with the tight security system for Freeman MacNeil's trial in Halifax. [Print from ATV video tape.]

system that protected the guilty and made criminals out of victims. "Look at this! I never seen nothing fuckin' like it. A fuckin' travesty of justice! This isn't gonna end here, you hear me?" Everyone heard, but no-one responded. His shouts were loud enough to be heard in the courtroom, and security officers came out to restore order in the hall. Joey stepped away from the cameras and hollered at the men, aiming his hurt and anger at them: "Come on boys, right fuckin' now! You'll earn your fuckin' pay today, ya bastards! This fuckin' justice system sucks!" The guards kept their distance and let him blow off steam; they weren't looking for a physical confrontation.

I raced over to Neil Burroughs, Sr., who was standing silently near the front, staring out a window. "Neil, some strong emotions in there. What caused it?" Again, a simple question was enough to get him started; like his son, Burroughs complained about the system that he felt had mistreated his family. "We weren't going to hurt anyone," he said. "We're not like that animal in there. We don't go around killing people. There was no need of any of that!" Burroughs shook his fist as blood raced to his face, his rage continuing to build. In the weeks ahead, Neil's father, like many of the other relatives, would begin to grieve the loss all over again, a painful but ultimately healing process that would release his anger. But right now, only outrage, and a sense of violation, existed. I moved on to Olive Warren. She tried to talk, but couldn't; instead, she reached out, squeezed my arm, and said, "I'm sorry." Stuart and I approached Germaine MacNeil, who was weeping. "I don't know what to say. I just want to go home. I want to go home to Arlene."

As the people in the hallway began to settle down, the jury returned with its recommendation on the second-degree sentencing. They asked the judge to apply the maximum—no parole eligibility for twenty-five years—then quickly left the court through the side door. The judge would make a ruling on their recommendation in a few weeks. Stuart and I went to the media room, on the opposite side of the courtroom, where Kevin Coady was waiting for us; the defence attorney had agreed to talk to us in the relative security of the small room. Coady looked a bit dazed as he spoke, saying he understood the outpouring of emotion in the courtroom. He also confirmed my interpretation of the verdict—that the jury concluded Neil Burroughs had been struck by his client while Donna Warren was still being confined, that MacNeil had taken part in the confinement, and that the confinement ended when Donna was killed. That was why MacNeil was found guilty of first-degree murder in Burroughs's death and second-degree murder in the case of Jimmy Fagan. I asked him if it would be possible to speak with Mrs. MacNeil, but Coady simply shook his head; she had already been taken out the side door and away from the commotion.

I knew some of Neil's and Jimmy's brothers were planning to go to the underground parking garage to wait for the prison van, so I headed there to talk to them. The Burroughs brothers had decided to leave, and the Fagan brothers, who had declined to comment for eighteen months, said they still didn't want to say anything. Stuart put his camera down, and I just stood there talking with the Fagans for a while. After a few minutes of venting their anger privately, they decided it would be all right for them to speak on camera after all. The five young men stood in a row, expressing their pain and anger. "That was no robbery gone bad. They were executed." "We wanted to put this behind us, but I guess we never will now. It's just not over, not like this." "We wanted to see it through for Jimmy. But now, well, it's just not right." "That scumbag rat Freeman MacNeil gets all the protection in the world." "I don't know what that jury was thinking. It should have been first-degree murder."

I thanked them, and we raced back to the station. Forty minutes until the 1 p.m. news, and I had to try to package all that emotion into a reasonable report. As the van backed out, I turned to look at the strange scene behind us—five powerfully built young men, staring blankly at each other or down at their feet. They had lost their brother, they had seen their sister completely out of control, they had watched their mother cry, and they too had cried—but they still felt empty and powerless. There was absolutely nothing they could do to help their mother or sister; there was absolutely nothing they could do to avenge their lost brother. Slowly they made their way towards their cars and left the court building, a place that, to them, could never offer justice. Their story was a powerful one, and it needed to be told, but I knew it would take more than the two-and-a-half minutes I would be allotted on the evening news.

In the weeks between the verdicts and the sentencing on the second-degree conviction, I was given the opportunity to tell that story, and more. The network agreed that the emotional trials and the grisly murders warranted a deeper examination. A thirty-minute news special would be built around the case, and I was asked to write and produce it, so back I went to Cape Breton to meet with the parents of the victims.

Gary Mansfield and I walked with Olive Warren through the graveyard where Donna was buried. We looked at the ornate head-stone bearing the graduation picture of the pretty young woman, as Olive spoke, saying that the murder had changed her life forever. "I'm not the same person," she said. "Nothing is the same. I have hate in my heart now, and that's something I never thought I'd have." Then she described her daily visits to the graveyard. "I come here and I sit and talk to her. I told her how the trials were going and what was hap-pening in court. When I get up to leave, I can hear her asking me, 'Why are you leaving me alone?' It breaks my heart every time I walk away from here." During the outburst in Halifax, I had been too busy and too pressured by time to react to what was happening, but that morning, looking at Donna's grave, there was time to reflect. My eyes filled, and tears ran down my face. Gary was concentrating on Olive Warren, and I was relieved that my emotion was going unnoticed. The story would show her grief; my tears had no place in it.

Later, Theresa and Al Fagan were kind enough to open their home to me, and we spent some time looking at photographs of a young, smiling Jimmy and the big, happy family—before it was ripped apart

Olive Warren and the author share a quiet moment near Donna Warren's grave, which her mother visits every day. [Print from ATV video tape.]

by a murder. They cried as they recalled their happiest, most fun-loving child, who now lay in a grave they visited frequently. "Jimmy was a great one at special occasions," Al said. "Oh, they're all good, but Jimmy had something special about him when it came to gifts. He always managed to find something for you that you knew you needed as soon as you opened it. You might not have known before, but once he gave it to you, well, you just knew. He was great like that.

"Even if I was having a club meeting," Theresa Fagan offered, "if Jimmy was home, he'd come and sit on that chair and talk to them all. He wouldn't stay long, now, but he'd say a little something to everyone. He just loved people."

Al Fagan was still angry. There was no way that what happened in Sydney River was a robbery gone bad, he said; it was an execution, carried out by people who wanted to know what it was like to kill, to shoot people in the head.

In the evening, Gary and I visited the hospital where Arlene MacNeil was still fighting to gain more control over her body. Her parents beamed as they predicted that she would walk again, someday. Arlene was already able to crawl, and she was growing stronger every day. The MacNeils also described the renovations being done at their house, which was being modified to meet Arlene's special needs. Soon she would be home to stay. Germaine cried as she described her daughter's old dreams for the future, and wondered aloud what that future might hold now. And Arlene? She captured my heart once again, showing a spark of delightful humour that only slightly embarrassed her mother. When I asked what she would do when she finally got home, Arlene looked at her mom, grinned, and said: "Get drunk!" She reached out and grabbed my hand, as she had done months earlier. Her grip was stronger now, and she seemed to understand more of what was happening around her. As the interview ended and I thanked her, Arlene squeezed my hand.

"I love you," she said.

"I love you too, sweetheart. I love you."

Carmel and Neil Burroughs decided not to participate in the news special; they felt they had been through enough. I told them I understood, and promised Carmel I would try to convey her feelings as best I could. Julia Burroughs, too, preferred not to discuss her loss in public.

In the process of preparing the special, I was able to obtain the RCMP video tapes of the crime scene, the re-enactment of events provided by Freeman MacNeil, and the lie-detector test taken by

Darren Muise. I wanted Gary to edit those tapes, so I had them with me in Sydney. Gary copied the tapes and edited the crime-scene video to remove all traces of the bodies—a very painful experience for him. The last time he had seen Donna Warren was when she served him at the Sydney River McDonald's. He remembered her smile and her friendly manner. Now he looked at the monitor and saw her lying on her back, a trail of blood streaming from her head, her eye blackened by gunpowder.

The news special was ready as the date for Freeman MacNeil's last court appearance approached. The November 12 hearing was only a formality: MacNeil had already been sentenced to the maximum term allowable under Canadian law, and nothing done at the hearing could change that; any other sentences would run concurrently. A number of the victims' relatives didn't even bother to attend this final hearing—they had no more rage to express—and those who did come were in an altogether different mood than before. Even when they were taken aside and asked to give a personal undertaking to remain calm in the court, they agreed without showing a trace of rancour. At the end of the hearing, Justice Gruchey made it clear to the families that he did not feel the death of Jimmy Fagan was any less significant

Arlene MacNeil with her parents, Germaine and Howard MacNeil, in the rehabilitation unit of the Sydney Mines hospital. [Print from ATV video tape.]

than that of Neil Burroughs or Donna Warren. Then, he imposed the term the jury had recommended—life in prison with no parole eligibility for twenty-five years. It was only the second time in Canada that a second-degree conviction had brought the maximum; this was a major victory in the esoteric world of legal precedent, but it meant very little to the people affected by the crime that brought the sentence. And it meant nothing to the young man who faced the extraordinary second-degree sentence. He could not seek parole for twenty-five years in any case.

Two days later, the ATV special aired, and among those who watched it closely were the prisoners at the maximum-security federal prison in Renous, New Brunswick—now home to Freeman Mac-Neil, Darren Muise, and Derek Wood. At the conclusion of the program, part of which showed how the three men had implicated each other in the crime, a chorus of jeers rang down "the range"—the row of cells where the killers were being held.

"Don't fuckin' worry about twenty-five years, hamburglers, you're not gonna live that long!"

"Ya fuckin' rats!"

"Squealers—we'll hear ya fuckin' squeal!"

An unwritten code had been broken, and inmates were promising revenge. The threats prompted prison authorities to continue to segregate the three men for their own protection. This decision angered some of the relatives of the victims, who said the killers were getting special treatment; their hopes had been that prison justice might do what civil justice had not—avenge their loss. Joey Burroughs was not a violent person, but he said he hoped the prison terms would be very hard on Wood, Muise, and MacNeil, who instead were being put into private rooms, like students in a university dormitory. But others, like Al Fagan, said it was time to forget the three young men who had caused so much pain. "We can't go on worrying about what happens to them in that jail," Fagan told me. "They're gone, and that's all that matters. We have to get on with our lives."

● ● ●

AT THE START of the Derek Wood trial, many of the victims' relatives expected to feel some sense of relief when the final trial was over. That never happened. Instead, they were left with a jaded view of the criminal justice system. Olive Warren and Carmel Burroughs responded to the disillusionment by directing their energy towards changing the system they had come to despise. The two women began circulating petitions in Cape Breton, calling on Parliament to reintroduce capital punishment, or, as an alternative, introduce consecutive jail terms for cases of multiple murder. As they pointed out to people who looked at the petition, in Canada every murder after the first one is a freebie. As word of the petition spread, a juror from the MacNeil trial called me, asking how to get a copy and saying that another juror also wanted to sign.

The decision to start a petition aimed at increasing the punishments handed out in Canadian courts showed how the McDonald's murders had changed the Warren and Burroughs families. Olive Warren was filled with hate, something she said was never part of her character before her daughter was murdered. She did not like what she felt, but she had a strong desire to act on those feelings, and the reaction to the petition in the Cape Breton community showed that many shared her sentiments. Very few people refused to sign and, in a matter of months, Olive Warren and Carmel Burroughs had obtained thousands of signatures from Cape Bretoners who felt the McDonald's murder trials had shown there were serious flaws in the justice system. Freeman MacNeil and Derek Wood had been given the stiffest sentences allowed under Canadian law, but many felt this fell far short of what was appropriate. The biggest issue was the lack of consecutive jail terms: many people approached by the two women said they could not support capital punishment, but Olive Warren noted that those who objected to the death penalty agreed to sign on the other side of the petition, which dealt with lengthier jail terms for cases of multiple murder.

Another campaign, started by relatives of Neil Burroughs, showed a whole different viewpoint in Cape Breton. Neil Burroughs's sister, Cathy Sellars, asked McDonald's of Canada to close and demolish the Sydney River restaurant in honour of the victims. The presence of the restaurant made it difficult for her and her family to get on with their lives, she said; driving to and from Sydney meant passing the crime scene. McDonald's offered instead to erect a monument in a local park to pay tribute to the four workers shot during the robbery. Cathy said that was not enough, but many Cape Bretoners said they did not feel the demolition of the restaurant was warranted—or even desirable. Garfield Lewis, for example, pointed to the number of young people who looked to his restaurants for employment. He could not afford to build a new restaurant in Sydney River if the old one was torn down, and he knew the Cape Breton economy was not strong enough for McDonald's International to take on the capital cost. His restaurants were just not that profitable. In the months after the shootings, many people avoided going to the Sydney River McDonald's, but by the summer of 1993, Lewis said that business was returning to normal, and that people were beginning to put the horrible events of May 1992 behind them.

For the families of Freeman MacNeil, Darren Muise, and Derek Wood, that was a difficult, if not impossible, task. Like the victims' families, they faced constant reminders of what had happened. Local media reports on the petition and the campaign to raze the restaurant meant the story was still in the public eye. Yet the character of the people of Cape Breton has been a blessing for the relatives of the three young men. Gail Muise believes she would not have been able to make it through the ordeal without the love and support of her friends and neighbours. They reacted as Cape Bretoners always have to tragedy—they supported the people in need of help, rather than blame Gail or her husband for what Darren had done. For Gail and Sandy Muise, the tragedy will never go away, although they try not to discuss it, even at home alone. Two years after the events, just raising the subject brings tears to Gail's eyes as she continues to ask herself the question with no real answers: how did her son end up inside that restaurant? Gail Muise says she will never recover, and that her life will never be what it once was.

And there are other people closely connected to the case who feel their lives have changed forever. Some even look to the positive effects after such a tragedy. Ken Haley, for example, says he is more confident now in his ability to perform his job as a prosecutor. He believes the successful prosecution of the McDonald's case has prepared him for any job, no matter how big. RCMP public affairs officer Dave Roper believes the case has given a similar sense of confidence to the Mounties who protect the people of Cape Breton County. The strong team effort that brought about the arrests and convictions showed the members of the Sydney RCMP subdivision that they are capable of handling the worst in big-city crime—although they hope, of course, that they are never called on to do so again.

● ● ●

WHEN THE LAST TRIAL was over, prosecutors Ken Haley and Brian Williston began to look at the question that many in Cape Breton had been
asking them. Why would three seemingly normal young men commit such a horrible act? Haley also tried to understand why the three
never really showed emotion during their trials. He had taken the
time to observe Derek Wood, Darren Muise, and Freeman MacNeil,
and hoped to see something in them that would show they were capable of normal human emotion. He was angry that they not only
committed such terrible crimes, but also sat in open court, day after
day, surrounded by anger, grief, and pain, without showing the slight-
est sign of being moved by what they had done.

The prosecutors also thought about the behaviour of the three
young men after the crime, during the interrogations and trials, and
behind bars. Not long after his arrest, Freeman MacNeil developed a
reputation with guards at the Cape Breton County Correctional Centre. They considered MacNeil a real pain in the ass, a prisoner who
knew what he was entitled to and insisted on getting everything he
could. If he wanted to write a letter, he demanded paper and a pen,
and privacy to write. Derek Wood also adapted quickly to prison life.
A few weeks after the murders, Constable Pat Murphy served papers
on Wood at the jail and talked with him for a while; he needed to hear
Wood's voice in case he had to identify the wiretapped voices in court.
Wood told the officer he was happy to talk with him, and then, to
Murphy's shock, suggested that police check first the next time they
decided to pay him a visit. It was movie day, he said, and he didn't
care to miss the show. As for Darren Muise, he too seemed relatively
content in prison, and talked as though he had everything in hand.

Dr. Akhtar, the forensic psychiatrist who testified at MacNeil's trial, put forward one theory that might enlighten those perplexed by
the young men's actions. He offered the so-called group dynamic as a
possible explanation. Alone, Freeman MacNeil, Darren Muise, and
Derek Wood probably would not have killed. Nothing in their background suggested they would become violent criminals. But, after
convincing each other they were big-time criminals, none of them
wanted to be seen as the weak link in the chain. Once the killing started, the young men felt compelled to show they were worthy of the
group by taking part in what was happening. In a sense, that theory
explained why all three became involved in the killing once it started,
but it didn't address the question of why the first shot was fired. What
went through Derek Wood's mind before he pulled the trigger? Was

he afraid to show the others that he was weak? Or was he caught up in the power he possessed at that moment? Did he feel that he was in complete control, and that no-one could stop him from doing whatever he decided to do?

Then there was the three men's behaviour in jail—behaviour Dr. Akhtar described as typical of people suffering from sociopathic personality disorders. Sociopaths are antisocial individuals in whom conscience has ceased to function; such people often thrive in the strictly controlled environment of a prison. But it would be an incredible co-incidence if all three of these average teenagers, who just happened to strike up a friendship, turned out to be sociopaths. Another possibility is that the three young men do have consciences, but for one reason or another do not feel guilt about what happened at McDonald's—perhaps they have displaced their guilt, as often happens in a group. It's a lot easier to lower one's own level of guilt by transferring it to the others involved, something Freeman MacNeil did when he incriminated Muise and Wood in his early statements to police.

The conditions in Cape Breton at the time of the crime may also have played a role. Criminologists have noted a strong correlation between crime and economic conditions. All three killers were living an essentially aimless existence, believing, as many kids do in an economically depressed area, that they had no future—nothing to live for and nothing to lose. An attitude like that can lead people to commit horrible acts. If Darren Muise, Freeman MacNeil, and Derek Wood all had steady jobs with promising futures, it is highly unlikely they would have been inside the Sydney River McDonald's on the morning of May 7, 1992. Perhaps they would have exhibited antisocial traits in other areas of their lives. But then, many successful business people and community leaders show such traits, usually referred to as white-collar crime.

Ever since I was called to cover the McDonald's murder in the early morning of May 7, 1992, I have probably been asked at least once a week why I think it happened. I myself have put the same question to everyone involved in the case, and no-one—not the police, the prosecutors, the defence lawyers, or the relatives of either the victims or the killers—can come up with an answer. Friends of the three killers still wonder how they became involved. One of Darren Muise's closest friends told me he has spent many sleepless nights trying to answer that question: he maintains that nothing Darren ever did as a child or young adult gave any kind of warning that he was capable of such brutal violence. Nor have the friends and neighbours of the other two young men found anything to suggest that they were monsters, or time bombs waiting to go off. Other teenagers in the Cape Breton area have told me that petty crime is often seen as acceptable behaviour. There are not enough jobs to go around, and stealing from cars or from homes is one way to make up for the lack of employment. These young people are quick to point out that violence is not a part of this crime of necessity, which they try to justify by saying that the insurance companies can always replace what's been stolen. It is interesting to note that other young adults living in the tough economic climate of Cape Breton strongly disagree with what some of their friends are doing. Many, including the young employees at McDonald's, still believe they can, and will, make a living and have a future at home, where they want to be.

A short time after the MacNeil trial ended, I was parked in a drive-through line outside a McDonald's near Halifax. It was early on a Friday evening, and I was startled when three young men stepped in front of my car. They were laughing and joking and pushing one another. As I watched them walk across the parking lot and jump in a car, I couldn't help wondering what made them different from Freeman MacNeil, Darren Muise, and Derek Wood. The McDonald's killers had walked and joked in a similar parking lot; they too had driven around their city on a Friday night. What made them commit a crime that the people of Sydney will never forget? As I drove away, I began to think about why the murders had left such deep scars on the residents of my home town. Partly, it was because of the place where the crime had occurred. McDonald's was one of the first fast-food chains to come to Sydney; an entire generation had grown up with it as part of their lives. We went there as children; we returned as teens, to hang out on a Friday night; and now we bring our own children there.

The words of Father Stanley MacDonald came back to me: the community, he said, had lost a gathering place. It was true. In some way, the murders had been a violation of a place that was part of all of us. We walked on those floors, which were later stained with the blood of innocent young people. We knew those kids with the striped uniforms, the silly hats, and the bright smiles.

The Sydney River McDonald's murders were a terrible tragedy. The legacy of pain left from the seven shots fired that night will continue to be felt for many years, as Justin Burroughs grows up with no father, as Arlene MacNeil grows old as a disabled adult, as the people who love all four victims continue to ask the question with no answer, and as those who love the men convicted try to deal with their grief and ask the same question. Why did it have to happen at all?

We must also ask ourselves if there is anything that can be done to change the dismal economic realities that left three bright young men convinced that their only hope was a life of crime. Cape Breton is not unique in its plight; there are many economically depressed areas. How many other young adults are there who feel there is nothing to lose, nothing to stop them from pulling a trigger again and again?